**Open Source Software**

Making Business Applications accessible

Els **Van Vossel**

Fabien **Pinckaers**

# Streamline your Manufacturing Processes with
# Open ERP

## A Simple Approach to Manage the Manufacturing and Supply Chain Complexity

Open Object Press

Open Source Software
Making Business Applications accessible to All Companies

# Open ERP

Streamline your Manufacturing Processes with OpenERP:

A Simple Approach to Manage the Manufacturing and Supply Chain Complexity

by Els Van Vossel and Fabien Pinckaers

First Edition

Many of the designations used by manufacturers and suppliers to distinguish their products are claimed as trademarks. Where those designations appear in this book, and Open Object Press was aware of a trademark claim, the designations have been printed in initial capitals.

While every precaution has been taken in the preparation of this book, the publisher and the authors assume no responsibility for errors or omissions, or for damages resulting from the use of the information contained herein.

Open Object Press

**Open Object Press** is a division of **OpenERP S.A.** (www.openerp.com)

Copyright © 2011 Els Van Vossel and Fabien Pinckaers

First edition July 2011          **ISBN :** 978-2-9600876-3-5

# Open ERP

## Open Object Press

40, Chaussée de Namur
1367 Grand-Rosière
http://openerp.com/

*Special Thanks to Marc Laporte, Olivier Laurent,
Gary Malherbe and Grégory Dethier*

# *Open* ERP

Open Object Press

40, Chaussée de Namur
1367 Grand-Rosière
http://openerp.com/

*From the same Editor*

**OpenERP for Retail and Industrial Management – Steps towards
Sales, Logistics and Manufacturing Integration, 2009,
Fabien Pinckaers and Geoff Gardiner, ISBN: 978-2-9600876-0-4**

**Drive your Sales & Marketing Activities with OpenERP –
Close Leads, Automate Marketing Campaigns and Get Accurate
Forecasts , 2011, Els Van Vossel and Fabien Pinckaers,
ISBN: 978-2-9600876-1-1**

**Integrate your Logistic Processes with OpenERP – Efficient
Warehouse Management with Sales and Purchases Integration,
2011, Els Van Vossel and Fabien Pinckaers,
ISBN: 978-2-9600876-2-8**

*The Authors: Els Van Vossel and Fabien Pinckaers*

# Contents

## II  Advanced Features in Purchase Quotation Management      47

## III  Managing your Warehouse      69

# IV   Streamlining your Manufacturing         137

## 6   Defining your Master Data         139

## V   On Site installation                            179

# Foreword

Information Systems have played an increasingly visible role over the past several years in improving the competitiveness of business. They are more than just tools for handling repetitive tasks; they will guide and advance all of a company's daily activities. Integrated Management Software is today very often a key source of significant competitive advantage.

## Open Source Software: Making Business Applications accessible

Some may look at the Business Application market as a mature market dominated by a few large key players, with no new business opportunities.

This would be ignoring the market reality. So many customers are frustrated by their experience with existing vendors; so many companies around the world need to have access to business applications, but cannot afford them.

OpenERP believes that business applications should not be a luxury. That any company, anywhere in the world, should be able to afford the best tools to professionally expand business. That is one of the reasons why OpenERP needs to break the existing rules of the ERPs and the Business Applications market.

Customers should use their budget smartly and invest in customizing the application to their specific needs, rather than paying expensive license fees. OpenERP is committed to the Open Source Business Model precisely because Open Source allows for this. Open Source is a disruptive model, as it creates more value for the customers.

For decades, customers have developed applications which remained specific to their own needs, and in the end proved extremely expensive to maintain. Open Source means that customers can benefit from past developments of other companies. Also by contributing to the evolution of the software, the users will enjoy the guarantee that their development will be included in future versions of the software. One of the major advantages is that such a *Community* brings a wealth of new functionality.

Open Source also allows us to engage with our customers differently. Since there is no licensing cost, any potential customer can download, test and use the software. OpenERP has no need for an expensive sales force to promote the product. OpenERP just needs to make the best product and make it available to customers.

Open Source allows for many barriers in this industry to be broken. The software is available to many companies who could otherwise not afford expensive business applications license fees. The OpenERP solution allows customers to use their money smartly and tailor the software to their individual needs. OpenERP leverages from its customer base to enrich the software and finally eradicate any lock-in to allow customers to use and even drop the software freely.

# The OpenERP Solution

OpenERP can build a new breed of business applications, more modular, more customer-friendly, fully web-based, which others cannot due to the heritage of their legacy systems.

OpenERP is a comprehensive suite of business applications including Sales, CRM, Project management, Warehouse management, Manufacturing, Financial management, and Human Resources, just to name a few. More than 1000 OpenERP modules are available from the OpenERP Apps market place (http://apps.openerp.com/).

The key to continued logistics success is effective Purchase, Sales, Warehouse & Manufacturing Management, and these are precisely the main topics of the book you are reading. OpenERP's Purchase, Sales, Warehouse & Manufacturing features are flexible and highly developed to assist you in managing all aspects of manufacturing.

OpenERP allows you to create bills of materials and use properties allowing your salespeople to easily select what they need to sell. Purchase proposals and sales forecasts can easily be created from OpenERP. In a few clicks, your sales person can transfer necessary information to the customer about the current and virtual stock.

# Structure of this book

In part One, *Configuring your OpenERP* (page 3) we will show you how to set up an OpenERP database. A step-by-step approach will guide you through a complete workflow to discover OpenERP's features.

Part Two, *Advanced Features in Purchase Quotation Management* (page 47), guides you from price request to purchase proposal and order, and goods receipt. Several advanced purchase features will also be explained.

Part Three, *Managing your Warehouse* (page 69), explains the principles of OpenERP's double-entry stock management. The book will provide you with ways to manage inventories, both on a physical and a financial level. Upstream and Downstream traceability and extensive reporting will be discussed as well.

Part Four, *Defining your Master Data* (page 139), guides you the manufacturing process, explaining several advanced features.

Part Five, *On Site installation* (page 179), explains the basic steps to install OpenERP on site. Both Linux and Windows installations will be described.

To manage your manufacturing, you do not need all the elements described in this book. But we find it very important to include an integrated flow, from the first quotation to the final billing of the suppliers including all the steps: quotation, order, receiving goods, inventory, manufacturing and billing. In some examples, we will also talk about the sales part, although advanced sales features will not be included in this book.

# About the authors

## Fabien Pinckaers

Fabien Pinckaers was only eighteen years old when he started his first company. Today, over ten years later, he has founded and managed several new technology companies, all based on Free / Open Source software.

He originated Tiny ERP, now OpenERP, and is the director of two companies including OpenERP S.A., the editor of OpenERP. In a few years time, he has grown the Tiny group from one to sixty-five employees without loans or external fund-raising, and while making a profit.

He has also developed several large scale projects, such as Auction-in-Europe.com, which became the leader in the art market in Belgium. Even today people sell more art works there than on ebay.be.

He is also the founder of the LUG (Linux User Group) of Louvain-la-Neuve, and of several free projects like OpenReport, OpenStuff and Tiny Report. Educated as a civil engineer (polytechnic), he has won several IT prizes in Europe such as Wired and l'Inscene.

A fierce defender of free software in the enterprise, he is in constant demand as a conference speaker and he is the author of numerous articles dealing with free software in the management of the enterprise.

Follow Fabien on his blog http://fptiny.blogspot.com/ or on twitter fpopenerp.

## Els Van Vossel

Els Van Vossel always had a dedication to both written and spoken word. Clear and explicit communication is crucial.

Educated as a Professional Translator in Antwerp, she worked as an independent translator on the localization of major ERP software. Els acquired ERP knowledge and decided to start working as a functional ERP consultant and a Technical Communicator for ERP software.

As such, the world of OpenSource software became more and more attractive. She started working with OpenERP software in her free time and doing so, Els really wanted to meet Fabien Pinckaers to share thoughts about documentation strategy. Now Els is reviewing and writing the OpenERP Books.

Being an author of several Software Manuals, she finds it exciting to work on the OpenERP documentation and continuously take it to a higher level. Please note that this is a hell of a job, but Els finds great pleasure in doing it!

Follow Els on her blog http://training-openerp.blogspot.com/ or on twitter elsvanvossel.

# Acknowledgements

*From Els Van Vossel*

Thank you Fabien, for offering me the opportunity to work with OpenERP. I thank all OpenERP team members for their support and understanding. My special thanks to my family who encouraged me to write this book.

*From Fabien Pinckaers*

I address my thanks to all of the team at OpenERP for their hard work in preparing, translating and re-reading the book in its various forms. My particular thanks to Laurence Henrion and my family for supporting me throughout all this effort.

# Part I

# First Steps: Driving a Purchase/Warehouse/Manufacturing Flow

*To manage your manufacturing, you do not need all the elements described in this book. But we find it very important to include an integrated flow, from the first quotation to the final billing of the suppliers including all the steps: quotation, order, receiving goods, inventory, manufacturing and billing.*

# Configuring your OpenERP 1

In this chapter, you can start exploring OpenERP through a basic configuration, with the modules that are discussed in this book. As mentioned before, we want to show an integrated flow, not just manufacturing management. Where appropriate, we will also talk about the sales part. For information about advanced sales features, please refer to the book `Integrate your Logistic Process with OpenERP – Efficient Warehouse Management with Sales and Purchases Integration`.

Use a web browser of your choice to connect to OpenERP Web.

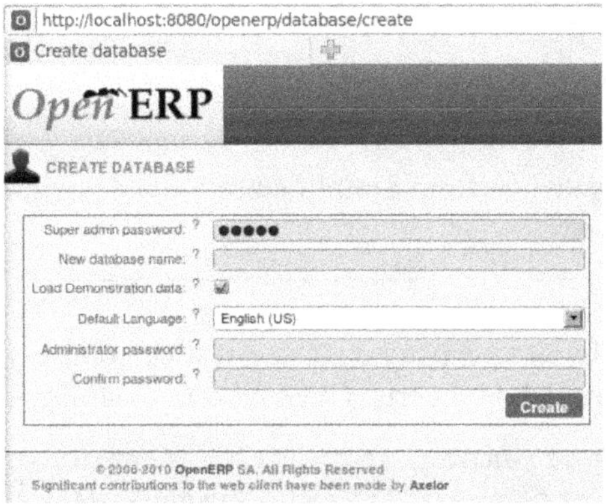

Figure 1.1: *Web Client at Startup*

Start by creating a new database from the *Welcome* page by clicking *Databases* and then completing the following fields on the *Create Database* form.

- *Super admin password* : by default it is `admin` , if you or your system administrator have not changed it,

- *New database name* : `DemoCompany` ,

- *Load Demonstration data* checkbox: `checked`,

- *Default Language* : `English (US)`,

- *Administrator password* : `admin` (because it is the easiest to remember at this stage, but obviously completely insecure),

- *Confirm password* : `admin` .

Press *Create* to start creating the database.

OpenERP suggests that you configure your database using a series of questions. In the software, these series of questions are managed through so-called `Configuration Wizards`.

Click the `Start Configuration` button to continue.

The next configuration wizard will help you to decide what your user interface will look like, whether the screens will only show the most important fields - `Simplified` - or whether you also want to see the fields for the more advanced users, the `Extended` view. Select `Extended` and click *Next* to continue.

In the next wizard, you can fill your company data, select your company's base currency and add your company logo which can be printed on reports. Click *Next* to continue.

Select the `Warehouse Management`, `Purchase Management`, `Sales Management`, `Manufacturing` and `Accounting & Finance` business applications for installation and click *Install*. Now OpenERP will start to install these five applications, allowing you to do a complete cycle, from sales / warehouse / purchase to invoice. You will have to wait for the next configuration wizard to be displayed (*Loading* will appear).

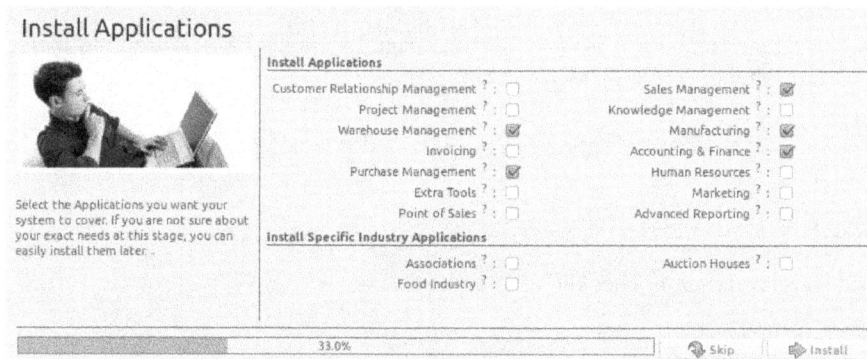

Figure 1.2: *Selecting the Required Functionality*

OpenERP's modularity enables you to install a single Business Application (such as Purchase) if that is all you need. Of course, you can choose to install extra applications such as Sales Management, to handle quotations, sales orders and sales invoices as well. For now, please install `Warehouse Management`, `Purchase Management`, `Sales Management`,

`Manufacturing` and `Accounting & Finance`, as these five Business Applications will be discussed in this book.

---

💡 **Reconfigure**

Keep in mind that you can change or reconfigure the system any time, for instance through the *Reconfigure* option in the main bar.

---

When you choose a business application for installation, OpenERP will automatically propose to add or configure related (smaller) applications to enrich your system. When you install Sales, OpenERP will also ask you whether you want to install Invoicing Journals for instance.

The figure *Selecting Accounting Configuration* (page 5) shows the Accounting Application Configuration screen that appears when you select `Accounting & Finance` to be installed.

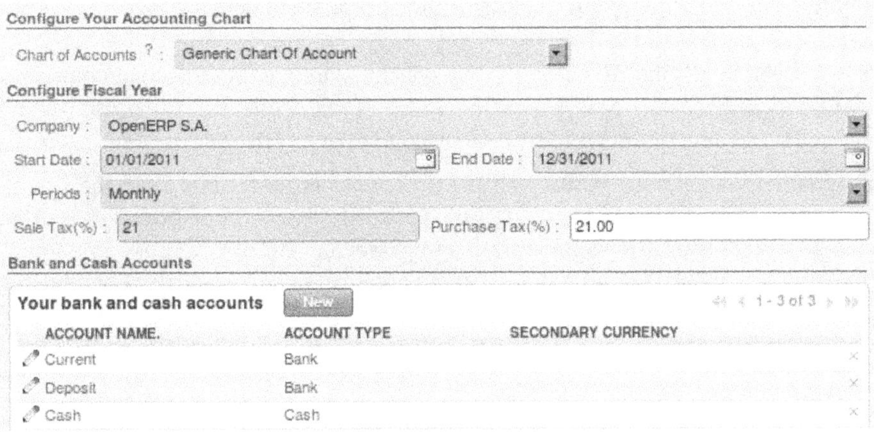

Figure 1.3: *Selecting Accounting Configuration*

Select the *Generic Chart of Account* and fill in the Sale Tax (%) applicable in your country. The Purchase Tax will automatically be set as well. Click one of the disk icons in front of the bank accounts to confirm the bank accounts to be created. Then click *Configure* to continue the configuration.

OpenERP Logistics & Manufacturing Management offers lots of features. You can easily manage your address book (customers, suppliers, ...), keep track of procurements and sales, manage your warehouse and inventory, and much more.

The figure *Selecting Purchase Configuration* (page 6) shows the Purchases Application Configuration screen that appears when you select `Purchase Management` to be installed.

Simply click `Configure` to continue the database creation.

The following wizards will appear:

- Configure your *Sales Management* application: click `Configure` to accept the default settings (no options checked).

---

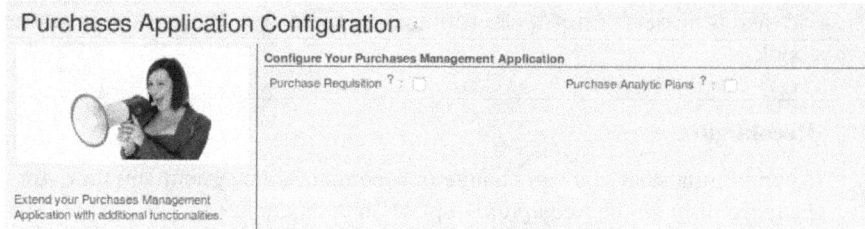

Figure 1.4: *Selecting Purchase Configuration*

- Configure your *MRP Application Configuration* application: click `Configure` to accept the default settings.

- Configure your *Accounting* application: click `Configure` to accept the default settings.

- Configure *Sales Order Logistics*: click `Next` to accept the default settings.

OpenERP's menu will be displayed, because your system is now ready for actual configuration. In the next chapter *Complete Example: Sell, Check the Stock, Manufacture and Purchase* (page 7) you will start working in the Manufacturing application in a step-by-step approach.

As your business is growing and evolving all the time, your requirements as to the use of OpenERP are likely to change. To sustain your growth, you can easily extend your Logistics & Manufacturing Management with other OpenERP business applications, such as HR or CRM, to name some. OpenERP offers this flexibility; you can start with one business application and gradually complete OpenERP to suit your ever changing needs!

# Complete Example: Sell, Check the Stock,

# Manufacture and Purchase $2$

In this chapter, we will show you a complete Sales / Purchase / Manufacturing / Warehouse flow. We will explain how to create a product, create a sales order, have an automatic purchase proposal and / or production order, produce and receive the goods, deliver to the customer, and get sales and purchase invoices in a step-by-step scenario.

First you will get an explanation about the scenario (what Thomas or one of his colleagues is supposed to do). Then the *Notes* will learn you how Thomas (or a colleague of his) enters the information in OpenERP. For the simplicity of the use case, we will do all of the steps under the Admin user. Please note that we will not discuss all elements in detail in this chapter. Later in the book, you will find all required information (apart from the advanced sales features).

> **Simplified or Extended View**
>
> In OpenERP your user interface will look slightly different according to the User Preferences. In `Simplified` view, the screens will only show the most important fields / tab pages. To see also the fields for the more advanced users, you should switch to the `Extended` view. You can easily switch from *Simplified* to *Extended* view by changing your *User Preferences* through the *Edit Preferences* button. For this use case, please switch to *Extended* view.

Your company will have a stand at the House & Design Fair to promote a series of products. Thomas, the salesman, shows the new products to the visiting prospects and customers.

1. Create a new customer

John Smith from the company Clarkson Ltd. visits your stand and decides to order the brandnew Desk and Chair you are promoting. Thomas will have to create this new customer in OpenERP.

> **New Customer**
>
> To create a new customer, Thomas clicks the Sales button in OpenERP's main screen. Then he goes to *Sales → Address Book → Customers* and clicks the *New* button. The name of a customer is in blue, because it is a mandatory field, so Thomas enters *Clarkson* in that field. He notices that the *Customer* check box is already checked. Thomas enters *John Smith* in the `Contact Name`, he selects the *Default* address type. In the `Street` field, Thomas enters London Street 40; he also enters the City *London* and the Country *United Kingdom* as shown in the screenshot below. He takes a look at the other three tabs and decides to keep the default values. Thomas then clicks the `Save` button to store the new customer.

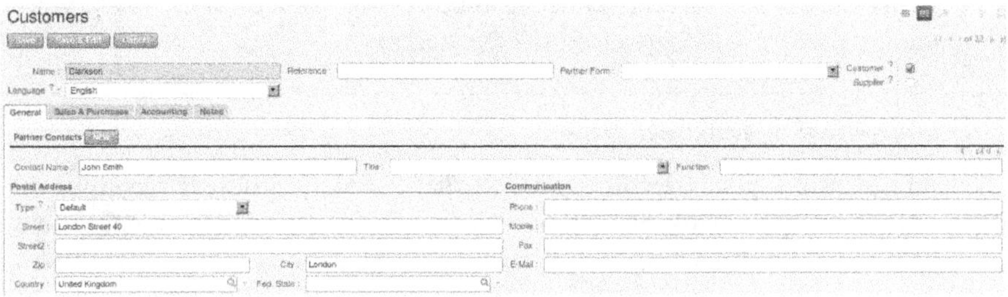

Figure 2.1: *New Customer*

2. Create a new product category and product

Because the desk and the chair from the new OfficeSecrets series do not yet exist in OpenERP, Mitchell, the Product Manager, will create this brandnew desk as a Make to Order product that will be bought directly from the supplier concerned. He will have to create a new product category for the OfficeSecrets series too.

> **Configuring Products**
>
> For more information about configuring products, please refer to the next chapter *Creating Products and their Categories* (page 34).

> **Product Category**
>
> Product categories do have an effect on the products assigned to them, and a product may belong to only one category. To create a new product category, Mitchell goes to *Warehouse*, selects the menu *Configuration → Product → Products Categories* and clicks *New* to get an empty form for defining a product category. Mitchell enters OfficeSecrets in the *Name* field and adds it to the parent category All products / Sellable. He leaves the other fields as such, and clicks *Save*.

Then Mitchell will create three new products. Note that he could also have created the new product category directly from the Product form.

**Product**

To create a new product, Mitchell goes to *Warehouse* → *Product* → *Products* and clicks the *New* button. The name of a product is in blue, because it is a mandatory field, so he enters *1600 Desk Wave Right-hand W1600x D1200x H725mm Maple* in that field. He notices that the *Can be Sold* and *Can be Purchased* check boxes are already checked by default. Mitchell selects the *Stockable Product* product type, because he wants to keep track of the stock movements of the desks. In the `Procurement Method` field, Mitchell selects *Make to Order*, because the company decided to only buy the product at the supplier when there is a sales order for it. The `Supply Method` will be *Buy*. He sets the Cost Price to 300 and the Sales Price to 541.25, as shown in the screenshot *Product* (page 11). Mitchell selects the product category `OfficeSecrets`. Now he just has to add the supplier from whom he will buy the desks. He clicks the `Suppliers` tab, then clicks `New`. He clicks the Magnifying glass to get a list of suppliers, from which he selects *Wood y Wood Pecker*. He sets the minimal quantity to 1 and clicks the `Save & Close` button. He takes a look at the other tabs and decides to keep the default values. He then clicks the `Save` button to store the new product.

To create the component to be included in the Bill of Material, Mitchell clicks the *Duplicate* button to duplicate the Desk (available when a product is not in Edit mode). He changes the name to *Leather for Chair* in that field. He unchecks the Can be Sold checkbox. Mitchell changes the `Procurement Method` to *Make to Stock*, because the company needs a permanent stock of leather to be able to fulfil the customer's demands. He sets the Cost Price to 20 and the Sales Price to 0. Mitchell then clicks the `Save` button to store the new product.

To create another component to be included in the Bill of Material, Mitchell clicks the *Duplicate* button to duplicate the Leather for Chair. He changes the name to *Chair Frame* in that field. He sets the Cost Price to 100. Mitchell then clicks the `Save` button to store the new product.

To create the finished product, Mitchell goes to the list of products, opens the Desk product and clicks the *Duplicate* button to duplicate the Desk (available when a product is not in Edit mode). He changes the name to *Leather Operator Chair* in that field. In the `Procurement Method` field, Mitchell selects *Make to Order*, then he changes the `Supply Method` to *Produce*. He sets the Cost Price to 200 and the Sales Price to 325.50. From the supplier tab, Mitchell deletes the supplier by clicking the black cross. He then clicks the `Save` button to store the new product.

3. Add Minimum Stock Rules

To make sure the leather and the frame is always in stock, Mitchell has to define minimum stock rules, telling OpenERP how many goods have to be ordered to keep a good stock level.

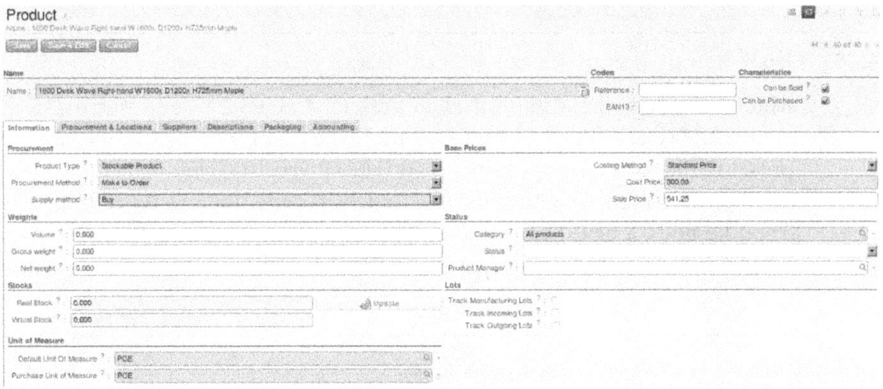

Figure 2.2: *Product*

---

**Minimum Stock Rules**

To enter minimum stock rules for the *Leather for Chair* product, he clicks the Minimum Stock Rules action, and clicks the New button. Mitchell notices that the product is already preset in the form. He selects the *OpenERP S.A.* warehouse and notices that the *Stock* location is automatically set. As a minimum quantity, he adds 10 and the maximum quantity will be 40. He then clicks the Save button to store the minimum stock rules, as shown in the screenshot *Minimum Stock Rules* (page 11). Do the same for the frame.

---

Figure 2.3: *Minimum Stock Rules*

4. Create a Bill of Material

To produce the chair from the frame and the leather seat, Mitchell has to create a Bill of Material for the finished product (the Chair). This way, he will tell OpenERP which components are required to produce the Chair.

---

**BoM**

You can also create a Bill of Materials from the *Manufacturing → Master Data → Bill of Materials*. More information on Bills of Material will be provided in the next chapters.

5. Warehouse and locations

Now Thomas will have a look at how the warehouse and the locations have been organised.

**Configuring locations**

We will not create a warehouse and configure locations in this chapter. For more information, please refer to the chapter *Managing your Warehouse* (page 69) later in this book. Just have a look at the list of locations defined with the demo data.

**Warehouse and Location Structure**

OpenERP has three predefined top-level location types: `Physical Locations` which define where your stock is physically stored, `Partner Locations` for the customer and supplier stock and `Virtual Locations` representing counterparts for procurement, production and inventory. Thomas clicks *Warehouse → Configuration → Warehouse Management → Locations* to display a list view of the locations.

6. Create a sales quotation

The customer *Clarkson* asked to receive a quotation for two Office Desks and two chairs from the OfficeSecrets series. Thomas enters the sales quotation.

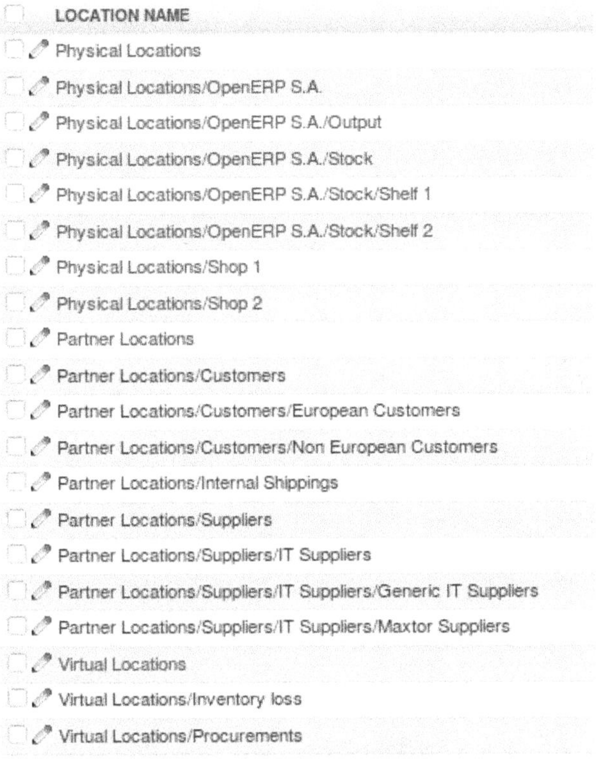

| | LOCATION NAME |
|---|---|
| ☐ ✎ | Physical Locations |
| ☐ ✎ | Physical Locations/OpenERP S.A. |
| ☐ ✎ | Physical Locations/OpenERP S.A./Output |
| ☐ ✎ | Physical Locations/OpenERP S.A./Stock |
| ☐ ✎ | Physical Locations/OpenERP S.A./Stock/Shelf 1 |
| ☐ ✎ | Physical Locations/OpenERP S.A./Stock/Shelf 2 |
| ☐ ✎ | Physical Locations/Shop 1 |
| ☐ ✎ | Physical Locations/Shop 2 |
| ☐ ✎ | Partner Locations |
| ☐ ✎ | Partner Locations/Customers |
| ☐ ✎ | Partner Locations/Customers/European Customers |
| ☐ ✎ | Partner Locations/Customers/Non European Customers |
| ☐ ✎ | Partner Locations/Internal Shippings |
| ☐ ✎ | Partner Locations/Suppliers |
| ☐ ✎ | Partner Locations/Suppliers/IT Suppliers |
| ☐ ✎ | Partner Locations/Suppliers/IT Suppliers/Generic IT Suppliers |
| ☐ ✎ | Partner Locations/Suppliers/IT Suppliers/Maxtor Suppliers |
| ☐ ✎ | Virtual Locations |
| ☐ ✎ | Virtual Locations/Inventory loss |
| ☐ ✎ | Virtual Locations/Procurements |

Figure 2.4: *Location Structure*

---

**Sales Quotation / Order**

Thomas goes to *Sales → Sales → Sales Orders*. He clicks the *New* button, to make a quotation. He enters *Clarkson* in the Customer field. Now he can enter the products he will be selling. Next to Sales Order Lines, Thomas clicks the New button to enter sales order lines. He selects the *Desk* product and changes the quantity to 2 as specified in the screenshot *Sales Order* (page 14). Thomas clicks the Save & New button to add a second line. He adds 2 chairs and notices that a message is displayed saying that there is no stock. Thomas clicks the Save & Close button. Then he clicks Compute to see the total price of the quotation. He opens the Other Information tab, because he wants the sales invoice to be created from the picking. So he changes the Shipping Policy to Invoice from the Picking. To print the quotation, he clicks *Quotation / Order* in the *Reports* section at the right side of the screen.

---

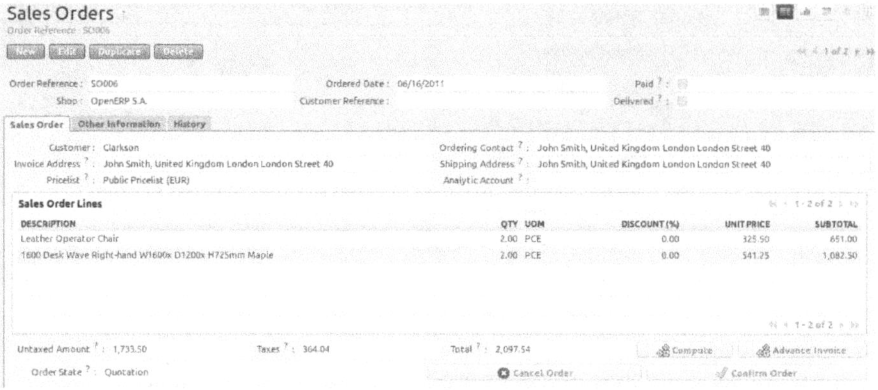

Figure 2.5: *Sales Order*

---

**Price Lists**

In this chapter, the *Public Pricelist* will be used. Later on, you will learn more about creating price lists.

---

7. Confirm the sales order

John Smith calls Thomas to tell him that he agrees with the quotation. Thomas now confirms the sales order.

---

**Sales Quotation / Order**

Thomas goes to *Sales → Sales → Sales Orders*. He enters *Clarkson* in the Customer field and then clicks Search. Thomas clicks the sales order to open it. He clicks the Confirm Order button to make a sales order from the quotation. To print the sales order, he clicks *Quotation / Order* in the *Reports* section at the right side of the screen.

---

**Order Confirmation**

When you click Confirm Order, red text will be displayed at the top of the screen depending on the parameters of the sales order. In our example, you will see two text lines, one about the quotation conversion and another one about the delivery order. You can click the second line to be directed to the delivery order. You can also open the delivery order from the History tab of the sales order.

---

8. Run the scheduler

---

The goods have to be produced and delivered to the customer, but Thomas notices that the desks and chairs are not available in stock. Because the Desk was defined as a Make to order & Buy product, OpenERP will automatically create a procurement order on confirmation of a sales order, allowing you to directly generate a purchase order. The same will be done for the Leather.

OpenERP has a scheduler that will run by default every day. In this case, Jason, your company's Purchaser, will run the scheduler manually.

---

**Scheduler**

Jason goes to *Warehouse → Schedulers*. He clicks Compute Schedulers because he needs to purchase material and wants to check whether anything needs to be added. In the Wizard, Jason clicks Compute Schedulers to start the computation.

---

**Procurement Exceptions**

Jason can also run the procurement for each product from the *Warehouse → Schedulers → Procurement Exceptions*. The procedurement exceptions menu also includes procurements that have not been scheduled yet.

---

9. Change the purchase request and confirm it

Now OpenERP will have created procurements (in this example purchase requests) for the products that need to be supplied.

---

**Purchase Requests**

Jason goes to *Purchases → Purchase Management → Request for Quotation*. He notices three purchase requests for *Wood y Wood Pecker*. He selects these three purchase requests by clicking the checkbox in front of them, then clicks the Merge Purchase Orders action at the right to order all products in one go. He clicks the yellow pencil to open the merged purchase request in Edit mode. Now he decides to purchase some extra desks, because Luke, the Sales Manager, told him he expects more sales. To do this, he clicks the yellow pencil in front of the order line and changes the quantity to 10. He clicks the Save & Close button, then he clicks Compute to see the total price of the quotation. From the Delivery & Invoicing tab, he specifies that the invoice has to be created from the picking (Invoicing Control *From Picking*). To confirm the purchase order, he just has to click the Convert to Purchase Order button.

---

10. Receive the products

The supplier Wood y Wood Pecker sends the goods to your company. Jason receives the goods and enters this receipt in OpenERP.

---

> **Incoming Shipments**
>
> Jason goes to *Warehouse → Warehouse Management → Incoming Shipments*. He notices the incoming shipment for Wood y Wood Pecker, and clicks the green arrow to start receiving the products. He clicks the `Validate` button to confirm that all products have been received from the supplier. From the `Incoming Shipments` list view, he notices that the Delivery order for the customer is now ready to process (red text at the top of the screen), at least for the desks. He wants to check the stock of Desks and goes to *Warehouse → Product → Products*. In the `Name` field, Jason types *desk*, then clicks Search. The real stock is 10, the virtual stock is 8, because of the confirmed sales order for two desks.

> **List versus Form view**
>
> You can receive / deliver goods from both list and form view. You can also receive / deliver goods by product instead of by complete order.

11. Create the draft purchase invoice

Because the purchase order was set to be invoiced from the picking, Jason can now create the draft invoice, which allows for easy invoicing control.

> **Draft Purchase Invoice**
>
> Jason returns to *Warehouse → Warehouse Management → Incoming Shipments* and clicks Clear. He opens the extended filters and clicks the `To Invoice` button. He ticks the check box in front of the incoming shipment to be invoiced and then clicks the `Create Invoice` action in the Reports section at the right side of the screen. He selects the Purchase Journal and clicks `Create` to generate the draft invoice. The screen with the supplier invoice will open. We will get back to this later.

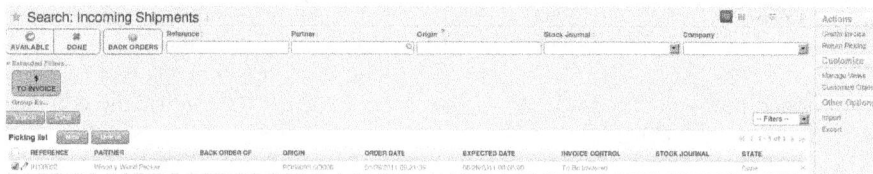

Figure 2.6: *Create Invoice from Incoming Shipments*

12. Run the scheduler again

---

To tell the system that the procurements have been received and that the raw materials are now in stock, so that the production order can be generated, Jason has to run the scheduler again.

> **Scheduler**
>
> Jason goes to *Warehouse → Schedulers*. He clicks Compute Schedulers. In the Wizard, Jason clicks Compute Schedulers to start the computation.

> **Just in Time**
>
> You can also install the mrp_jit (Just in Time) so that this is computed in real time. In a production environment, however, you would typically have the scheduler run.

13. Start manufacturing

Jason checks his list of manufacturing orders which are ready to produce. He notices the leather operator chair and decides to start manufacturing it.

> **Manufacturing or Production Orders**
>
> Jason goes to *Manufacturing → Manufacturing → Manufacturing Orders* and selects the order to start producing the chairs. He opens it by clicking the yellow pencil, then clicks the Start Production button. He notices the products to be consumed. He assembles the frame and the leather for both chairs. When he has finished, he clicks the Produce button. He keeps the default settings and clicks Confirm, then Cancel to close the window. He clicks the Save button to see the changes.

14. Deliver the goods to the customer and create draft sales invoice

The Chairs are now also available in stock and the complete order can be delivered to the customer. In the warehouse, they check the open delivery orders.

> **Delivery**
>
> Randy from the warehouse goes to *Warehouse → Warehouse Management → Delivery Orders* to check the goods ready for delivery. He clicks the yellow pencil to open the delivery order. He clicks the Process button to deliver the 2 desks and chairs, then he clicks Validate.

15. Create the sales invoice

Thomas now checks whether the goods have been delivered to his customer. He can check this from the sales order, or he can tell from the status of the delivery order.

> **Creating a Sales Invoice**
>
> To create the draft sales invoice, Thomas has several possibilities.
>
> He opens *Sales → Invoicing → Deliveries to Invoice* and selects the corresponding delivery for invoicing by ticking the check box and clicking the `Create Invoice` action in the Reports section at the right of the screen.
>
> He goes to *Warehouse → Warehouse Management → Delivery Orders*, and clicks the `Create Invoice` button.
>
> He goes to the list of sales orders, and opens the sales order concerned. Thomas clicks the *History* tab, clicks the picking list and then the `Create Invoice` button. He selects the *Sales Journal* and clicks the `Create` button.
>
> The draft invoice is now displayed in list view. Thomas opens the invoice and clicks the `Validate` button. To print the invoice, he clicks the `Print Invoice` button, or the `Invoices` action in the Reports section at the right of the screen. The printed invoice will automatically be added as pdf document to Attachments.

16. Confirm the purchase invoice

Robin, the accountant, now receives the invoice from his supplier. He can do the invoicing control according to the picking directly from the Purchase Invoices screen.

> **Invoice Control**
>
> Robin goes to *Accounting → Suppliers → Supplier Invoices* and opens the Wood y Wood Pecker invoice. Robin verifies whether the invoice from the supplier matches this draft invoice created from the picking order. The invoice indeed matches and he clicks the `Approve` button to confirm the invoice and assign a document number to it.

> **Purchaser**
>
> The purchaser can also do the invoice matching from *Purchases → Invoice Control → Supplier Invoices to Receive*.

Below you find a graphical representation of the sales flow we explained before; the part from quotation to invoice. This view is available in OpenERP. You can open this *Process view* by clicking the question mark next to the *Sales Order* title.

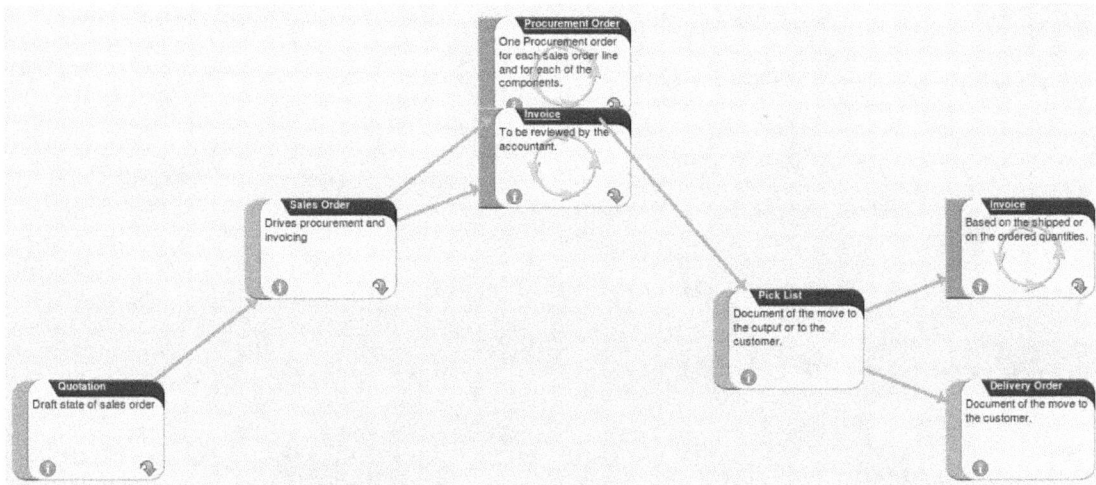

Figure 2.7: *From Quotation to Invoice*

# Let's get Started and Configure a New

# Instance                                              3

*Now that you have discovered some of the many possibilities of OpenERP from a tour of the demonstration database, you will develop a real case. An empty database provides the starting point for testing a classic workflow from product sales to purchase, completing your guided tour and your getting familiar with OpenERP.*

A database loaded with demonstration data is very useful to understand OpenERP's general capabilities. But to explore OpenERP through a lens of your own company's needs, you should start with an empty database. You will work in this chapter on a minimal database containing no demonstration data, so that there is no confusion about what you created. You will keep the database you have created, to allow you to build on it throughout the rest of this book if you want to.

You will develop a real case through the following phases:

1. Specify a real case;

2. Describe the functional needs;

3. Configure the system with the essential modules;

4. Carry out the necessary data loading;

5. Test the system with your database.

The case is deliberately simple to provide you with a foundation for the more complex situations you might have to handle in your company. Throughout this chapter, we assume that you access OpenERP through its web interface. And it is also assumed (as in the rest of this book) that you are using the latest download of OpenERP version 6, the stable production version at the time of writing (not the trunk version, which is likely to have new and potentially unstable features).

## 3.1 Business Example

In this example, you will configure a system that enables you to:

- buy products from a supplier,

- stock the products in a warehouse,

- sell these products to a customer.

The system should support all aspects of invoicing, payments to suppliers and receipts from customers.

## 3.2 Basic Settings

For this business case, you will have to model:

- accounts and account types,
- the suppliers and a supplier category,
- the customers and a customer category,
- some products and a product category,
- an inventory,
- a purchase order,
- a sales order,
- invoices,
- payments.

To test the system, you will need at least one supplier, one customer, one product, a warehouse, a minimal chart of accounts and a bank account.

## 3.3 Get your Database Up and Running without Demo Data

Please note that the new database you have to create, will *not* include demo data and only the minimally required functionality as a starting point. You will need to know your super administrator password for this – or you will have to ask your ICT manager for the password to be able to create this database.

Please refer to *Configuring your OpenERP* (page 3) for more information about how to create a new database that you will give the name of your company.

As a reminder, please find the steps below, without further explanation.

Start by creating a new database from the *Welcome* page by clicking *Databases* and then completing the following fields on the *Create Database* form.

- *Super admin password* : by default it is admin , if you or your system administrator have not changed it,
- *New database name* : YourCompany,
- *Load Demonstration data* checkbox: unchecked,
- *Default Language* : English (US),
- *Administrator password* : admin,
- *Confirm password* : admin.

Press *Create* to start creating the database.

OpenERP suggests that you configure your database using a series of questions. In the software, these series of questions are managed through so-called `Configuration Wizards`.

Click the `Start Configuration` button to continue.

The next configuration wizard will help you to decide what your user interface will look like, whether the screens will only show the most important fields - `Simplified` - or whether you also want to see the fields for the more advanced users, the `Extended` view. Select `Extended` and click *Next* to continue.

---

**User Preferences**

You can easily switch from Simplified to Extended view by changing your *User Preferences*.

---

In the next wizard, you can fill your company data, select your company's base currency and add your company logo which can be printed on reports. Fill out the required data and click *Next* to continue.

Select the `Warehouse Management`, `Purchase Management`, `Sales Management`, `Manufacturing` and `Accounting & Finance` business applications for installation and click *Install*. Now OpenERP will start to install these five applications, allowing you to do a complete cycle, from sales / warehouse / purchase / manufacturing to invoice. You will have to wait for the next configuration wizard to be displayed (*Loading* will appear).

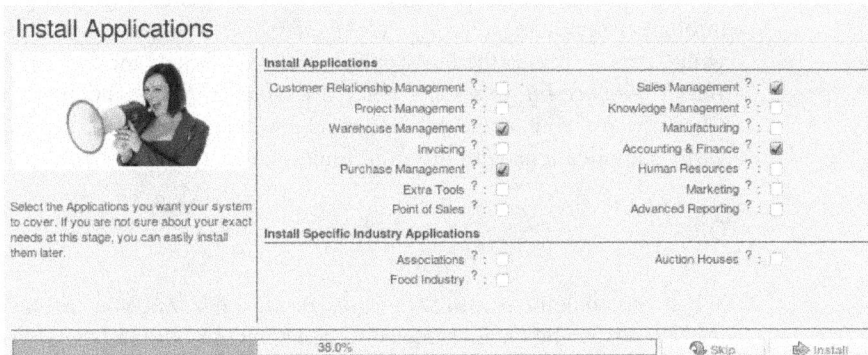

Figure 3.1: *Selecting the Required Functionality*

---

**Reconfigure**

Keep in mind that you can change or reconfigure the system any time, for instance through the *Reconfigure* option in the main bar.

---

When you choose a business application for installation, OpenERP will automatically propose to add or configure related (smaller) applications to enrich your system. When you install Sales, OpenERP will also ask you whether you want to install Invoicing Journals for instance.

*Skip* the step that asks you to configure your Accounting Chart, because you will learn how to create accounts.

In the Purchases Application Configuration screen, simply click `Configure` to continue the database creation.

The following wizards will appear:

- Configure your *Sales Management* application: click `Configure` to accept the default settings (no options checked).

- Configure your *MRP Application Configuration* application: click `Configure` to accept the default settings.

- Configure your *Accounting* application: click `Configure` to accept the default settings.

- Configure *Sales Order Logistics*: click `Next` to accept the default settings.

OpenERP's menu will be displayed, because your system is now ready for actual configuration.

> **Setup Wizard**
>
> You will have to go through the Setup wizard in steps. You have two options:
>
> 1. If you click the *Start Configuration* button, OpenERP guides you through a series of steps to: *Configure Your Interface* - proceed with `Simplified` (the other option is `Extended`); and *Configure Your Company Information* - enter a *Company Name* and select a *Currency* for your company. Then OpenERP helps you to install various applications with different functionality through wizards.
>
> - OR -
>
> 2. When you click the button *Skip Configuration Wizards*, you can have the screen as shown in screenshot *Starting the minimal database* (page 25). Then you can start working with this minimal database (*we will not use this option here*).

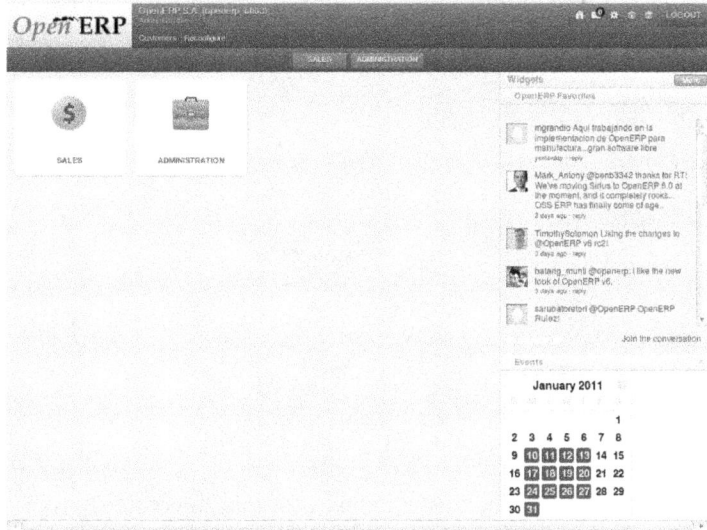

Figure 3.2: *Starting the minimal database*

## 3.4 Fit your Needs

Functional needs can be provided by core modules from OpenERP. You just have to decide which functionality you want in your system. As explained before, you can click the *Check Box* of the corresponding application. Another way of installing modules, is to go the *Administration → Modules → Modules* menu. Here you will find a list of all modules available in OpenERP. You can also check our website http://apps.openerp.com/ for more information about modules.

To manage your manufacturing, you do not need all the elements described in this book. But we find it very important to include an integrated flow, from first quotation to the payment of the supplier including all the steps: quotation, order, receiving goods, inventory, manufacturing.

To manage such a flow, we need at least the following applications:

- Manufacturing (the `mrp` module),

- Warehouse Management (the `stock` module),

- Accounting & Finance (the `account` module),

- Purchase Management (the `purchase` module),

- Sales Management (the `sale` module).

When you log on, OpenERP will display the opening screen with all selected business applications installed.

You will create all the elements in the database that you need to carry out the use case. These are specified in the functional requirements.

Figure 3.3: *Database with all Required Functionality for this Example*

---

**Examples**

Of course, we will provide examples for you to configure your database, such as customers and suppliers. Make sure to use your own data instead.

---

### 3.4.1 Configuring Accounts

You need to start with a minimal set of accounts, and therefore you will need a couple of account types to determine the account's use, how it will be transferred at year closing, and what category it belongs to. You can structure your accounts into a chart at any time (and, in fact, you can structure them into several additional charts at the same time as you will see in the on line chapter of the OpenERP book), so you do not need to be concerned unduly about structure.

**Account Types**

To create account types, go to *Accounting → Configuration → Financial Accounting → Accounts → Account Types* and click the *New* button. You will need the following six types, the first of which is shown in figure *New Account Type* (page 27). Click *Save* to confirm each account type.

Table 3.1: Defining Account Types

| Acc. Type Name | Code | P&L / BS Category | Deferral Method |
|----------------|---------|-------------------|-----------------|
| View | view | / | None |
| Income | income | Profit & Loss (Income Accounts) | None |
| Expense | expense | Profit & Loss (Expense Accounts) | None |
| Cash | cash | Balance Sheet (Assets Accounts) | Balance |
| Receivable | receiv | Balance Sheet (Assets Accounts) | Unreconciled |
| Payable | pay | Balance Sheet (Liability Accounts) | Unreconciled |

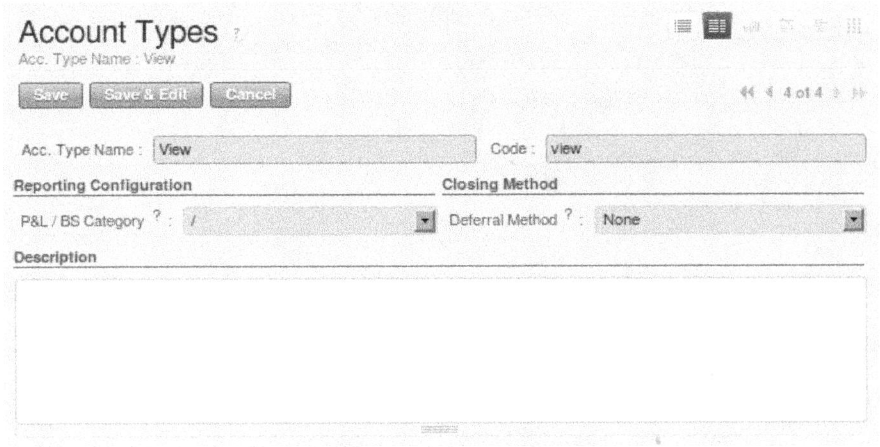

Figure 3.4: *New Account Type*

## Accounts

To create accounts, go to *Accounting → Configuration → Financial Accounting → Accounts → Accounts* and click the *New* button.

You need accounts to keep track of your customers and suppliers, two more to sell and buy goods, and one for the payment and receipt of funds. And also one 'organizing' account that is just a view of the other five. So basically you will need at least the following six accounts, one of which is shown in *New Account* (page 28). Click *Save* to confirm each account.

> **Chart of Accounts Structure**
>
> When you create a chart of accounts, you should always start with the main view account to define the chart, as shown in the table (Minimal Chart). This will allow you to easily link new accounts to the correct chart directly.

Table 3.2: Defining Accounts

| Name | Code | Parent | Internal Type | Account Type | Reconcile |
|------|------|--------|---------------|--------------|-----------|
| Minimal Chart | 0 | | View | View | unchecked |
| Payable | AP | 0 Minimal Chart | Payable | Payable | checked |
| Receivable | AR | 0 Minimal Chart | Receivable | Receivable | checked |
| Bank | B | 0 Minimal Chart | Liquidity | Cash | unchecked |
| Purchases | P | 0 Minimal Chart | Regular | Expense | unchecked |
| Sales | S | 0 Minimal Chart | Regular | Income | unchecked |

The *Account Type* entry is taken from the list of types that you just created. Although it looks a bit like a text box, it does not behave in quite the same way. A single Del or Backspace keystroke is all you need to delete the whole text, and when you type the name (or part of the name), you still need to

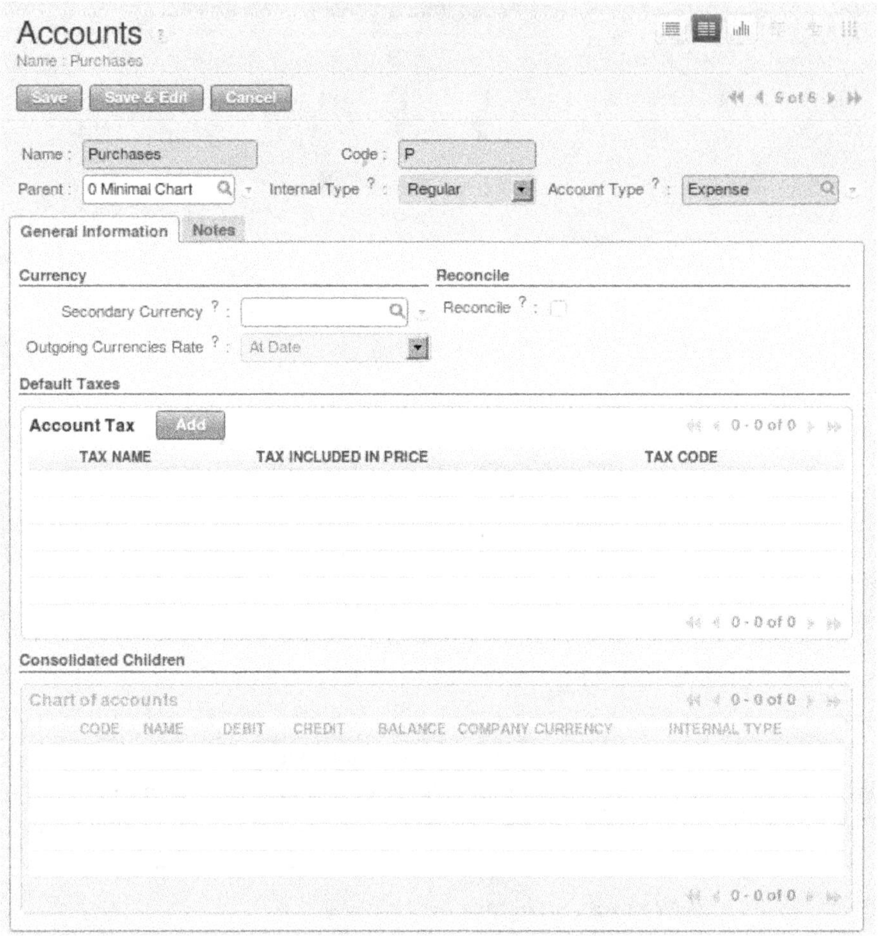

Figure 3.5: *New Account*

associate that text with the entry by clicking the *Tab* or *Enter* key to confirm your selection. You can also use the *Search* icon to open a list of available account types.

## Properties

You now define some default properties, so that you do not have to think about which account is used for a certain transaction every time you do something. The main new properties are the four that associate accounts payable and receivable to partners, and expenses and income to product categories.

Create properties using *Administration → Configuration → Parameters → Configuration Parameters* and then clicking the *New* button. This menu is only available in Extended view.

> **Selecting the correct field**
>
> When you have several fields with the same name, make sure to select the field for which the *Field Name* corresponds to the property name you are defining. Note that you can also duplicate properties and then change the required fields.

Table 3.3: Defining Properties

| Name | Field | Type | Value |
|------|-------|------|-------|
| property_account_payable | Account Payable | Many2One | (account.account) AP Payable |
| property_account_receivable | Account Receivable | Many2One | (account.account) AR Receivable |
| property_account_expense_categ | Expense Account | Many2One | (account.account) P Purchases |
| property_account_income_categ | Income Account | Many2One | (account.account) S Sales |

To check the result of your configuration, you can go to *Accounting* → *Customers* → *Customers* and open the form containing your company data. On the `Accounting` tab, you will notice that both the default account receivable and account payable have been filled.

> **Mistakes in configuring accounts and properties**
>
> It is easy to make mistakes in configuring accounts and their properties, but the consequences are not immediately obvious. You will mostly discover mistakes when trying to make a Purchase or Sales Order (see later, for example, *Driving your Purchases* (page 49)), where the accounts are required fields or, if you are diligent, when you set up Partners.
>
> If you configure them correctly at this stage, then fields will be completed automatically and you will never know a thing. If you do not configure all this correctly, then you will not be able to save the order form until you have corrected the problem or until you manually set the accounts.
>
> Since this configuration is quite tedious, you would do best by finding a certified Chart of Accounts that has already been set up to meet your needs, and adapt the predefined chart if necessary.

## 3.4.2 Configuring Journals

You will also need to configure some journals, which are used to record the transactions from one account to another when invoices are raised and then paid. Create journals from the menu *Accounting* → *Configuration* → *Financial Accounting* → *Journals* → *Journals* and then click the *New* button.

> **Default Values**
>
> Notice that when you select the journal type, the Display Mode will already be preset. An entry sequence for the journal will be created automatically when you save the journal. The default debit and credit account will be used as a counterpart when encoding manual journal entries. Debit and credit accounts are mandatory for bank journals.

Table 3.4: Defining Journals

| Journal Name | Code | Type | Display Mode | Default Debit Account | Default Credit Account |
|---|---|---|---|---|---|
| Purchase Journal | PUJ | Purchase | Sale/Purchase Journal View | P Purchases | P Purchases |
| Sales Journal | SAJ | Sale | Sale/Purchase Journal View | S Sales | S Sales |
| Bank Journal | BNK | Bank and Cheques | Bank/Cash Journal View | B Bank | B Bank |

In this example, validating a Purchase Order creates a draft invoice (see later, again for example, *Driving your Purchases* (page 49)), where a journal is required.

As with accounts and properties, if you configure them correctly at this stage, the fields will be completed automatically and you will never know a thing. If you do not configure all this correctly, there will be errors with the order form or corresponding draft invoice, until you have corrected the problem or until you manually set the journal.

## 3.4.3 Configuring the Main Company

In case you had chosen to *Skip Configuration Wizards* when you first created the database, you may configure your company information in the following manner. Start configuring your database by typing your company's name in the *Main Company*. When you print standard documents such as quotations, orders and invoices you will find this configuration information used in the document headers and footers.

To do this, click *Sales* → *Address Book* → *Customers* and click the name of the only company there, which is YourCompany . This gives you a read-only form view of the company, so make it editable by clicking the *Edit* button to the upper left of the form.

Change the contact name to match your first name and name. The company name and the contact name below are just an example.

- *Name* : Ambitious Plumbing Entreprises.

- *Contact Name* : George Turnbull.

Before you save this, look at the partner's accounting setup by clicking the *Accounting* tab. The fields *Account Receivable* and *Account Payable* have account values that were taken from the account properties you just created. You do not have to accept those values: you can enter any suitable account you like at this stage, although OpenERP limits the selection to accounts that make accounting sense.

Back at the first tab, *General*, change any other fields you like, such as the address and phone numbers, then click *Save*. This changes one Contact for the Partner, which is sufficient for the example.

From the *MAIN MENU*, click *Administration → Companies → Companies* and edit the only entry there. Please note that you have to keep your own company data, but for the example we use the Ambitious Plumbing company.

- *Company Name*: AmbiPlum,

- *Partner*: should already show Ambitious Plumbing Enterprises,

- *Report Header*: Ambitious Plumbing,

- *Report Footer 1*: type your slogan, i.e. Best Plumbing Services, Great Prices,

- *Report Footer 2*: type your company details, such as bank account or Ambitious - our Registered Company Details.

Figure *Changing Company Details* (page 32) shows the effect of this. You can also change various other company-wide parameters for reports and scheduling in the other tabs, and you can upload a company logo of a specific size for the reports. Click *Save* to store the changes.

You can leave the currency at its default setting of EUR for this example. Or you can change it in this Company and the two default Pricelists (*Sales → Configuration → Pricelists → Pricelists*) if you did not set the correct company currency in the Configuration Wizard.

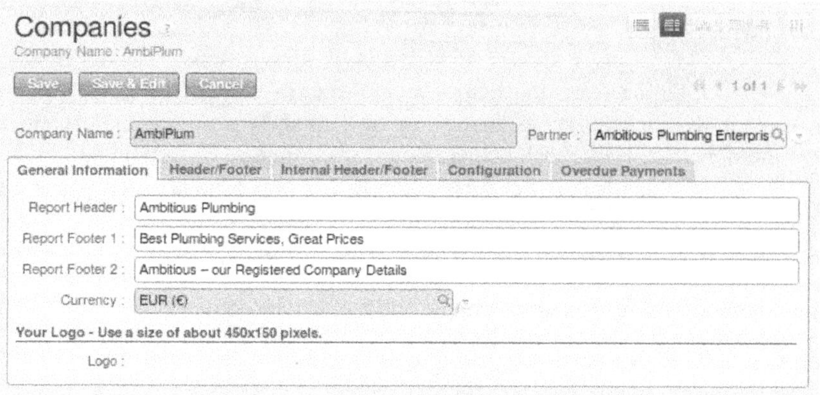

Figure 3.6: *Changing Company Details*

## 3.4.4 Creating Partner Categories, Partners and their Contacts

You will now create a supplier category and a customer category. Partner categories are useful for organizing groups of partners, but have no special behaviour that affects partners, so you can assign them as you like. Then you will define one supplier and one customer, with a contact for each.

To do this, go to the menu *Sales → Configuration → Address Book → Partner Categories* and click *New* to open a new form for defining *Partner Categories*. Define the two categories that follow by just entering their *Category Name* and saving them:

- Suppliers,

- Customers.

Then create two partners from the menu *Sales → Address Book → Customers*. OpenERP allows you to create both suppliers and customers from this menu. Please note that we provide some example data, but of course you should define your own customers and suppliers. Feel free to also complete the address, which we don't do in our example. Click the *New* button to open a blank form and then add the following data for the first partner:

- *Name* : Plumbing Component Suppliers,

- *Customer* checkbox : unchecked,

- *Supplier* checkbox : checked,

- *Contact Name* : Jean Poolley,

- *Address Type* : Default,

- click *Add* and select Suppliers to add the category to the *Partner Categories* field by selecting it from the Search Partner Categories list,

- then save the partner by clicking the *Save* button.

Figure 3.7: *New Partner Form*

Figure *New Partner Form* (page 33) shows the result.

> **Contact Types**
>
> If you have recorded several contacts for the same partner you can specify which contact is used for various documents by specifying the *Address Type*.
>
> For example, the delivery address can differ from the invoice address for a partner. If the Address Types are correctly assigned, OpenERP can automatically select the appropriate address during the creation of the document – an invoice is addressed to the contact that has been assigned the Address Type of Invoice, otherwise to the Default address.

For the second partner, proceed just as you did for the first, with the following data:

- *Name* : Smith and Offspring,

- *Customer* checkbox : checked,

- *Supplier* checkbox : unchecked,

- *Contact Name* : Stephen Smith,

- *Address Type* : Default,

- add Customers in the *Categories* field,

- *Save* the form.

To check your work, you can go to the menu *Sales* → *Configuration* → *Address Book* → *Partner Categories* and click on each category in turn to see the companies in the category.

---

**Multiple Partner Categories**

If this partner was also a supplier, then you would add Suppliers to the categories as well, but there is no need to do so in this example. You can assign a partner to multiple categories at all levels of the hierarchy.

---

## 3.4.5 Creating Products and their Categories

Unlike partner categories and their assigned partners, product categories do have an effect on the products assigned to them – and a product may belong to only one category. Under the main menu link *Warehouse* or *Sales*, select the menu *Configuration* → *Product* → *Products Categories* and click *New* to get an empty form for defining a product category.

Enter Radiators in the *Name* field. Click *Save*. You will see that other fields, specifically those in the *Accounting Properties* section, have been automatically filled in with values of accounts and journals. These are the values that will affect products – equivalent fields in a product will take on these values if they, too, are blank when their form is saved.

---

**Property Fields**

Properties have a rather unusual behaviour. They are defined by parameters in the menus in *Administration* → *Configuration* → *Parameters* → *Configuration Parameters*, and they update fields only when a form is saved, and only when the fields are empty at the time the form is saved. You can manually override any of these properties as you need.

Property fields are used throughout the OpenERP system and extensively in a multi-company environment. There, property fields in a partner form can be populated with different values depending on the user's company. For example, the payment conditions for a partner could differ depending on the company from which it is addressed.

---

> **UOM**
>
> UOM is an abbreviation for Unit of Measure. OpenERP manages multiple units of measure for each product: you can buy in tons and sell in kgs, for example. The conversion between each category is made automatically (so long as you have set up the conversion rate in the product form first).

> **Managing Double Units of Measure**
>
> The whole management of stock can be carried out with double units of measure (UOM and UOS – for Unit of Sale). For example, an agro-food company can stock and sell ham by piece, but buy and value it by weight. There is no direct relationship between these two units, so a weighing operation has to be done.
>
> This functionality is crucial in the agro-food industry, and can be equally important in fabrication, chemicals and many other industries.

Now create a new product through the *Warehouse* or *Sales* menu:

1. Go to *Products* → *Products* and click *New*.

2. Create a product – type `Titanium Alloy Radiator` in the *Name* field.

3. The *Product Type* field should be assigned as `Stockable Product`. The fields *Procurement Method*, *Supply method*, *Default Unit Of Measure*, and *Purchase Unit Of Measure* should stay at their default values. For more information about these methods, please refer to chapter *Procurement Methods – Make to Stock and Make to Order* (page 104).

4. Enter `57.50` into the *Cost Price* field and `132.50` into the *Sale Price* field.

5. Click the *Search* icon to the right of the *Category* field to select the *Radiators* category.

6. Click the *Accounting* tab, then click *Save* and observe that *Accounting Properties* here remain empty. When product transactions occur, the Income and Expense accounts that you have just defined in the Product Category are used by the Product unless an account is specified here, directly in the product, to override that.

7. Once the product is saved, it changes to a non-editable state. If you had entered data incorrectly or left a required field blank, an error message would pop-up, the form would have stayed editable and you would need to click from tab to tab to find a field colored red that would have to be correctly filled in.

## 3.4.6  Stock Locations

Click *Warehouse* → *Inventory Control* → *Location Structure* to see the hierarchy of stock locations. These locations have been defined by the minimal default data loaded when the database was created. You will use this default structure in this example.

---

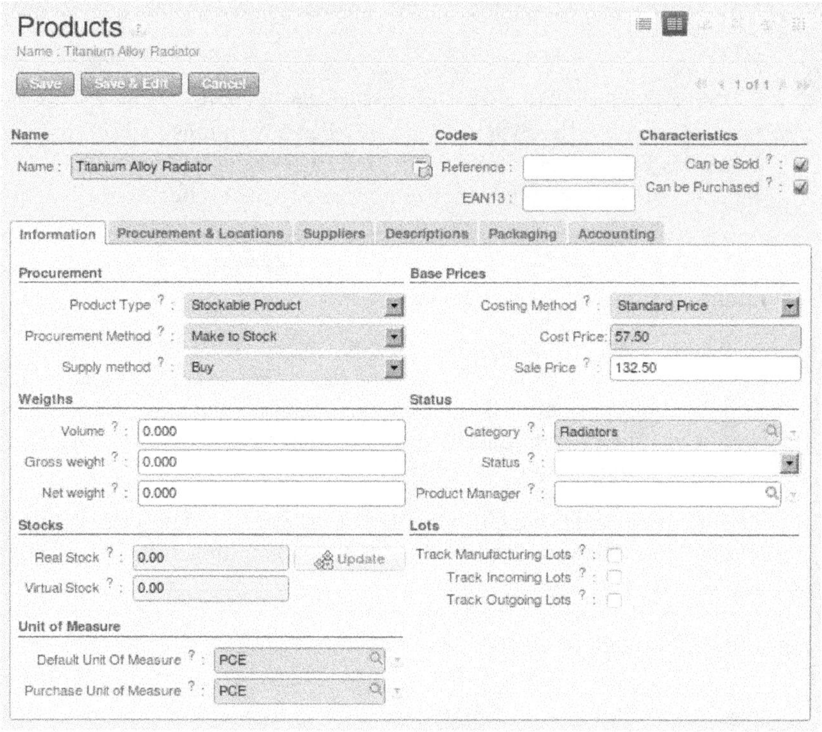

Figure 3.8: *Product Form*

OpenERP has three predefined top-level location types , `Physical Locations` and `Partner Locations` that act as their names suggest, and `Virtual Locations` that are used by OpenERP for its own purposes.

1. From the *Main Menu* click *Warehouse* → *Configuration* → *Warehouse Management* → *Locations* to reach a list view of the locations (not the tree view).

2. Click the `Clear` button to display a complete list of all predefined locations.

3. Click the name of a location, such as `Physical Locations/Ambitious Plumbing Enterprises` to open a descriptive form view. Each location has a *Location Type* and a *Parent Location* that defines the hierarchical structure. While you are here you might have to change the location's name to `Ambitious Plumbing Enterprises`.

4. From the *Main Menu* click *Warehouse* → *Configuration Warehouse Management* → *Warehouses* to view a list of warehouses. There is only the one at the moment, named after your company, or in the example `Ambitious Plumbing Enterprises` .

A Warehouse contains an input location, a stock location and an output location for sold products. You can associate a warehouse with a partner to give the warehouse an address. That does not have to be your own company (although it can be); you can easily specify another partner who may be holding stock on your behalf.

> **Location Structure**
>
> Each warehouse is composed of three locations *Location Input*, *Location Output*, and *Location Stock*. Your available stock is given by the contents of the *Location Stock* and its child locations.
>
> So the *Location Input* can be placed as a child of the *Location Stock*, which means that when *Location Stock* is interrogated for product quantities, it also takes into account the contents of the *Location Input*. *Location Input* could be used as a goods-in QC location. The *Location Output* must never be placed as a child of *Location Stock*, since items in *Location Output*, which can be considered to be packed ready for customer shipment, should not be thought of as available for sales elsewhere.

## 3.4.7 Setting up a Chart of Accounts

You can set up a chart of accounts during the creation of a database, but for this exercise you will start with the minimal chart that you created (just a handful of required accounts without hierarchy, tax or subtotals).

A number of account charts have been predefined for OpenERP, some of which meet the needs of national authorities (the number of those created for OpenERP is growing as various contributors create and freely publish them). You can take one of those without changing it if it is suitable, or you can take any chart as your starting point and design a complete chart of accounts to meet your exact needs, including accounts for inventory, asset depreciation, equity and taxation.

You can also run multiple charts of accounts in parallel – so you can put all of your transaction accounts into several charts, with different arrangements for taxation and depreciation, aggregated differently for various needs.

Before you can use any chart of accounts, you need to specify a Fiscal Year. This defines the different time periods available for accounting transactions.

Create a Fiscal Year manually from *Accounting → Configuration → Financial Accounting → Periods → Fiscal Years*.

- In the *Fiscal Year* field, type the name of the current fiscal year (e.g. 2011),

- In the *Code* field, type the code of the current fiscal year (e.g. 11 or 2011),

- In the *Start Date* field, type the starting date of your company's fiscal year (e.g. 01/01/2011),

- In the *End Date* field, type the ending date of your company's fiscal year (e.g. 12/31/2011),

- Click the *Create Monthly Periods* button, if you have monthly declarations or click the *Create 3 Months Periods* button for quarterly declarations,

- Usually you will also create an extra period *00* to post your opening balance and outstanding invoices. To do this, click the *New* button, then type *00/2011* as the Period Name, *00/2011* as the Code and the first day of your financial year as the Start of Period and the End of Period dates. Then check the Opening/Closing Period checkbox.

Click *Accounting → Charts → Charts of Accounts* to open a *Chart of Accounts* form where you define exactly what you want to see. Simply click *Open Charts* to accept the defaults and display a hierarchical structure of the accounts.

## 3.4.8 Make a Backup of the Database

If you know the super-administrator password, make a backup of your database using the procedure described below. Then restore it to a new database: testing .

As a super-administrator, you do not only have rights to create new databases, but also to:

- backup databases,

- delete databases,

- restore databases.

All of these operations can be carried out from the *Databases* button in the web client's *Login* screen.

---

**Backup (copy) a Database**

To make a copy of a database, go to the web *Login* screen and click the *Databases* button. Then click the *Backup* button, select the database you want to copy and enter the super-administrator password. Click the *Backup* button to confirm that you want to copy the database.

---

**Drop (delete) a Database**

To delete a database, go to the web *Login* screen and click the *Databases* button. Then click the *Drop* button, select the database you want to delete and enter the super-administrator password. Click the *Drop* button to confirm that you want to delete the database.

---

**Restore a Database**

To restore a database, go to the web *Login* screen and click the *Databases* button. Then click the *Restore* button, click the *Choose File* button to select the database you want to restore. Give the database a name and enter the super-administrator password. Click the *Restore* button to confirm that you want to install a new copy of the selected database. To restore a database, you need to have an existing copy, of course.

---

> **Duplicating a Database**
>
> To duplicate a database, you can:
>
> 1. make a backup file on your PC from this database.
>
> 2. restore this database from the backup file on your PC, and give it a new name.
>
> This can be a useful way of making a test database from a production database. You can try out the operation of a new configuration, new modules, or just the import of new data.

A system administrator can configure OpenERP to restrict access to some of these database functions so that your security is enhanced in normal production use.

This operation enables you to test the new configuration on testing so that you can be sure everything works as designed. Then if the tests are successful, you can make a new database from, perhaps called live or production, for your real work.

From here on, connect to this new testing database logged in as admin if you can. If you have to make corrections, do that on YourCompany and copy it to a new testing database to continue checking it.

Or you can just continue working with the YourCompany database to get through this chapter. You can recreate YourCompany quite quickly if something goes wrong and you cannot recover from it but, again, you would need to know your super-administrator password for that.

# 3.5 Testing a Complete Purchase Cycle according to an Example

To familiarize yourself with the system workflow, you will test a purchase-sales workflow in two phases.

The first consists of a product purchase, which requires the following operations:

1. Place a purchase order with Plumbing Component Suppliers for 10 Titanium Alloy Radiators at a unit price of 56.00.

2. Receive these products at your Goods In.

3. Generate a purchase invoice.

4. Pay your supplier.

Then, you will sell some of these products, using this sequence:

1. Receive a sales order for 6 Titanium Alloy Radiators from Smith and Sons, sold at a unit price of 130.00.

2. Dispatch the products.

3. Invoice the customer.

4. Receive the payment.

### 3.5.1 Purchase Order

To place a Purchase Order with your supplier, use the menu *Purchases* → *Purchase Management* → *Purchase Orders* and click the *New* button.

Complete the following field:

- *Supplier* : Plumbing Component Suppliers.

As you complete the *Supplier* field, OpenERP automatically completes the *Address* field and the *Pricelist* field from information it takes from the Partner record.

Enter the following information in the Purchase Order Lines (click *New*):

- *Product* : Titanium Alloy Radiator - type in part of this name then press the tab key to complete it, or click the *Search* icon at the end of the line to bring a search box (if product is previously configured)

When you have selected a product on the product line, OpenERP automatically completes the following fields from information it finds in the Product record:

- *Product UOM* : the unit of measure for this product,

- *Description* : the detailed description of the product,

- *Scheduled Date* : based on the product lead time,

- *Unit Price* : the unit price of the product,

- *Analytic account* : if any account is specified and if you belong to the User Group *Useability / Analytic Accounting* (see menu *Administration* → *Users* → *Users*) then it will appear on the order line (it is not in this example),

- *Taxes* : applicable taxes defined in the partner, if specified, otherwise in the product, if specified (there are no taxes in this example).

You can edit any of these fields to suit the requirements of the purchase order at the time of entry. Change the:

- *Quantity* : 10,

- *Unit Price* to 56.00.

Save the order line and close the *Order Line* window by clicking the *Save & Close* button. You can then save the whole one-line order by clicking *Save*, which makes the form non-editable.

It is now in a state of Request for Quotation. To approve the quotation, click *Convert to Purchase Order*, which corresponds to an approval from a manager or from Accounts within your own company and moves the order into Approved state.

If you click the *Delivery & Invoicing* tab you will see the delivery *Destination* is your own company's Stock location and that the invoice was created from the order. It is not entirely obvious at this stage, but the invoice is in a draft state so it can be edited and, crucially, it has no accounting impact yet: it is just ready for your accounting group to activate it.

## 3.5.2 Receiving Goods

After confirming the order, you would wait for the delivery of the products from your supplier. Typically this would be somebody in Stores, who would:

1. Open the menu *Warehouse → Warehouse Management → Incoming Shipments*.

> **From the Purchase Order**
>
> You could have clicked the *Receptions* link to the right of the Purchase Order to reach the same screen, but this would confuse the purchasing role with the stores role. That link is very useful during testing and training, however.

2. When the *Incoming Shipments* window appears, select the name of the entry in the list (IN/00001) to display the Packing List itself – you would usually do a search for the supplier name or order number in a list that was larger than this – then click *Process* to load the *Process Document* form.

3. Click *Validate* to indicate that you are receiving the whole quantity of 10 units.

At this point you have accepted 10 units into your company, in a location that you have already seen.

Using the menu *Purchases → Products → Products* you can find the product *Titanium Alloy Radiators* with *Real Stock* and *Virtual Stock* 10. Open the product form, and click the *Stock by Location* link at the right side of the screen to see the *Real Stock* and *Virtual Stock* of this product in various locations. Now select the checkbox in front of the Stock and Suppliers locations. The right side menu appears. Click the *Location Inventory Overview* report to see the inventory valuation for each of these two locations.

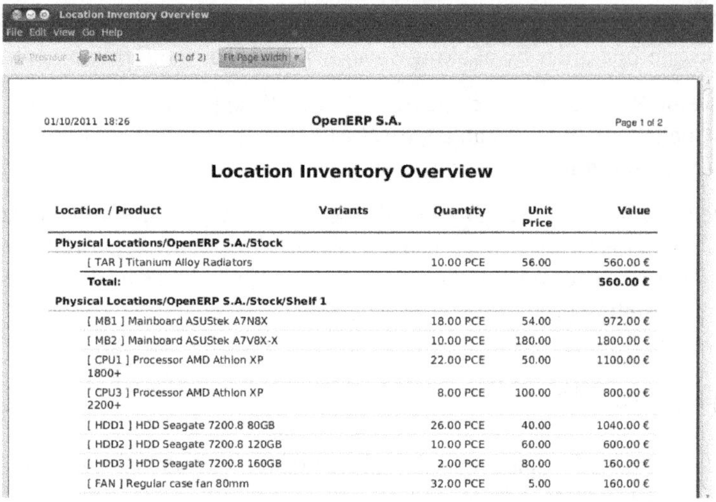

01/10/2011 18:26 OpenERP S.A. Page 1 of 2

**Location Inventory Overview**

| Location / Product | Variants | Quantity | Unit Price | Value |
|---|---|---|---|---|
| **Physical Locations/OpenERP S.A./Stock** | | | | |
| [ TAR ] Titanium Alloy Radiators | | 10.00 PCE | 56.00 | 560.00 € |
| **Total:** | | | | **560.00 €** |
| **Physical Locations/OpenERP S.A./Stock/Shelf 1** | | | | |
| [ MB1 ] Mainboard ASUStek A7N8X | | 18.00 PCE | 54.00 | 972.00 € |
| [ MB2 ] Mainboard ASUStek A7V8X-X | | 10.00 PCE | 180.00 | 1800.00 € |
| [ CPU1 ] Processor AMD Athlon XP 1800+ | | 22.00 PCE | 50.00 | 1100.00 € |
| [ CPU3 ] Processor AMD Athlon XP 2200+ | | 8.00 PCE | 100.00 | 800.00 € |
| [ HDD1 ] HDD Seagate 7200.8 80GB | | 26.00 PCE | 40.00 | 1040.00 € |
| [ HDD2 ] HDD Seagate 7200.8 120GB | | 10.00 PCE | 60.00 | 600.00 € |
| [ HDD3 ] HDD Seagate 7200.8 160GB | | 2.00 PCE | 80.00 | 160.00 € |
| [ FAN ] Regular case fan 80mm | | 32.00 PCE | 5.00 | 160.00 € |

Figure 3.9: *List of Products and their Stock Levels*

**Traceability in Double-Entry**

OpenERP operates a double-entry stock transfer scheme similar to double-entry accounting. Because of this you can carry out various analyses of stock levels in your warehouse, along with the corresponding levels in Partner Location at your Supplier. The double-entry system, similar to that of accounting, enables you to keep track of stock movements quite easily, and to resolve any errors that occur.

### 3.5.3 Invoice Control

When you have received an invoice from your supplier (which would usually be sent to your Accounts department), go to the menu *Accounting* → *Suppliers* → *Supplier Invoices* to open a list of supplier invoices waiting for receipt. These invoices enable your Accounts Department to match the the price and quantities ordered against the price and quantities on the supplier's invoice (and since it is not uncommon to receive an invoice showing details more favourable to the supplier than those agreed at the time of purchase, this is a useful function).

In this example, you created an invoice automatically when you confirmed the supplier's Purchase Order. That is because the *Invoicing Control* field on the order was set to `From Order` (the default option). Other options enable you to create invoices at the time of receiving goods or manually. The initial state of an invoice is `Draft` .

Now click the invoice for your order `PO00001` to display its contents. You can compare the goods that you have recorded there with the invoice received from your supplier. If there is a difference, it is possible to change the invoice lines to, for example, add a delivery charge. Select the correct *Invoice Date* and click *Approve* to confirm the invoice and put it into the `Open` state.

Accounting entries are generated automatically once the invoice is validated. You can check the entry from the Other Info tab, in the *Journal Entry* field. To see the effects on your chart of accounts, go to the menu *Accounting → Charts → Chart of Accounts*, and click *Open Charts* at the *Chart of Accounts* page to see that you have a debit of 560.00 in the Purchases account and a credit of 560.00 in the Payable account.

> **Invoice Control**
>
> Should your purchase invoice have to be checked by the purchaser first, he can go to the menu *Purchases → Invoice Control → Supplier Invoices to Receive* to check whether the invoice corresponds with the order (or the goods receipt according to the Invoice Control settings).

## 3.5.4 Paying the Supplier

Select the menu *Accounting → Suppliers → Supplier Invoices* and click the *Unpaid* button for a list of supplier invoices that have not yet been paid. In practice, you would search for the invoice by order number or, more generally, for invoices nearing their payment date. You can type PO00001 in the *Source Document* box to find the invoice.

Open the invoice and click the *Pay Invoice* button. It opens the *Pay Invoice* window in new tab with a description of the payment.

Supplier and Date comes automatically from invoice. You just have to enter the Payment Method (i.e. the corresponding bank journal). When you select the payment method, you will notice that the corresponding invoice is displayed in Supplier Invoices and Outstanding Transactions, and that the Amount is filled automatically. Then click the *Validate* button to post this entry and consider the invoice as Paid.

> **Payment of an Invoice**
>
> The method described here is for companies that do not use their accounting system to pay bills, but just to record the payments. If you are using the account module with all its features, other, more efficient, methods let you manage payments, such as entering bank statements, reconciling paperwork, using tools for preparing payments, interfacing with banks.

You can monitor the accounting impact of paying the invoice through the chart of accounts available from the menu *Accounting → Charts → Chart of Accounts*. OpenERP automatically creates accounting entries from the payment, and can reconcile the payment to the invoice. You now have a new transaction that has debited the Payable account with 560.00 and credited the Bank account.

If you look in *Accounting → Journal Entries → Journal Entries* you will see both accounting transactions, one in the Purchase Journal and another one in the Bank Journal, both with the Posted state.

# 3.6 Testing a Complete Sales Cycle according to an Example

## 3.6.1 Sales Order

In OpenERP, sales proposals and sales orders are managed using documents that are based on the same common functionality as purchase orders, so you will recognize the following documents in general but see changes to their detail and to their workflows. To create a new sales proposal, use the menu *Sales → Sales → Sales Orders* and click the *New* button which creates a new order as a `Quotation`, then:

1. Select the *Customer* `Smith and Offspring`. This has the effect of automatically completing several other fields: *Ordering Contact*, *Invoice Address*, *Shipping Address*, and the *Pricelist* `Public Pricelist (EUR)`. They are all only defaults, so these fields can be modified as you need.

2. Click the *New* button in *Sales Order Lines* section to open a *Sales Order Lines* window.

3. Select the product `Titanium Alloy Radiator`. Although the *Product* field is not itself required, it is used by OpenERP to select the specific product so that several other fields can be automatically completed on the order line of the quotation, such as *Description*, *Unit of Measure*, *Unit Price*, *Procurement Method*, *Delivery Lead Time*, and *Taxes*.

4. Change the *Quantity (UoM)* to 6 and the *Unit Price* to `130.00`. Then click *Save & Close* and the line appears on the quotation form.

5. On the *Other Information* tab of this Sales Order, select a *Picking Policy* of `Complete Delivery` and a *Shipping Policy* of `Invoice on Order After Delivery` from the dropdown menu lists.

6. Return to the first tab *Sales Order* and validate the document by clicking *Confirm Order* which calculates prices and changes the order's state from `Quotation` to `In Progress` as shown in screenshot *Sales Order Form* (page 44). If you were in negotiation with the prospective customer, you would click *Compute* and *Save*, to keep the document in `Quotation` state for as long as necessary.

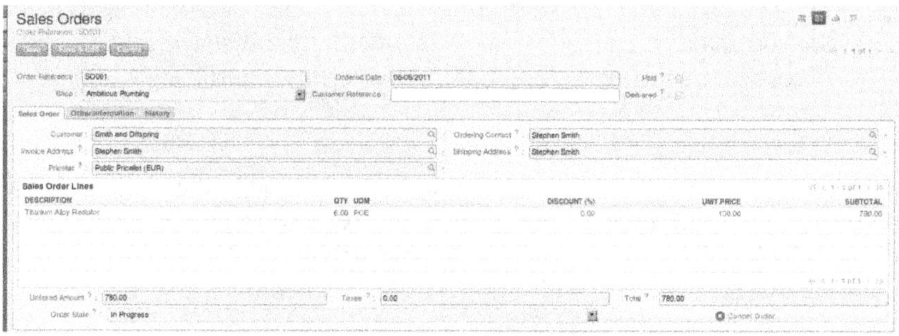

Figure 3.10: *Sales Order Form*

---

7. In the last tab of the order *History*, you can see the *Picking List* that has been created and you will be able to see any invoices that relate to this order when they are generated.

Go to *Sales → Products → Products* to display a list of products: just the one, `Titanium Alloy Radiator` , currently exists in this example. Its *Real Stock* still shows `10.00` but its *Virtual Stock* now shows `4.00` to reflect the new future requirement of 6 units for dispatch.

## 3.6.2 Preparing Goods for Shipping to Customers

The stores manager selects the menu *Warehouse → Warehouse Management → Delivery Orders* to get a list of orders to dispatch. For this example, find the Delivery Order related to the sales order which you have created. You should click the `Available` button, to see all delivery orders, because your delivery order will be in `Confirmed` state and not yet in `Available` state. Open the Delivery Order concerned.

> **Running Schedulers**
>
> At the moment, your Sales Order is waiting for products to be reserved to fulfil it. A stock reservation activity takes place periodically to calculate the needs, which also takes customer priorities into account. The calculation can be started from the menu *Warehouse → Schedulers → Compute Schedulers*. Running this automatically reserves products (i.e. the status will be set to Available if the products are in stock).
>
> If you do not want to have to work out your stock needs but have a lean workflow you can install the `mrp_jit` (Just In Time) module.

Although OpenERP has automatically been made aware that items on this order will need to be dispatched, it has not yet assigned any specific items from any location to fulfil it. It is ready to move `6.00 Titanium Alloy Radiators` from the *Stock* location to the *Customers* location, so start this process by clicking *Check Availability*. The *Move* line has now changed from the `Confirmed` state to the `Available` state.

Then click the *Process* button to reach the *Process Document* window, where you click the *Validate* button to transfer the 6 radiators to the customer.

To analyze stock movements that you have made during these operations, go to *Warehouse → Product → Products* and select the radiator by clicking the checkbox in front of it, then click the action *Stock by Location* which is at the right most side to see that your stocks have reduced to 4 radiators and the generic `Customers` location has a level of 6 radiators.

## 3.6.3 Invoicing Goods

Use the menu *Accounting → Customers → Customer Invoices* to open a list of Sales invoices generated by OpenERP. If they are in the `Draft` state, it means that they do not yet have any impact on the accounting system. You will find a draft invoice has been created for the order `SO001` once you have dispatched the goods because you had selected `Invoice on Order After Delivery`.

---

Once you confirm an invoice, OpenERP assigns it a unique number, and all of the corresponding accounting entries are generated. So open the invoice and click *Validate* to do that and move the invoice into an `Open` state with a number of `SAJ/2011/0001`.

You can send your customer the invoice for payment at this stage. Click *Print Invoice* to get a PDF document that can be printed or emailed to the customer.

The PDF of your invoice will automatically be added as an attachment. This gives you a permanent non-editable record of your invoice on the OpenERP system.

Review your chart of accounts to check the impact of these activities on your accounting. You will see the new revenue line from the invoice.

### 3.6.4 Customer Payment

Registering an invoice payment by a customer is essentially the same as the process of paying a supplier. From the menu *Accounting → Customers → Customer Invoices*, click the name of the invoice that you want to mark as paid:

1. Use the *Payment* button which opens a new window *Pay Invoice*.

2. Select the *Payment Method*, for this example select `Bank Journal` then validate the entry.

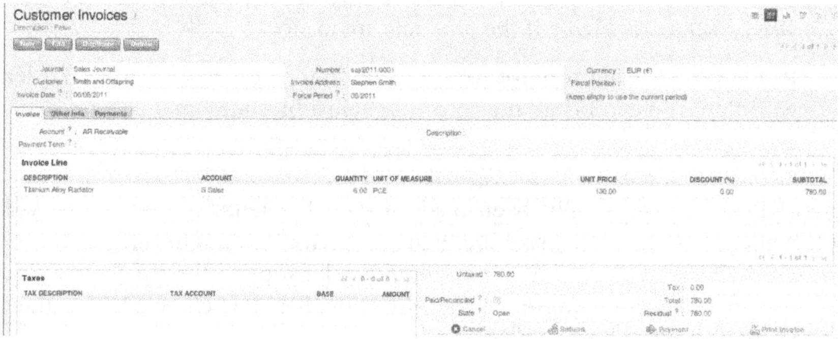

Figure 3.11: *Invoice Form*

Check your Chart of Accounts as before to see that you now have a healthy bank balance in the `Bank` account.

# Part II

# Advanced Features in Purchase Quotation Management

*To manage your manufacturing, you do not need all the elements described in this book. But we find it very important to include an integrated flow, from the first quotation to the final billing of the suppliers including all the steps: quotation, order, receiving goods, inventory, manufacturing and billing.*

# Driving your Purchases

4

*In the preceding chapters you saw how to use customer invoices and delivery notes in OpenERP. This chapter is about the management of purchases, the process ahead of these two operations. You will now see how OpenERP handles and simplifies this and the control of purchases from suppliers.*

For this chapter you can continue using the database already created or you should start with a fresh database that includes demonstration data, with `purchase` and its dependencies installed and no particular chart of accounts configured.

## 4.1 All the Elements of a Complete Workflow

The supplier or purchase order is the document that lets you manage price negotiations, control supplier invoices, handle goods receipts and synchronize all of these documents.

Let us start by looking at the following order workflow:

1. Price request to the supplier,

2. Confirmation of purchase,

3. Receipt and control of products,

4. Control of invoicing.

### 4.1.1 Setting up your Database

To set up a system for these examples, create a new database with demonstration data in it, and select the *Extended* interface when you log in as the *admin* user. You can enter your own company details when asked, or just use the default if you want. Then, using the Configuration Wizard, select *Purchase Management* in the *Install Applications* section to install the `purchase` module, which also installs several other modules as dependencies. Continue the remainder of this chapter logged in as the *admin* user.

### 4.1.2 Price Request from the Supplier

To enter data for a new supplier price request (i.e. request for quotation), use the menu *Purchases → Purchase Management → Request for Quotation*. When you click *New*, OpenERP opens a blank request for quotation form that you use for requesting prices from a supplier. This is shown in the figure *Data Entry for a Purchase Order* (page 50). If the price request came from an automatic procurement created by OpenERP, you will find a reference to the document that generated the request in the *Origin* field.

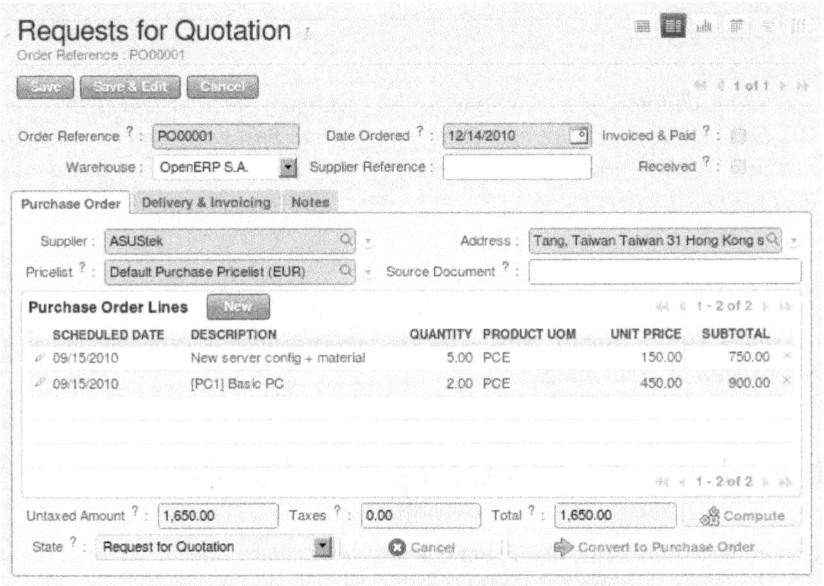

Figure 4.1: *Data Entry for a Purchase Order*

---

**Managing Alerts**

If you install the `warning` module, you will be able to define alerts that appear when the purchaser enters a price request or order. You can set alerts on the product and on the supplier.

---

The internal reference, the date and the warehouse the products should be delivered to, are completed automatically by OpenERP, but you can change these values if needed. Next, when you select a supplier, OpenERP automatically completes the contact address for the supplier. The pricelist is also automatically completed from the pricelist in the supplier form. This should bring in all of the conditions that you have negotiated with the supplier for a given period.

---

**Supplier Selection**

Searching for a supplier is limited to all of the partners in the system that have the *Supplier* checkbox checked. If you do not find your supplier, it might be worth checking the whole list of all partners to make sure that the supplier does not yet exist without the Supplier checkbox being checked.

---

Once the main body of the purchase order has been completed, you can enter the product lines.

When you have selected the product, OpenERP automatically completes the other fields in the form:

---

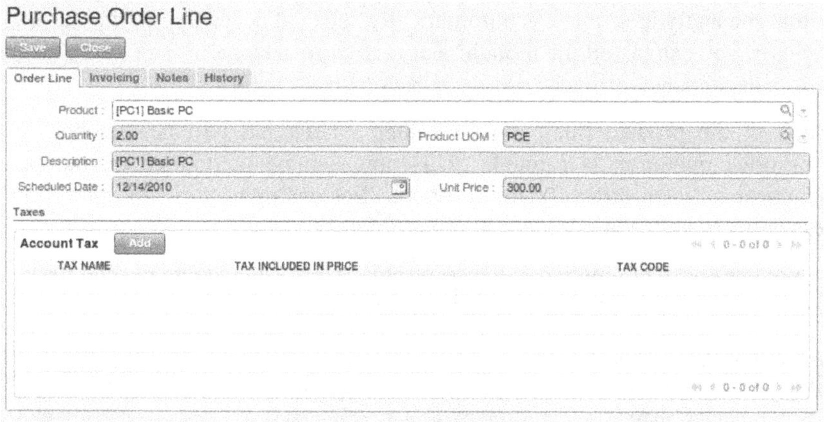

Figure 4.2: *Purchase Order Line*

- *Product UoM*, taken from the *Purchase Unit of Measure* field in the product form,

- The *Description* of the product in the supplier's language,

- *Scheduled Date*, calculated from the order date and the delivery lead time for the supplier (for the given product),

- *Unit Price*, taken from the supplier's pricelist,

- *Taxes*, taken from the information on the product form and partner form, depending on the rules seen in *Financial Analysis*.

---

**Product Wording and Code**

When you enter supplier names in the product form, you can set a name and a product code for each individual supplier. If you do that, OpenERP will then use those details instead of your own internal product names for that selected supplier.

---

If you work with management by case, you can also set the analytic account that should be used to report all the purchase costs. The costs will then be reported at the receipt of the supplier invoice.

---

**Management by Case**

Analytic accounts can be very useful for all companies that manage costs by case, by site, by project or by folder. To work with several analytic axes, you should install the module `purchase_analytic_plans`, by selecting *Purchase Analytic Plans* in the *Reconfigure* wizard and clicking *Configure*.

---

To make sure that the analytic account is automatically selected according to the partner, the date, the products or the user, you can install the module `account_analytic_default` (which is installed automatically as a dependency of `purchase_analytic_plans`).

In the *Notes* tab of the product line, you can enter a note that will be attached when the order confirmation or price quotation is printed. This note can be predefined on the product form to automatically appear on each order for that product. For example, you can enter "Do not forget to send by express delivery as specified in our contract reference 1234."

Once the document has been completed, you can print it as a price estimate to send to the supplier. You can set a note for the attention of the supplier in the form's third tab.

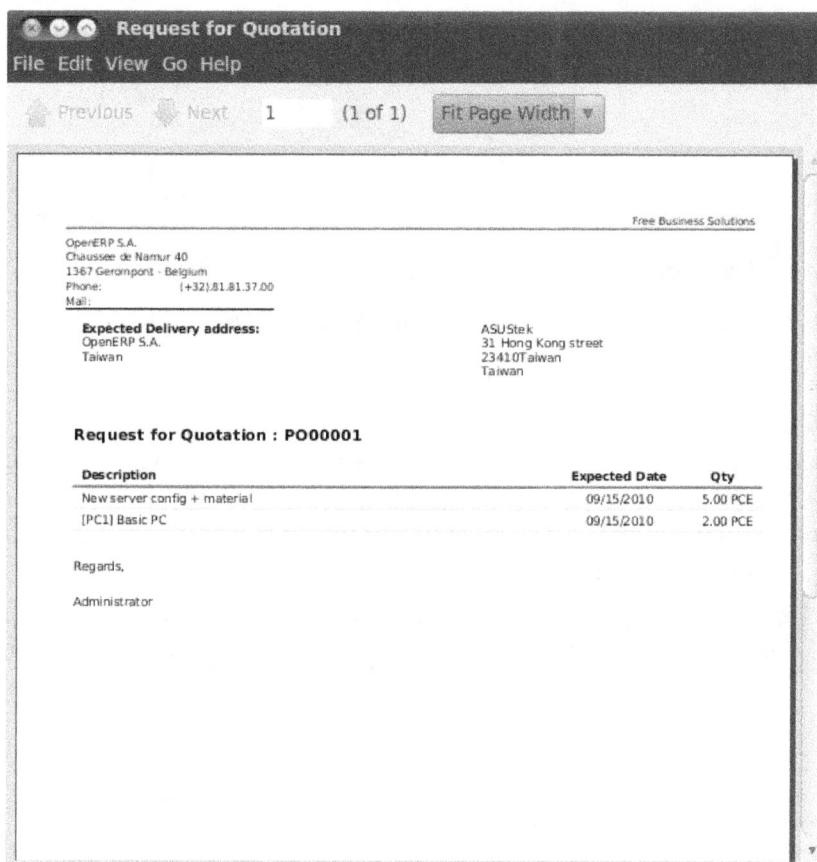

Figure 4.3: *Printing the Supplier Price Quotation*

Then leave the document in the `Request for Quotation` state. When you receive a response from the supplier, use the menu *Purchases → Purchase Management → Requests for Quotation*. Select the order and complete its details.

When you want to approve the order, use the button *Convert to Purchase Order*. The price request then passes into the `Approved` state. No further changes are possible.

Requests for Quotation (purchase.order)

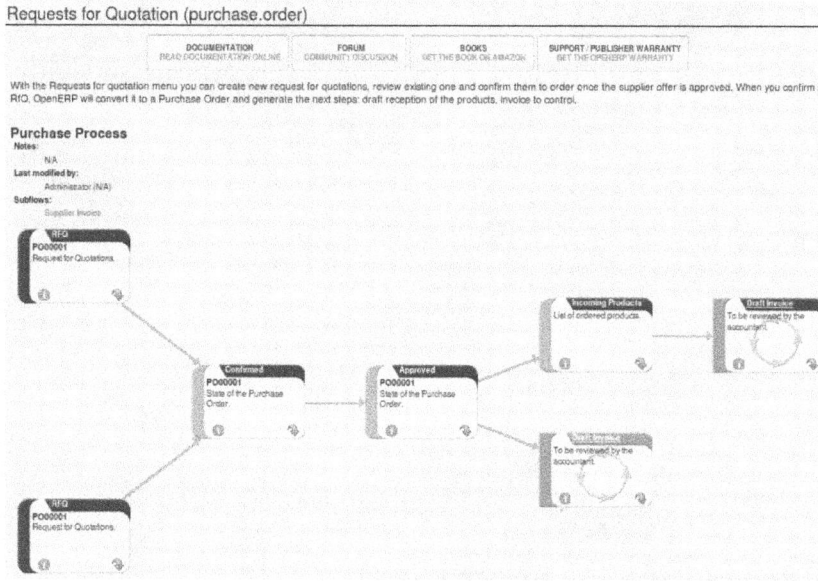

Figure 4.4: *Purchase Order Process*

## 4.1.3 Goods Receipt

Once the order has been approved, OpenERP automatically prepares the goods receipt order in the draft state for you. To get a list of the products you are waiting for from your suppliers, use the menu *Warehouse → Warehouse Management → Incoming Shipments*.

> **Purchasing Services**
>
> If you buy services from your supplier, OpenERP does not generate a goods receipt note. There is no service receipt equivalent to a goods receipt.

Select the document that corresponds to the item that you are receiving. Usually, the goods receipt note is found by making a search on the order reference or the supplier name. You can then confirm the receipt of the products.

As described in *Your Warehouse* (page 71), if you receive only part of the order, OpenERP manages the remainder of that order. A second receipt note is then automatically created for the goods not received. You can cancel it if you think that you will never receive the remaining products.

After receiving the goods, OpenERP will show you which orders are open and the state of their receipt and invoicing if you return to the list of orders.

## 4.1.4 Control of Invoicing

To control supplier invoicing, OpenERP provides three systems as standard, which can differ order by order:

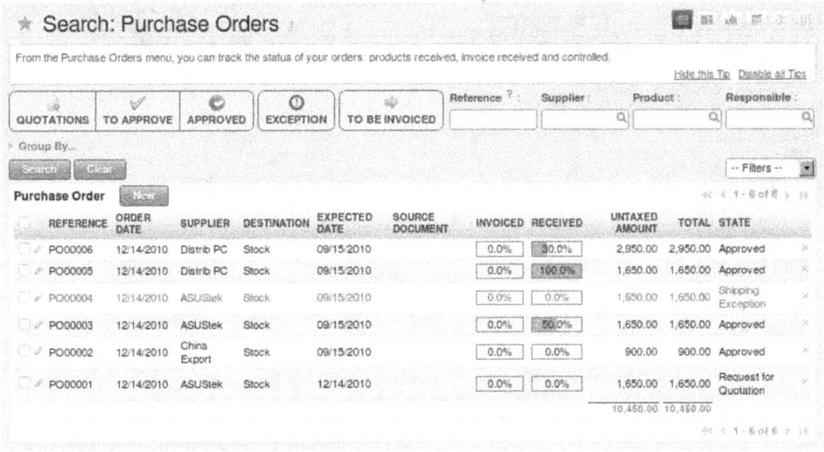

Figure 4.5: *List of Open Orders, and their Receipt and Invoice Status*

- *From Order* : invoicing based on quantities ordered,

- *From Picking* : invoicing based on quantities received,

- *Manual* : manual invoicing.

The mode of invoicing control is set in the second tab of the purchase order in the field *Invoicing Control*.

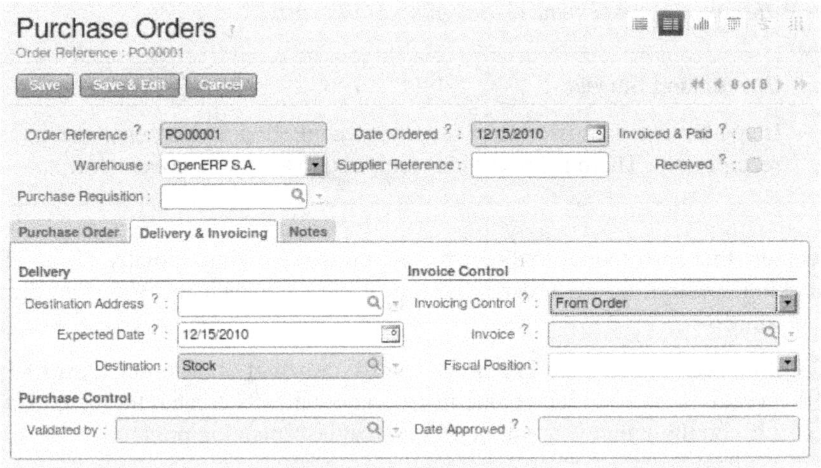

Figure 4.6: *Purchase Order, Invoice Control*

## 4.1.5 Control based on Orders

If you selected your invoicing control based on orders, OpenERP will automatically generate a supplier invoice in the draft state when the order is confirmed. You can obtain a list of invoices waiting using the menu *Accounting* → *Suppliers* → *Supplier Invoices* and enabling the `Draft` filter.

When you receive a paper invoice from your supplier, all you need to do is validate the invoice pre-generated by the system. Do not forget to check the price and the quantities. When the invoice is confirmed, the accounting entries represent the cost of purchase and are automatically entered into the system.

The supplier order is automatically set as `Paid` when you pay the supplier invoice.

This method of controlling invoices is often used in service companies, because the invoiced amounts correspond to the ordered amounts. In logistics, by contrast, you most often work with invoicing controlled by goods receipt.

## 4.1.6 Control based on Goods Receipt

To control your supplier invoices based on goods receipt, set the field *Invoicing Control* on the second tab of the order to *From Picking*.

In this case, no invoice, draft state or any other, is generated by the order. On the goods receipt note, the field *Invoice Control* is set to *To Be Invoiced*.

The storesperson can then receive different orders. If he wants to generate the draft invoice for a goods receipt, he can click the action *Create Invoice*. OpenERP then asks you for the journal for this invoice. It then opens that or the generated invoices (in the case of creating invoices for several receipts at one time) which enables you to modify it before confirming it.

This approach is useful when you receive the invoice at the same time as the item from the supplier. Usually, invoices are sent by post some days later. In this case, the storesperson leaves the item unchanged without generating an invoice. Then, once per day or once per week the accountant will create the draft invoices based on all the receipts for the day. To do that, he uses the menu *Purchases* → *Invoice Control* → *Purchase Lines Not Invoiced*. He clicks the action *Create invoices* to generate all draft invoices from the list of receipts that have not yet been invoiced. At that point, the accountant can decide if he wants to generate an invoice per item or group all items for the same partner into the same invoice.

Invoices are then handled just like those controlled from `On Order`. Once the invoice arrives at the accounting service, he just compares it with the invoices waiting to control what the supplier invoices you.

> **Delivery Charges**
>
> To manage delivery charges, install the module `delivery` using the *Reconfigure* wizard and selecting *Delivery Costs* in *Sales Application Configuration* section. This will automatically add delivery charges to the creation of the draft invoice as a function of the products delivered or ordered.

## 4.1.7 Tenders

To manage tenders, you should use the module `purchase_requisition`, installed via the *Purchase Requisition* option in the *Reconfigure* wizard. This lets you create several supplier price requests for a single supply requirement. Once the module is installed, OpenERP adds a new *Purchase Requisitions* menu in *Purchases → Purchase Management*. You can then define the new tenders.

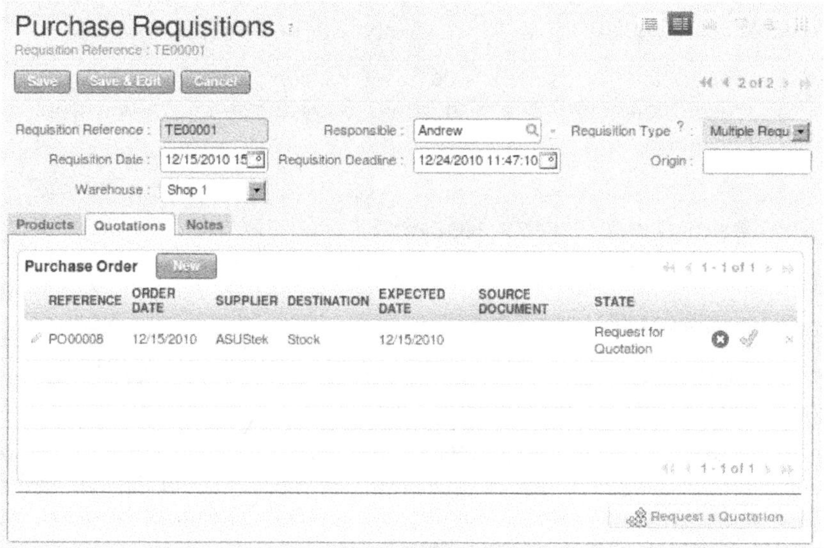

Figure 4.7: *Defining a Tender*

To enter data for a new tender, use the menu *Purchases → Purchase Management → Purchase Requisitions* and select *New*. OpenERP then opens a new blank tender form. The reference number is set by default and you can enter information about your tender in the other fields.

If you want to enter a supplier's response to your tender request, add a new draft purchase order into the list on the *Quotation* tab of your tender document. If you want to revise a supplier price in response to negotiations, edit any appropriate purchase order that you have left in the draft state and link that to the tender.

When one of the orders about a tender is confirmed, all of the other orders are automatically cancelled by OpenERP if you selected the Purchase Requisition (exclusive) type. That enables you to accept just one order for a particular tender. If you select Multiple requisitions, you can approve several purchase orders without cancelling other orders from this tender.

## 4.1.8 Price Revisions

OpenERP supports several methods of calculating and automatically updating product costs:

- Standard Price: manually fixed, and

- Standard Price: revalued automatically and periodically,

- Average Price: updated at each receipt to the warehouse.

This cost is used to value your stock and represents your product costs. Included in that cost is everything directly related to the received cost. You could include such elements as:

- supplier price,

- delivery charges,

- manufacturing costs,

- storage charges.

### Standard Price

The mode of price management for the product is shown in the tab *Information* on the product form. On each individual product, you can select if you want to work in `Standard Price` or on weighted `Average Price`.

> **Simplified Interface**
>
> If you work in the `Simplified` interface mode you will not see the field that lets you manage the price calculation mode for a product. In that case, the default value is `Standard Price`.

The `Standard Price` setting means that the product cost is fixed manually for each product in the field *Cost Price*. This is usually revalued once a year based on the average of purchase costs or manufacturing costs.

You usually use standard costs to manage products where the price hardly changes over the course of the year. For example, the standard cost could be used to manage books, or the cost of bread.

Those costs that can be fixed for the whole year bring certain advantages:

- you can base the sale price on the product cost and then work with margins rather than a fixed price per product,

- accounting is simplified because there is a direct relationship between the value of stock and the number of items received.

To get an automated periodic revaluation of the standard price you can use the action *Update* on the product form, enabling you to update prices of all the selected products. OpenERP then recalculates the price of the products as a function of the cost of raw materials and the manufacturing operations given in the routing.

## Average Price

Working with standard prices does not lend itself well to the management of the cost price of products when the prices change a lot with the state of the market. This is the case for many commodities and energy.

In this case, you would want OpenERP to automatically set the price in response to each goods receipt movement into the warehouse. The deliveries (exit from stock) have no impact on the product price.

---

**Calculating the Price**

At each goods receipt, the product price is recalculated using the following accounting formula: $NP = (OP * QS + PP * QR) / (QS + QR)$, where the following notation is used:

- NP: New Price,

- OP: Old Price,

- QS: Quantity actually in Stock,

- PP: Price Paid for the quantity received,

- QR: Quantity Received.

---

If the products are managed as a weighted average, OpenERP will open a window that lets you specify the price of the product received at each goods receipt. The purchase price is, by default, set from the purchase order, but you can change the price to add the cost of delivery to the various received products, for example.

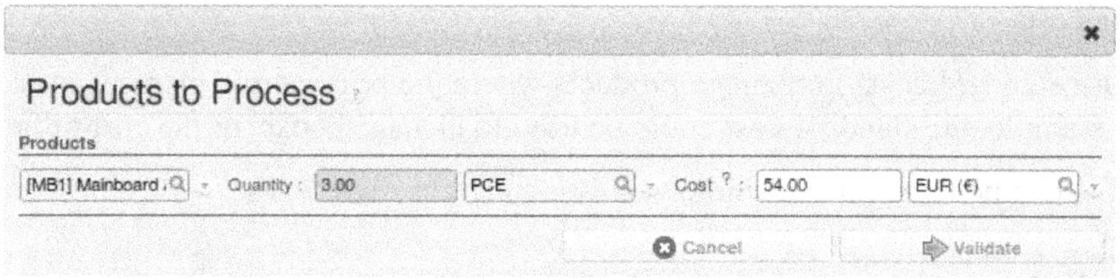

Figure 4.8: *Goods Receipt of Products managed in Weighted Average*

---

Once the receipt has been confirmed, the price is automatically recalculated and entered on the product form.

# 4.2 Purchase Analysis through Analytic Accounts

## 4.2.1 Powerful Statistics

OpenERP enables you to perform analysis of purchases by period (current year, current month, previous month), by state (quotations, orders), supplier, user, product, category, warehouse and so on. This is made possible through a search view accessed through the menu *Purchases → Reporting → Purchase Analysis*.

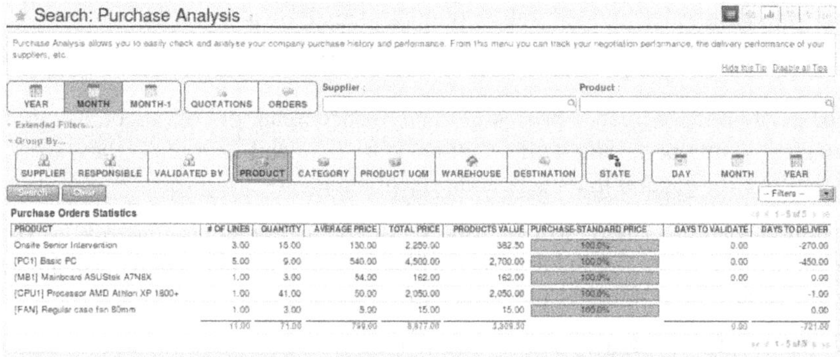

Figure 4.9: *Analysis of Purchases over the Month by Product*

This analysis is carried out on supplier orders and not on invoices or the quantities actually received. To get an analysis by product, use the module `product_margin`. The function of this module is described in detail in the chapter about sales (only in Logistics, not in Manufacturing).

To analyze the received quantities, you can use the statistical reports in Warehouse. To manage purchases by project, you should use analytic accounts. You can set an analytic account on each line of a supplier order. The analytic costs linked to this purchase will be managed by OpenERP from the goods receipt and confirmation of the supplier invoice. The `hr_timesheet_invoice` module lets you re-invoice the analytic costs automatically using parameters in the analytic accounts such as sale pricelist, associated partner company, and maximum amount.

So you can put an invoice order with a defined invoice workflow in place based on the analytic accounts. If you are working Make to Order, the workflow will be:

1. Customer Order,

2. Procurement Order on supplier,

3. Receive invoice and goods from the supplier,

4. Delivery and invoicing to the customer.

When re-invoicing based on costs you would get the following workflow:

1. Enter the customer contract conditions from the analytic accounts,

2. Purchase raw materials and write the services performed into the timesheets,

3. Receive the supplier invoice and the products,

4. Invoice these costs to the customer.

> **Analytic Multi-plans**
>
> If you want several analysis plans, you should install the module `purchase_analytic_plans`. These let you split a line on a supplier purchase order into several accounts and analytic plans.

Sitting at the heart of your company's processes, analytic accounts (or cost accounts) are indispensable tools for managing your operations well. Unlike your financial accounts, they are for more than accountants - they are for general managers and project managers, too.

You need a common way of referring to each user, service, or document to integrate all your company's processes effectively. Such a common basis is provided by analytic accounts (or management accounts, or cost accounts, as they are also called) in OpenERP.

Analytic accounts are often presented as a foundation for strategic enterprise decisions. But because of all the information they pull together, OpenERP's analytic accounts can be a useful management tool, at the center of most system processes.

There are several reasons for this:

- they reflect your entire management activity,

- unlike the general accounts, the structure of the analytic accounts is not regulated by legal obligations, so each company can adapt it to its needs.

> **Independence from General Accounts**
>
> In some software packages, analytic accounts are managed as an extension of general accounts – for example, by using the two last digits of the account code to represent analytic accounts.
>
> In OpenERP, analytic accounts are linked to general accounts but are treated totally independently. So you can enter various different analytic operations that have no counterpart in the general financial accounts.

While the structure of the general chart of accounts is imposed by law, the analytic chart of accounts is built to fit a company's needs closely.

Just as in the general accounts, you will find accounting entries in the different analytic accounts. Each analytic entry can be linked to a general account, or not, as you wish. Conversely, an entry in a general account can be linked to one, several, or no corresponding analytic accounts.

You will discover many advantages of this independent representation below. For the more impatient, here are some of those advantages:

- you can manage many different analytic operations,

- you can modify an analytic plan on the fly, during the course of an activity, because of its independence,

- you can avoid an explosion in the number of general accounts,

- even those companies that do not use OpenERP's general accounts can use the analytic accounts for management.

> **Who Benefits from Analytic Accounts?**
>
> Unlike general accounts, analytic accounts in OpenERP are not so much an accounting tool for Accounts as a management tool for everyone in the company. (That is why they are also called management accounts.)
>
> The main users of analytic accounts should be the directors, general managers and project managers.

Analytic accounts make up a powerful tool that can be used in different ways. The trick is to create your own analytic structure for a chart of accounts that closely matches your company's needs.

## 4.2.2 To Each Enterprise its own Analytic Chart of Accounts

To illustrate analytic accounts clearly, you will follow three use cases, each in one of three different types of company:

1. Industrial Manufacturing Enterprise.

2. Law Firm.

3. IT Services Company.

*Case 1: Industrial Manufacturing Enterprise*

In industry, you will often find analytic charts of accounts structured into the departments and products that the company itself is built on.

So the objective is to examine the costs, sales and margins by department and by product. The first level of the structure comprises the different departments, and the lower levels represent the product ranges that the company makes and sells.

**Analytic Chart of Accounts for an Industrial Manufacturing Company**

1. Marketing Department

2. Commercial Department

3. Administration Department

4. Production

   • Product Range 1

   • Sub-groups

   • Product Range 2

In daily use, it is useful to mark the analytic account on each purchase invoice. The analytic account is the one to which the costs of that purchase should be allocated. When the invoice is approved, it will automatically generate the entries for both the general and the corresponding analytic accounts. So, for each entry on the general accounts, there is at least one analytic entry that allocates costs to the department that incurred them.

Here is a possible breakdown of some general accounting entries for the example above, allocated to various analytic accounts:

Table 4.1: Breakdown of general and analytic accounting entries (Case 1)

| General accounts | | | | Analytic accounts | |
|---|---|---|---|---|---|
| Title | Account | Debit | Credit | Account | Value |
| Purchase of Raw Material | 600 | 1500 | | Production / Range 1 | -1 500 |
| Subcontractors | 602 | 450 | | Production / Range 2 | -450 |
| Credit Note for defective materials | 600 | | 200 | Production / Range 1 | 200 |
| Transport charges | 613 | 450 | | Production / Range 1 | -450 |
| Staff costs | 6201 | 10000 | | Marketing | -2 000 |
| | | | | Commercial | -3 000 |
| | | | | Administrative | -1 000 |
| | | | | Production / Range 1 | -2 000 |
| | | | | Production / Range 2 | -2 000 |
| PR | 614 | 450 | | Marketing | -450 |

The analytic representation by department enables you to investigate the costs allocated to each department in the company.

So, the analytic chart of accounts shows the distribution of the company's costs using the example above:

Table 4.2: Analytic chart of accounts (Case 1)

| Account | Total |
|---|---|
| Marketing Department | -2 450 |
| Commercial Department | -3 000 |
| Administration Department | -1 000 |
| Production | -6 200 |
| Product Range 1 | -3 750 |
| Product Range 2 | -2 450 |

In this example of a hierarchical structure in OpenERP, you can analyze not only the costs of each product range but also the costs of the whole of production. The balance of a summary account ( *Production* ) is the sum of the balances of the child accounts.

A report that relates both general accounts and analytic accounts enables you to get a breakdown of costs within a given department. An analysis of the Production / Product Range 1 department is shown in this table:

Table 4.3: Report merging both general and analytic accounts for a department (Case 1)

| **Production / Product Range 1** | |
|---|---|
| General Account | Amount |
| 600 – Raw Materials | - 1 300 |
| 613 – Transport charges | - 450 |
| 6201 – Staff costs | -2 000 |
| Total | -3 750 |

The examples above are based on a breakdown of the costs of the company. Analytic allocations can be just as effective for sales. That gives you the profitability (sales - costs) of different departments.

> **Representation by Unique Product Range**
>
> This analytic representation by department and by product range is usually used by trading companies and industries.
>
> A variant of this is not to break it down by sales and marketing departments but to assign each cost to its corresponding product range. This will give you an analysis of the profitability of each product range.
>
> Choosing one over the other depends on how you look at your marketing effort. Is it a global cost allocated in some general way, or does each product range have responsibility for its own marketing costs?

*Case 2: Law Firm*

Law firms generally adopt management by case, where each case represents a current client file. All of the expenses and products are then attached to a given file.

A principal preoccupation of law firms is the invoicing of hours worked, and the profitability by case and by employee.

Mechanisms used for encoding the hours worked will be covered in detail in the Human Resources chapter on line. Like most system processes, hours worked are integrated into the analytic accounting. Every time an employee enters a timesheet for a number of hours, that automatically generates analytic accounts corresponding to the cost of those hours in the case concerned. The hourly charge is a function of the employee's salary. So a law firm will opt for an analytic representation which reflects the management of the time that employees work on the different client cases.

---

***Example Representation of an Analytic Chart of Accounts for a Law Firm***

1. Absences

   - Paid Absences
   - Unpaid Absences

2. Internal Projects

   - Administrative
   - Others

3. Client Cases

   - Client 1
   - Case 1.1
   - Case 1.2
   - Client 2
   - Case 2.1

---

All expenses and sales are then attached to a case. This gives the profitability of each case and, at a consolidated level, of each client.

Billing for the different cases is a bit unusual. The cases do not match any entry on the general account and nor do they come from purchase or sale invoices. They are represented by the various analytic operations and do not have exact counterparts in the general accounts. They are calculated on the basis of the hourly cost per employee. These entries are automatically created on billing worksheets.

At the end of the month when you pay salaries and benefits, you integrate them into the general accounts but not in the analytic accounts, because they have already been accounted for in billing each account. A report that relates data from the analytic and general accounts then lets you compare the totals, so you can readjust your estimates of hourly cost per employee depending on the time actually worked.

The following table gives an example of different analytic entries that you can find for your analytic account:

Table 4.4: Analytic entries for the account chart (Case 2)

| Title | Account | Amount | General Account | Debit | Credit |
|---|---|---|---|---|---|
| Study the file (1 h) | Case 1.1 | -15 | | | |
| Search for information (3 h) | Case 1.1 | -45 | | | |
| Consultation (4 h) | Case 2.1 | -60 | | | |
| Service charges | Case 1.1 | 280 | 705 – Billing services | | 280 |
| Stationery purchase | Administrative | -42 | 601 – Furniture purchase | 42 | |
| Fuel Cost -Client trip | Case 1.1 | -35 | 613 – Transports | 35 | |
| Staff salaries | | | 6201 – Salaries | | 3 000 |

You will see that it allows you to make a detailed study of the profitability of different transactions. In this example, the cost of Case 1.1 is 95.00 (the sum of the analytic costs of studying the files, searching for information and service charges), but has been invoiced for 280.00, which gives you a gross profit of 185.00.

But an interest in analytical accounts is not limited to a simple analysis of the profitability of different cases.

This same data can be used for automatic recharging of the services to the client at the end of the month. To invoice clients, just take the analytic costs in that month and apply a selling price factor to generate the invoice. Invoicing mechanisms for this are explained in greater detail in *ch-services*. If the client requires details of the services used on the case, you can then print the service entries in the analytic account for this case.

> **Invoicing Analytic Costs**
>
> Most software that manages billing enables you to recharge for hours worked. In OpenERP, these services are automatically represented by analytic costs. But many other OpenERP documents can also generate analytic costs, such as credit notes and purchases of goods.
>
> So when you invoice the client at the end of the month, it is possible for you to include all the analytic costs, not just the hours worked. So, for example, you can easily recharge the whole cost of your journeys to the client.

*Case 3: IT Services Company*

Most IT service companies face the following problems:

- project planning,

- invoicing, profitability and financial follow-up of projects,

- managing support contracts.

To deal with these problems, you would use an analytic chart of accounts structured by project and by contract. A representation of that is given in the following example:

1. Internal Projects

    - Administrative and Commercial
    - Research and Development

2. Client Projects

    - Client 1
    - Project 1.1
    - Project 1.2
    - Client 2
    - Project 2.1
    - Project 2.2

3. Support Contracts – 20h

    - Customer X
    - Customer Y

The management of services, expenditures and sales is similar to that presented above for lawyers. Invoicing and the study of profitability are also similar.

But now look at support contracts. These contracts are usually limited to a prepaid number of hours. Each service posted in the analytic accounts shows the remaining available hours of support. For the management of support contracts, you would use the quantities and not the amounts in the analytic entries.

In OpenERP, each analytic line lists the number of units sold or used, as well as what you would usually find there – the amount in currency units (USD or GBP, or whatever other choice you make). So you can sum the quantities sold and used on each analytic account to determine whether any hours of the support contract remain. To differentiate services from other costs in the analytic account, you use the concept of the analytic journal. Analytic entries are then allocated into the different journals:

- service journal,
- expense journal,
- sales journal,
- purchase journal.

So to obtain the detailed breakdown of a support contract, you only have to look at the service journal for the analytic account corresponding to the contract in question.

Finally, the analytic account can be used to forecast future needs. For example, monthly planning of staff on different projects can be seen as an analytic budget limited to the service journal. Accounting entries are expressed in quantities (such as number of hours, and numbers of products), and in amounts in units of currency (USD or GBP perhaps).

So you can set up planning on just the basis of quantities. Analyzing the analytic budget enables you to compare the budget (that is, your plan) to the services actually carried out by month end.

---

**Cash Budgets**

Problems of cash management are amongst the main difficulties encountered by small growing businesses. It is really difficult to predict the amount of cash that will be available when a company is young and rapidly growing.

If the company adopts management by case, then staff planning can be represented on the analytic accounts report, as you have seen.

But since you know your selling price for each of the different projects, you can see that it is easy to use the plan in the analytic accounts to more precisely forecast the amounts that you will invoice in the coming months.

---

# Part III

# Managing your Warehouse

# Your Warehouse

5

*OpenERP's stock management is at once very simple, flexible and complete. It is based on the concept of double entry that revolutionized accounting. The system can be described by Lavoisier's maxim "nothing lost, everything changed" or, better, "everything moved". In OpenERP you do not talk of disappearance, consumption or loss of products: instead you speak only of stock moves from one place to another.*

Just as in accounting, the OpenERP system manages counterparts to each of its main operations such as receipts from suppliers, deliveries to customers, profit and loss from inventory, and consumption of raw materials. Stock movements are always made from one location to another. To satisfy the need for a counterpart to each stock movement, the software supports different types of stock locations:

- Physical stock locations,

- Partner locations,

- Virtual locations as counterparts for procurement, production and inventory.

Physical locations represent warehouses and their hierarchical structure. These are generally the locations that are managed by traditional stock management systems.

Partner locations represent your customers' and suppliers' stocks. To reconcile them with your accounts, these stores play the role of third-party accounts. Reception from a supplier can be shown by the movement of goods from a partner location to a physical location in your own company. As you see, supplier locations usually show negative stocks and customer locations usually show positive stocks.

Virtual locations as counterparts for production are used in manufacturing operations. Manufacturing is characterized by the consumption of raw materials and the production of finished products. Virtual locations are used for the counterparts of these two operations.

Inventory locations are counterparts of the stock operations that represent your company's profit and loss in terms of your stocks.

The figure *Location Structure when OpenERP has just been installed* (page 72) shows the initial configuration of the locations when the software is installed (*Warehouse → Warehouse Management → Locations*).

---

**Hierarchical Stock Locations**

In OpenERP, locations are structured hierarchically. You can structure your locations as a tree, dependent on a parent-child relationship. This gives you more detailed levels of analysis of your stock operations and the organization of your warehouses.

---

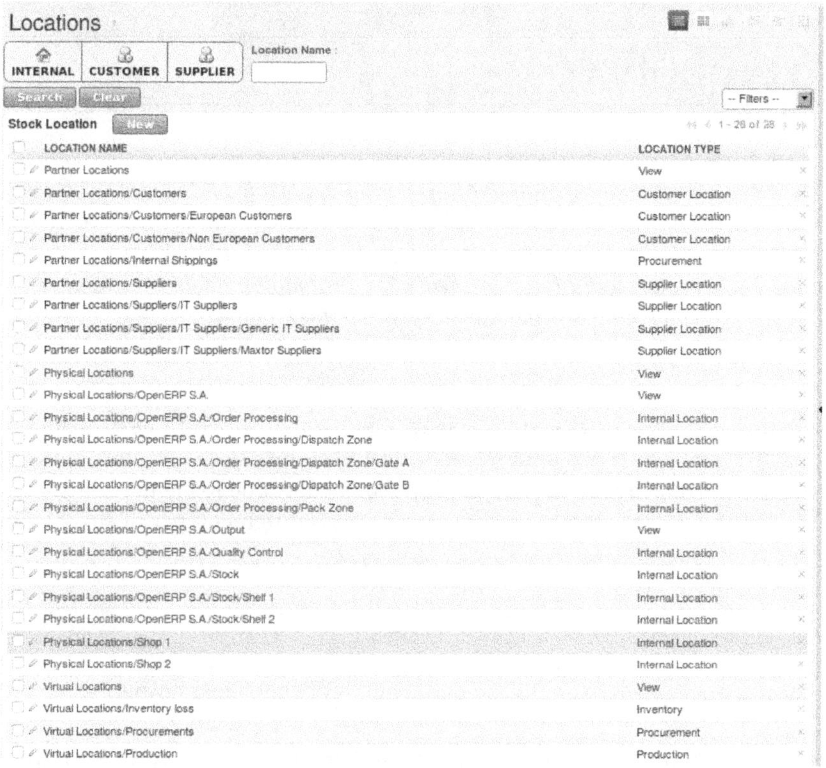

Figure 5.1: *Location Structure when OpenERP has just been installed*

---

**Locations and Warehouses**

In OpenERP a **Warehouse** represents the place where your physical stock is stored. A warehouse can be structured into several locations at multiple levels. Locations are used to manage all types of storage places, such as at the customer and production counterparts.

---

For this chapter you can continue using the database with demo data from a previous chapter or start with a fresh database that includes demo data, with Warehouse Management and its dependencies installed and any chart of accounts configured.

In this chapter, the following modules will be used:

Table 5.1: List of modules

| Name | Description |
|------|-------------|
| stock | to handle the stock functions |
| stock_planning | to define planning on products |
| stock_location | to define pull and push flows |
| delivery | to define delivery methods and costs |
| account_anglo_saxon | to illustrate the valuation according to the anglo-saxon principles |
| sale_journal | to handle stock by journal |
| mrp_jit | to illustrate the just-in-time functionality |
| sale_supplier_direct_delivery | to directly deliver the product from the supplier to the customer |

# 5.1 Understanding Double-Entry Stock Management

To illustrate this concept of stock management, see how stock moves are generated by the following operations:

- Receiving products from a supplier,

- Delivery to a customer,

- Inventory operation for lost materials,

- Manufacturing.

The structure of stock locations is shown by the figure *Location Structure when OpenERP has just been installed* (page 72). Stocks are assumed to be totally empty and no operation is in progress nor planned.

If you order '30 bicycles' from a supplier, OpenERP will do the following operations on receipt of the products:

Table 5.2: Stock Move Operation from Suppliers to Stock

| Location | Products |
|----------|----------|
| Partner Locations > Suppliers | -30 bicycles |
| Physical Locations > OpenERP S.A. > Stock | +30 bicycles |

If you deliver 2 bicycles to a European customer, you will get the following transactions for the delivery:

Table 5.3: Stock Move Operation from Stock to European Customers

| Location | Products |
|----------|----------|
| Physical Locations > OpenERP S.A. > Stock | -2 bicycles |
| Partner Locations > Customers > European Customers | +2 bicycles |

When the two operations are complete, you will see the following stock in each location:

Table 5.4: Resulting Stock Situation

| Location | Products |
|---|---|
| Partner Locations > Suppliers | -30 bicycles |
| Physical Locations > OpenERP S.A. > Stock | +28 bicycles |
| Partner Locations > Customers > European Customers | +2 bicycles |

So you can see that the sum of the stocks of a product in all the locations in OpenERP is always zero. In accounting you would say that the sum of the debits is equal to the sum of the credits.

Partner locations (customers and suppliers) are not located under your company in the hierarchical structure, so their contents are not considered as part of your own stock. So if you just look at the physical locations inside your own company, those two bicycles are no longer in your company. Although they are no longer in your own physical stock, it is still very useful to see them in your customer's stock, because that will help when you carry out detailed stock management analysis.

**Consignment Stock**

To manage Consignment Stock, you need to define the location for the consignment customer or supplier as part of your own stock and not as a partner location.

**Accounts**

In managing stock, a gap between the data in the software and real quantities in stock is difficult to avoid. Double-entry stock management gives twice as many opportunities to find an error. If you forget two items of stock, this error will automatically be reflected in the counterpart's location.

You can make a comparison with accounting, where you will easily find an error because you can look for an anomaly in an account or in the counterparts: if there is not enough in a bank account then that is probably because someone has forgotten to enter a customer's invoice payment. You always know that the sum of debits must equal the sum of the credits in both accounting and OpenERP's stock management.

In accounting, all documents lead to accounting entries that form the basis of management accounting. If you create invoices or enter statements of account, for example, the results of the operations are accounting entries on accounts. And it is the same for stock management in OpenERP. All stock operations are carried out as simple stock moves. Whether you pack items, or manufacture them, or carry out a stock inventory operation, stock moves are carried out every time.

You have seen a fairly simple example of goods receipt and product delivery, but some operations are less obvious – a stock inventory operation, for example. An inventory operation is carried out when you compare the stock shown in software with real stock numbers counted in the stores. In OpenERP, with its double-entry stock management, you would use stock moves for this inventory operation. That helps you manage your stock traceability. Suppose there are 26 bicycles in real stock, but OpenERP shows 28 in the system. You then have to reduce the number in OpenERP to 26. This reduction of 2 units is considered as a loss or destruction of products and the correction is carried out as in the following operation:

Table 5.5: Inventory Operation to Adjust Stock

| Location | Products |
| --- | --- |
| Physical Locations > OpenERP S.A. > Stock | -2 bicycles |
| Virtual Locations > Inventory Loss | +2 bicycles |

The product stock under consideration then becomes:

Table 5.6: Real and Counterpart Stocks when Operations are Completed

| Location | Products |
| --- | --- |
| Partner Locations > Suppliers | -30 bicycles |
| Physical Locations > OpenERP S.A. > Stock | +26 bicycles |
| Partner Locations > Customers > European Customers | +2 bicycles |
| Virtual Locations > Inventory Loss | +2 bicycles |

This example shows one of the great advantages of this approach in terms of performance analysis. After a few months, you can just make a stock valuation of the location *Inventory Control → Location Structure → Virtual Locations → Inventory Loss* to give you the value of the company's stock losses in the given period.

Now see how the following manufacturing operation is structured in OpenERP. To make a bicycle you need two wheels and a frame. This means that there should be a reduction of two wheels and a frame from real stock and the addition of a bicycle there. The consumption / production is formalized by moving products out of and into physical stock. The stock operations for this are as follows:

Table 5.7: Stock Situation Resulting from Manufacturing

| Location | Products | Step |
| --- | --- | --- |
| Physical Locations > OpenERP S.A. > Stock | -2 Wheels | Consumption of raw materials |
| Virtual Locations > Production | +2 Wheels | Consumption of raw materials |
| Physical Locations > OpenERP S.A. > Stock | -1 Frame | Consumption of raw materials |
| Virtual Locations > Production | +1 Frame | Consumption of raw materials |
| Virtual Locations > Production | -1 Bicycle | Manufacture of finished products |
| Physical Locations > OpenERP S.A. > Stock | +1 Bicycle | Manufacture of finished products |

So now you have got the outcome you need from the consumption of raw materials and the manufacturing of finished products.

> **Assessing Created Value**
>
> You might already have noticed a useful effect of this approach: if you do a stock valuation in the `Virtual Locations > Production` location you get a statement of value created by your company (as a negative amount). Stock valuation in any given location is calculated by multiplying quantities of products in stock by their cost. In this case, the raw material value is deducted from the finished product value.

# 5.2 Managing Physical Inventory Structure

## 5.2.1 Warehouse

Warehouses are designed for physical locations from which you can deliver to the customer, and to which you receive raw materials. When you buy products from a supplier, you should take account of the Warehouse you use for this purchase. This also enables the end user to not have to choose from a list of locations, but simply a real warehouse. Use the menu *Warehouse → Configuration → Warehouse Management → Warehouses*, then click New to configure a new warehouse.

A warehouse is defined by a link between three locations:

- The *Location Stock* field shows the place of products available for delivery to a customer directly from this warehouse. Availability is given by all the products in that location and any child locations.

- The *Location Input* field shows where ordered products are received from a supplier in that warehouse. It can be the same as the stock location if, for example, you want to do a quality control operation on your incoming raw materials.

- The *Location Output* field (called `Output` in the demonstration database) is designed as a buffer zone in which you store all the items that have been picked, but not yet delivered to a customer. You are strongly advised not to put this location within the stock hierarchy but instead at a higher level or at the same level.

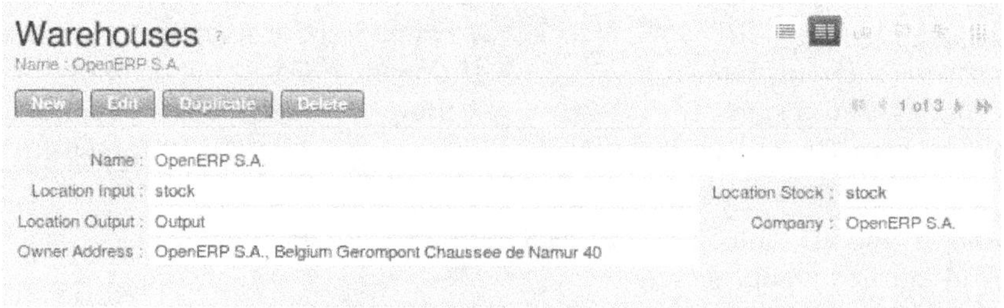

Figure 5.2: *Warehouse Parameters*

You can also set an address for the warehouse. This address should ideally be an address of your company. Once the warehouse has been defined, it can be used in:

- Minimum stock rules,

- Supplier orders,

- Customer orders (using the definition of a point of sale, which is linked to a warehouse).

### Automatic Procurement

Several methods of automatically procuring products can be carried out by OpenERP:

- the workflow used by products that have the procurement method *Make to Order*,

- using minimum stock rules for *Make to Stock* products,

- using the master production schedule for *Make to Stock* products.

The last two methods are described below.

### Minimum Stock Rules

To automatically make stock replenishment proposals, you can use minimum stock rules. Go to the menu *Warehouse → Automatic Procurements → Minimum Stock Rules*.

The rule is the following: if the virtual stock for the given location is lower than the minimum stock indicated in the rule, the system will automatically propose a procurement to increase the level of virtual stock to the maximum level given in the rule.

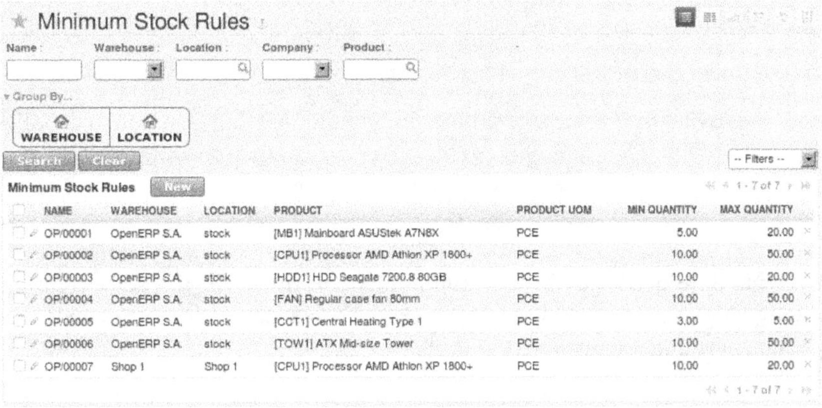

Figure 5.3: *List of Minimum Stock Rules*

**Conflict Resolution**

You may find draft production or procurement orders to be created although they should not exist. That can happen if the system is badly configured (for example, if you have forgotten to set the supplier on a product).

To check this, look at the list of procurements in the exception state in the menu *Warehouse* → *Schedulers* → *Procurement Exceptions*. More details about processing these exceptions is given in *ch-mnf*.

We underline that the rule is based on *virtual* quantities and not just on real quantities. It takes into account the calculation of orders and receipts to come.

Take the following example:

- Products in stock: 15

- Products ordered but not delivered: 5

- Products in manufacturing: 2

The rules defined are:

- Minimum stock: 13

- Maximum stock: 25.

Once the rules have been properly configured, the purchasing manager only needs to look at the list of orders for confirmation with the supplier using the menu *Purchases* → *Purchase Management* → *Requests for Quotation*.

**Procurement**

Note that the procurement does not require that you buy from a supplier. If the product has a *Supply Method* `Produce`, the scheduler will generate a Manufacturing order instead of a supplier order.

You can also set multiple quantities in the minimum stock rules. If you set a multiple quantity of 3 the system will propose procurement of 15 pieces, and not the 13 it really needs. In this case, it automatically rounds the quantity upwards.

> **Maximum Quantity**
>
> Pay attention to the fact that the maximum quantity is not the maximum you will have in stock. If we take the following situation: a company has 10 pieces of product with minimum stock rules defined for this product by *Min quantity = 10*, *Max quantity = 30* and *Qty multiple = 12*. If an order of 2 pieces comes, a purchase of 24 pieces order will be executed. The first 12 pieces will be ordered to reach the minimum quantity and the other 12 to reach the maximum quantity. At the end, the stock of this product will be equal to 32 pieces.

In a minimum stock rule, when you indicate a warehouse, it suggests a stock location by default in that warehouse. You can change that default location when the scheduler completes.

## 5.2.2 Location

A location is one component of the warehouses that is used to managed all types of storage places, such as at the customer's and production counterparts.

There are different types of locations that allow you to structure your warehouses according to your needs. Locations are structured hierarchically to account for the subdivision of a warehouse into sections, aisles, and/or cupboards. The hierarchical view also enables you to structure virtual locations such as production counterparts. That gives you a finer level of analysis. Go to the menu *Warehouse → Configuration → Warehouse Management → Locations*, then click New to define new locations.

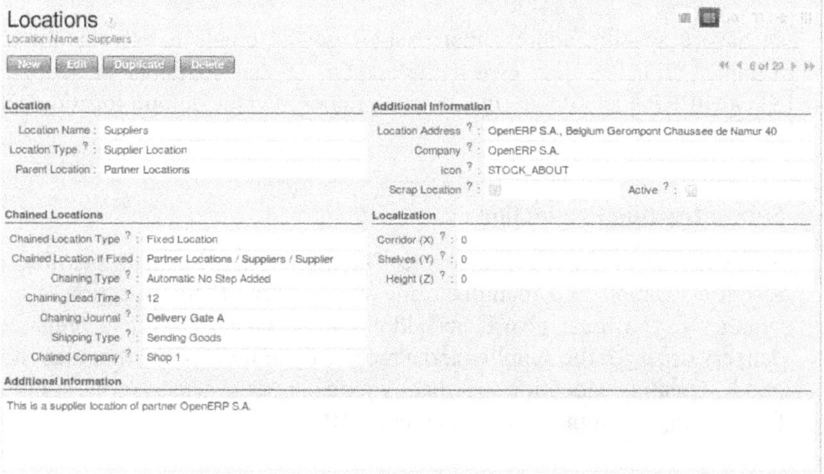

Figure 5.4: *Defining a new Stock Location*

Here are the different available types of locations:

- `Supplier Location`: virtual location representing the source location for products received

---

from suppliers,

- View: shows that the location is only an organizational node for the hierarchical structure, and cannot be involved in stock moves itself. The view type is not made into a leaf node in a structure – it usually has children.

- Internal Location: physical location inside your own stock,

- Customer Location: virtual location representing the destination for products sent to customers,

- Inventory: virtual location serving as the counterpart for inventory operations used to correct stock levels (physical inventories),

- Procurement: virtual location serving as temporary counterpart for procurement operations when you do not yet know the source (supplier or production). Products in this location should be zero after the scheduler run completes,

- Production: virtual counterpart location for production operations; consuming raw material and sending finished products,

- Transit Location for Inter-Companies Transfers: used as an intermediate location in a multi-company environment.

You can have several locations of the same type. In that case, your product, supplier and warehouse configurations determine the location that is to be used for any given operation.

## Location Addresses

Each location can have a specific address that enables you to create a location for a customer or a supplier, for example. You can then give it the address of that customer or supplier. Go to the partner form to tell OpenERP it should use this location rather than the default location given to partner deliveries.

> **Subcontracting Production**
>
> You will see in the on line chapter Manufacturing that it is possible to assign a location to a manufacturing workcenter. If this location is at a supplier's, you must give it an address so that OpenERP can prepare a delivery order for the supplier and a receive operation for the manufactured goods. Creating a location specifically for a partner is also a simple solution for handling consigned stocks in OpenERP.

> **Consigned Stock**
>
> Consigned stock is stock that is owned by you (valued in your accounts), but is physically stocked by your supplier. Or, conversely, it could be stock owned by your customer (not valued by you), but stocked in your company. Make sure that you create consignment locations as part of your internal stock.

To enable you to easily consolidate at a higher level, the location definition is hierarchical. This structure is given by the field `Parent Location`. That also enables you to manage complex cases of product localization.

For example, you could imagine the following scenario: **One Company with Two Warehouses**

A company has a warehouse in Paris and in Bordeaux. For some orders, you have to deliver the products from Paris, and for others from Bordeaux. But you should also specify a fictitious warehouse that OpenERP uses to calculate whether it should deliver products from Paris or from Bordeaux. To do this in OpenERP, you would create a third warehouse 'France' which consolidates the warehouses in Paris and Bordeaux. You create the following physical locations:

- Company
  - Output
    * Warehouses France
      · Warehouse Paris
      · Warehouse Bordeaux

OpenERP will then deliver the goods from the warehouse that has the ordered product in stock. When products are available in several warehouses, OpenERP will select the nearest warehouse. To formalize the notion of distance between warehouses you should use the geographic co-ordinates (X, Y, Z) of the different stores to enable OpenERP to search for the nearest goods. The same co-ordinates could also be used to structure the shelves, aisles and interior rooms in a warehouse.

## Linked Locations

Locations in OpenERP can be linked between each other to define paths followed by products. So you can define rules such as: all products that enter the warehouse should automatically be sent to quality control. The warehouse and quality control are represented by two different locations.

Then when a product arrives in a location, OpenERP can automatically suggest that you send the product to another linked location. Three link modes are available:

- Manual Operation,
- Automatic Move,
- Automatic No Step Added.

The *Manual Operation* mode will create an internal move order to the linked location once products arrive in the source locations. This order will wait for a confirmation of the move by a user. This enables you to have a list of moves to do, proposed by the system and confirmed by the storesperson.

The *Automatic Move* mode will do the same, but will not wait for a confirmation from the user. Products will automatically be sent to the linked location without any intervening manual operation to do. This corresponds to the case where, for simplicity, you delete a step in the process so the end user can set off the process automatically.

The *Automatic No Step Added* mode will not include the additional stock move, but will change the destination move transparently to assign the linked location. You could then assign a destination location to which you send all the products that arrive in your warehouse. The storesperson will modify the goods receipt note.

---

**Product Logistics**

The module `stock_location` lets you generate paths to follow, not just at the level of locations, but also at the level of products. It then enables you to manage default locations for a given product or to refer to the products as a function of operations such as quality control, supplier receipt, and after-sales service.

A more detailed explanation of this module, with examples, is given at the end of this chapter.

---

If there is linking to do, the **Chained Location Type** field allows you to determine the destination location. If the field is set to 'Customer', the location is given by the properties of the partner form. If the field is set to *fixed*, the destination location is given by the field **Chained Location If Fixed**.

Some operations take a certain time between order and execution. To account for this lead time, you can set a value in days in the field **Chaining Lead Time**. Then the extra move (automatic or not) will be carried out several days after the original move. If you use the mode *Automatic No Step Added*, the lead time is inserted directly into the initial order. In this way, you can add security lead times at certain control points in the warehouse.

## Structuring Locations

In the next part, you will see that by linking locations you can manage a whole series of complex cases for efficient production management:

- Handling multiple operations for a customer order,

- Tracking import and export by sea transport,

- Managing a production chain in detail,

- Managing rented products,

- Managing consigned products.

To show these concepts, different cases of structuring and configuring these locations are given below. Many other configurations are possible according to company needs.

Examples:

- **Handling customer orders**

Customer orders are usually handled in one of two ways:

- item note (or preparation order), confirmed when the item is ready to send,

- delivery order (or freight note), confirmed when the transporter has delivered the item to a customer.

You use the following stock move in OpenERP to simulate these operations:

- Packing Note: Stock > Output,

- Delivery Order: Output > Customer.

The first operation is automatically generated by the customer order. The second one is generated by the stock management, showing that the Output location is linked to the Customer location. The two operations will be displayed in *Waiting* status. If the Output location is not situated beneath the stock location, you then have to move the item from stock to the place where the item is prepared.

Some companies do not want to work in two steps, because it just seems like extra work to have to confirm a delivery note in the system. You can then set the link mode to 'Automatic' to make OpenERP automatically confirm the second step. It is then assumed all the items have automatically been delivered to the customer.

- **Linked production**

The `stock_location module` enables you to manage the linkages by product in addition to doing that by location. You can then create a location structure that represents your production chain by product.

The location structure may look like this:

- Stock
    - Level 1
    - Level 2
        * Link 1
            · Operation 1
            · Operation 2
            · Operation 3
            · Operation 4

You can then set the locations a product or a routing must go through in the relevant form. All products that enter the production chain will automatically follow the predetermined path. You can see the location structure using *Warehouse → Inventory Control → Location Structure*.

## 5.2.3 Shop

The counterparts for procurement, inventory and production operations are given by the locations shown in the product form. The counterparts of reception and delivery operations are given by the locations shown in the partner form. The choice of stock location is determined by the configuration of the warehouse, linked to a Shop, which can be defined using *Sales → Configuration → Sales → Shop*.

Once a shop is defined, you will be able to make sales orders from this shop. You need at least one shop in order to be able to make sales orders.

## 5.2.4 Stock

In the Product form, the `Stock by Location` action will give you the stock levels of the various products in any selected location. If you have not selected any location, OpenERP calculates stocks for all of the physical locations. When you are in the Stock by Location view, click the Print button to print the Location Content or the Location Inventory Overview reports.

---

**Availability of Stock**

Depending on whether you look at the product from a customer order, or from the menu of a product form, you can get different values for stock availability. If you use the Product menu, you get the stock in all of the physical stock locations. Looking at the product from the order you will only see the report of the warehouse selected in the order.

---

In this respect, two important fields in the product form are:

- Real Stock: Quantity physically present in your warehouse,
- Virtual Stock: Calculated as follows: real stock – outgoing + incoming.

---

**Virtual Stock**

Virtual stock is very useful because it shows what the salespeople can sell. If the virtual stock is higher than the real stock, this means products will be coming in. If virtual stock is smaller than real stock, certain products are reserved for other sales orders or work orders.

---

**Detail of Future Stock**

To get more details about future stock, you can click `Stock Level Forecast` to the right of the product form to get the report Forecast Stock Levels as illustrated below. OpenERP shows a graph of the changes in stock in the days to come, varying as a function of purchase orders, confirmed production and sales orders.

---

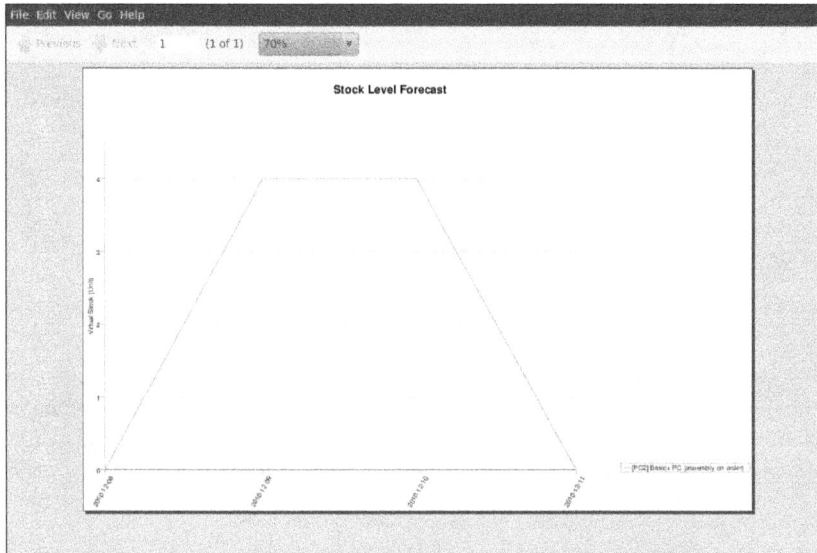

Figure 5.5: *Printout of forecast stock levels*

---

**Filter Stock by Location**

By default, in Product list view, the columns Real Stock and Virtual Stock show the stock figures for all stock locations where a product is stored. Use the *Extended Filters* to enter a specific stock location, if you want to only see the stock in a specific location.

---

## Lead Times and Locations

The tab **Procurement & Locations** in the Product form contains information about different lead times and locations. Three lead time figures are available:

- **Customer Lead Time**: lead time promised to the customer, expressed in number of days between the order and the delivery to the customer,

- **Manufacturing Lead Time**: lead time, in days, between a production order and the end of production of the finished product,

- **Warranty (months)**: length of time in months for the warranty of the delivered products.

---

**Warranty**

The warranty period is used in the *Repairs management and after-sales service*. You can find more information on this subject in the on line chapter about Manufacturing.

---

Fields in the section *Storage Localisation* are for information only; they do not have any impact on the management of stock.

*Counter-Part Locations Properties* are automatically proposed by the system, but the different values can be modified. You will find counterpart locations for:

- Procurement,

- Production,

- Inventory.

A procurement location is a temporary location for stock moves that have not yet been finalized by the scheduler. When the system does not yet know if procurement is to be done by a purchase or production, OpenERP uses the counterpart location Procurement. In this location, you will find everything that has not yet been planned by the system. The quantities of product in this location cancel each other out.

### Initial Inventory

Once a product has been defined, use an initial inventory operation to put current quantities into the system by location for the products in stock. Go to the menu *Warehouse → Inventory Control → Physical Inventories* to do your initial inventory.

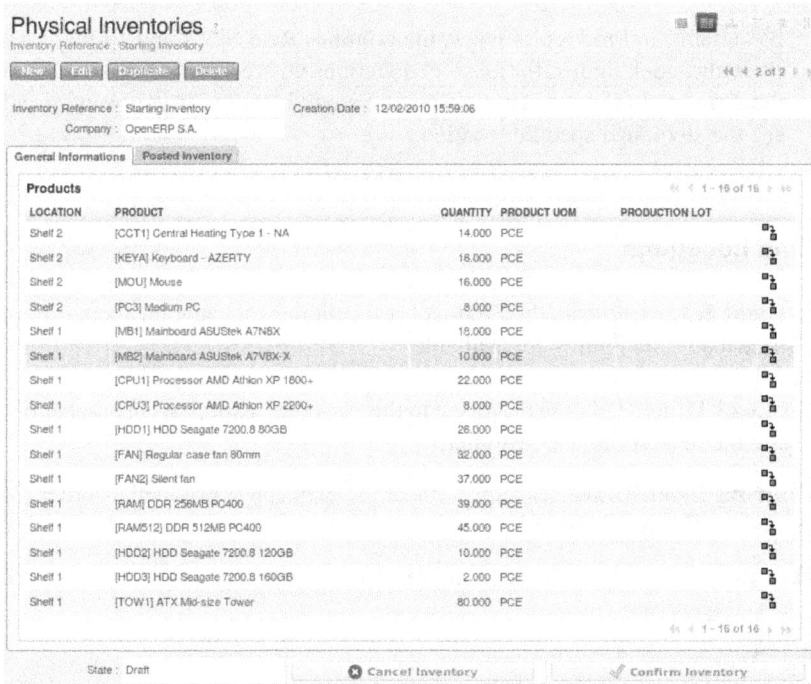

Figure 5.6: *Defining a New Inventory Operation*

---

Give a name (for example Initial Inventory or Lost Product XYZ ) and a date (proposed by default) for each inventory operation.

You have three ways of doing an inventory.

- Click the Import Inventory action and select the location concerned. You can choose to include child locations and set the inventory to zero (especially useful to ensure the count is done correctly).

- You can update the inventory from the Product form. Go to the Information tab, Stocks section, and click the Update button. On confirmation, OpenERP will create a Physical Inventory.

- You can manually add inventory lines. You can then enter data about the quantities available for each product by location. Start by entering the location, for example Stock , and then select the product. OpenERP automatically completes the quantity available for that product in the location shown. You can then change that value to correct the value in stock.

Enter data for a single line in your inventory:

- Location : Stock,

- Product : PC1 Basic PC,

- Quantity : 23 Units.

When your inventory operation is finished, you can confirm it using the Confirm Inventory button to the bottom right of the form. OpenERP will then automatically create the stock moves to close the gaps, as mentioned at the start of this chapter. You can verify the moves generated using the Posted Inventory tab of the inventory operation form.

The correct levels of your product are now in your stock locations. A simple way of verifying this is to reopen the product form to see the quantities available in stock.

---

**Periodical Inventory**

You are usually legally required to do a stock check of all your products at least once a year. As well as doing a complete annual stock check, OpenERP also supports the method of periodical inventory.

That means you can check the stock levels of a proportion of your products every so often. This system is accepted in France as long as you can guarantee that all of your products have been counted at least once per year. To see the last inventory count per product, use the report *Warehouse → Reporting → Last Product Inventories*.

You can do this the same way for all products and all locations, so you only carry out small inventory operations through the year, rather than a single large stock check at one point in the year (which usually turns out to be at an inconvenient time).

---

# 5.3 Keeping Track of Stock Movements

## 5.3.1 Goods Receipts

In OpenERP, you have the choice between three ways to receive goods from suppliers.

The first method is to manually enter the information in the incoming shipment. To receive the products through this method, you have to go to *Incoming Shipments* section in the *Warehouse Management* submenu, click New and then you enter the information about the receipt.

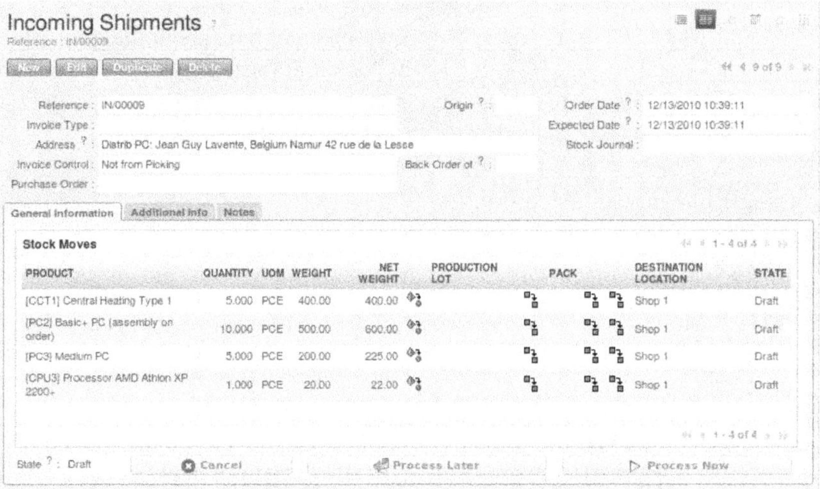

Figure 5.7: *Manual Data Entry for Product Receipt*

The second method is to receive products from a generated incoming shipment. To achieve the reception using this method, you have to go to *Incoming Shipments* section in the *Warehouse Management* submenu. You will find the list of waiting incoming shipments.

The third method is to receive products by waiting products without looking at the shipment document. You can validate the reception by products in *Receive Products* section in the :guilabel:' Product Moves' submenu. With this method, you will be able to receive one product, regardless of the document which is attached to this product.

### Receipt of a Supplier Order by Purchase Order

If you use Purchase Orders in OpenERP, product receipts are automatically generated by the system when the purchase order is confirmed. You do not have to enter any date, just confirm that the quantities ordered match the quantities received.

Incoming Shipments forms are automatically prepared by OpenERP from the purchase management process. You will find a list of all the awaited receipts in the menu *Warehouse* → *Warehouse Management* → *Incoming Shipments*. Use the order number or the supplier name to find the right goods receipt form for confirmation of a goods-in. This approach enables you to control quantities received by referring to the quantities ordered.

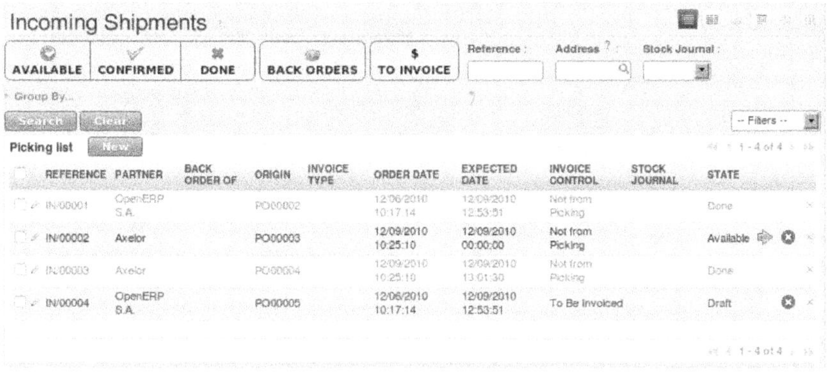

Figure 5.8: *List of Items Waiting*

You can also do goods-in data entry manually if there is no order, using the same menu by clicking the *New* button.

A new goods-in data entry form opens. Enter the supplier data in the *Address* field and type the reference number from your supplier in the field *Origin*. You should then enter data about the products received in the lines.

The source location is already completed by default because of your supplier selection. You should then give the destination location where you will place the products. For example, enter Stock. At this stage, you can set a lot number for traceability (this function will be described later in this chapter, so leave this field empty for the moment).

Once the form has been completed, you can confirm the receipt of all the products at the same time using the *Process Now* button. If you want to enter data for a goods receipt that you are still waiting for, click the button *Process Later*.

**Partial or Complete Reception**

When you process the incoming shipment, you can choose between partial or complete.

If you have to validate a partial incoming shipment, click `Process now` and change the number of items according to the quantity received.

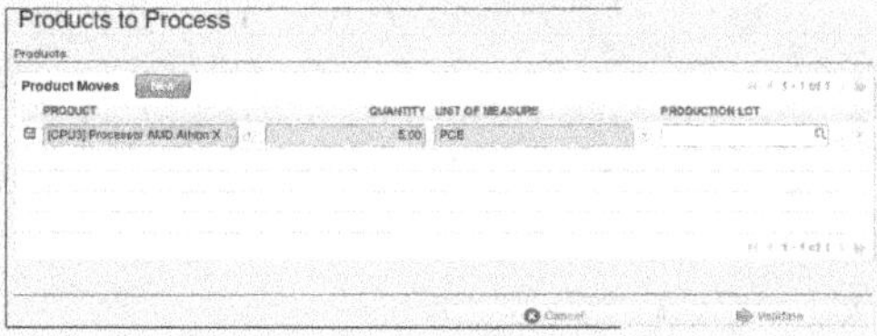

Figure 5.9: *Confirm partial reception*

Another object will be generated with a back order reference equal to the `Reference` number of the incoming shipment already confirmed.

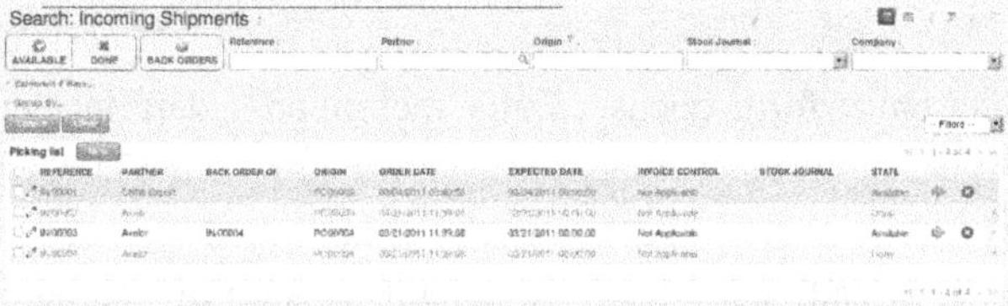

Figure 5.10: *Process a Partial Incoming Shipment*

Once the rest of the order has arrived and has been processed, both orders will be merged.

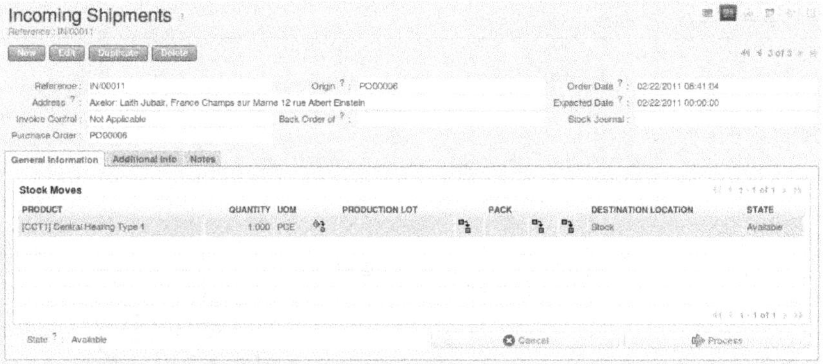

Figure 5.11: *Form for Entering Goods received from a Supplier Order*

The products then arrive in stock and should reflect the quantities shown on the product form.

In the *Incoming Shipments* form, the field *Invoice Control* lets you influence the way you send invoices to suppliers. If this is set to `To be invoiced`, a supplier invoice will now be generated automatically in the draft state, based on the goods received. Your accountant then has to confirm this pre-invoicing once the supplier's invoice is received. This enables you to verify that the invoiced quantities correspond to the quantities received.

> **Print the Packing List**
>
> In order to print the packing list of an incoming shipment, select the incoming shipment of which you need the details and click `Packing List` in the panel at the right side of the screen.
>
> This link is available in the `Internal Moves` and `Delivery Orders` sections.

In case you received damaged or wrong products, you can return them to the supplier. In the `Incoming shipment` form, click the `Return Products` button. A window will open that lets you choose the invoicing process to follow. Once you click `Process`, a stock move is generated with the same reference number and *return* to specify that this is a return move.

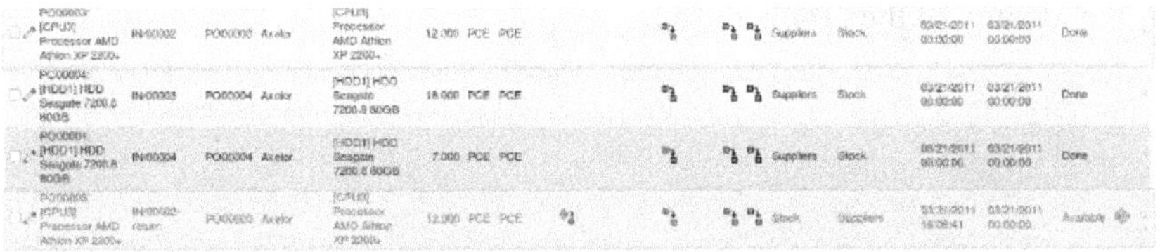

Figure 5.12: *Stock Move for Returned Products*

## Receipt of a Supplier Order by Product

The approach shown above is very useful if goods receipts correspond to the original orders. If your suppliers deliver items that do not necessarily coincide with the orders, however, it is easier to work by products received rather than by orders.

From this version on, you can also handle receptions by product, even from List view. Go to *Warehouse → Products Moves → Receive Products*.

Filters allow you to easily select receipts to be done, and so on. One way to quickly receive products is to Group by *Supplier* and select *To Do*.

This is very useful functionality when your supplier sends the goods for several purchase orders at a time. You can now just receive the products, regardless of the purchase order they come from, simply by clicking the green arrow at the right side of the screen.

The List view offers great flexibility and allows you to rapidly receive products by keeping full functionality! Of course, you can handle both partial and complete receptions, and you can add information about the production lots and packs.

This can be also accomplished from Form view.

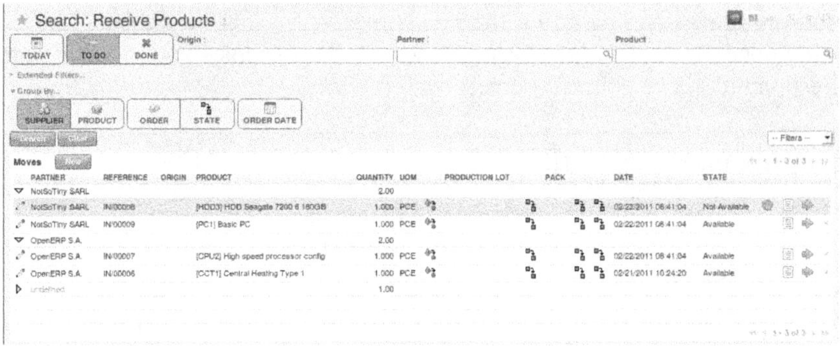

Figure 5.13: *Receipt of a Supplier Order using Group By*

## 5.3.2 Internal Stock Moves

You should install the `stock_location` module (from the list of modules, or through Reconfigure wizard, Advanced Routes) if routing products to customers, from suppliers or in your warehouse is determined by the identity of the product itself.

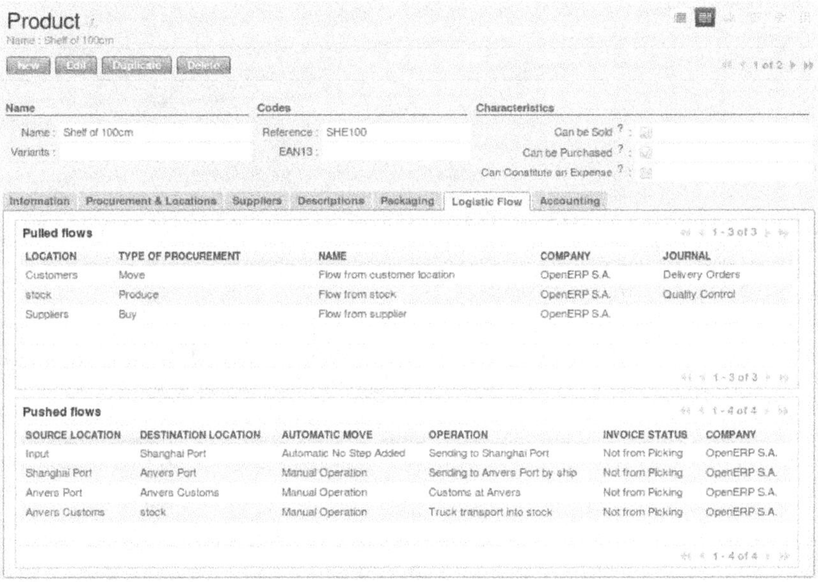

Figure 5.14: *Managing the Paths from one Location to Another in a Product Form*

This will let you configure logistics rules individually for each product. For example, when a specific product arrives in stores, it can automatically be sent to quality control. In this case, it has to be configured as a Push Flow with rules in the Product form. The fields that make up those rules are:

- **Source Location**: the rule only applies if a product comes from this location,

- **Destination Location**: the rule only applies if a product ends up in this location,

- **Automatic Move**: `Automatic Move, Manual Operation, Automatic No Step Added,`

- **Delay (days)**,

- **Operation**: a free text field which will be included in the automatic stock move proposed by OpenERP.

There are two main logistic flows:

- **Pushed Flows**

- **Pulled Flows**

*Push* flows are useful when the arrival of certain products in a given location should always be followed by a corresponding move to another location, optionally after a certain delay. The original Warehouse application already supports such Push flow specifications on the Locations themselves, but these cannot be refined per product. *Pull* flows are a bit different from Push flows, in the sense that they are not related to the processing of product moves, but rather to the processing of procurement orders. What is being pulled is a need, not directly products. You will now see some examples of using these locations and logistics by product through Pushed Flows for:

- A rentable product,

- A product bought in China, following its freight by ship from port to port,

- A product that you want to send to quality control before putting it in stocks.

We will develop the third scenario: **the quality control**.

You can configure the system to put a given product in the Quality Control bay automatically when it arrives in your company. To do that, you just configure a rule for the product to be placed in the Quality Control location rather than the Input location when the product is received from the supplier.

Table 5.8: Rule to Move Products manually from Input to Quality Control

| Field | Value |
|---|---|
| Source location | Stock |
| Destination location | Quality Control |
| Automatic Move | Manual Operation |
| Shipping Type | Getting Goods |
| Delay (days) | 0 |
| Operation | Quality Control |

Once this product has been received, OpenERP will automatically manage the request for an internal movement to send it to the Quality Control location. If you want to do this automatically without having to confirm it, in the `Automatic Move` field, select *Automatic Move* or *Automatic No Step Added*.

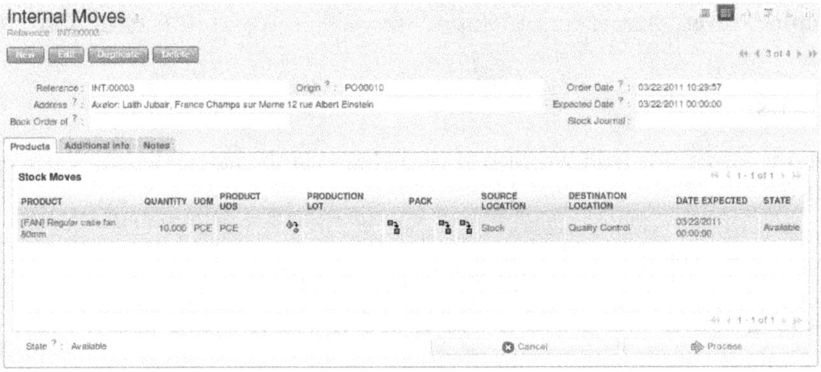

Figure 5.15: *Manual Stock Move to Quality Control*

With the configuration described in the table above, you will have to confirm the stock move manually once you have received the goods.

If you do not want to confirm the stock move manually, but you want to see the move *Suppliers –> Stock* then *Stock –> Quality Control*, change the `Automatic Move` field and select *Automatic Move*. With this configuration, you will see the two stock moves.

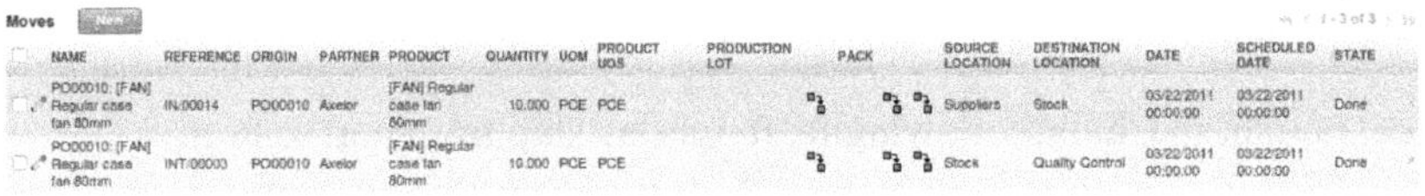

Figure 5.16: *Automatic Stock Move to Quality Control*

If you select `Automatic Move No Step Added`, you will only see one stock move: *Suppliers –> Quality Control*

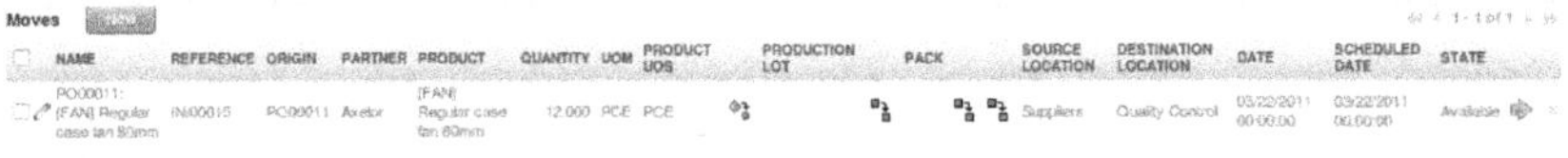

Figure 5.17: *Automatic Stock Move to Quality Control (No Step Added)*

## 5.3.3 Shipping of Goods

In the same way as delivering goods, you can ship goods in three different ways:

- manually enter data,

- deliver goods according to a sales order,

- deliver goods by product.

Everything about goods receipt can also be done manually in the same way for a customer delivery. This time, use the automated product delivery processes based on customer orders. Install the `sale` module (*Reconfigure* wizard, *Sales Management*), so that you can proceed further in this section of the chapter.

Now create a new sales order from the menu *Sales → Sales → Sales Orders*. Enter the following data in this order:

- *Shop* : `OpenERP S.A.`
- *Customer* : `Agrolait`
- *Sales order lines* :
    - *Product* : `[PC2] Basic+ PC (assembly on order)`,
    - *Quantity (UoM)* : 3,
    - *Product UoM* : `PCE`,
    - *Procurement Method* : `from stock`.

You have already seen that OpenERP shows the available product stock in list view. The real stock is equal to the virtual stock because you have nothing to deliver to customers and you are not waiting for any of these products to be received into stock. The salesperson then has all the information needed to take orders efficiently.

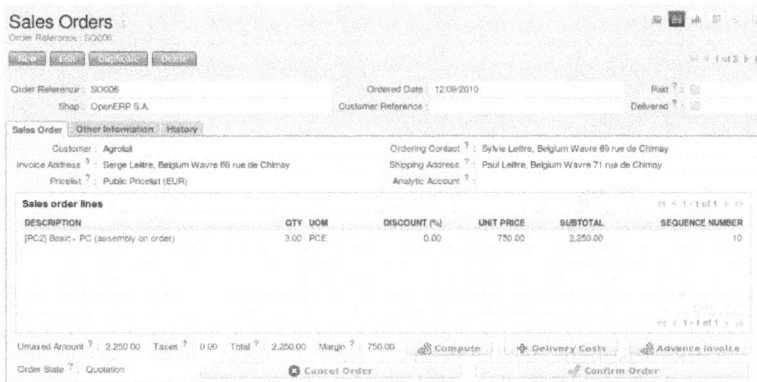

Figure 5.18: *Entering an Order for Three Computers*

Then confirm the quotation to convert it to an order. If you return to the product form, you will see the virtual stock is now smaller than the real stock.

Start the scheduler through the menu *Warehouse → Schedulers → Compute Schedulers*. Its functionality will be detailed in *ch-mnf*. This manages the reservation of products and places orders based on the dates promised to customers, and the various internal lead times and priorities. Three products will be reserved in the order that you created, so they cannot be sold to another customer.

> **Just in Time**
>
> Install the module `mrp_jit` to schedule each order in real time after it has been confirmed. This means that you do not have to start the scheduler or wait for its periodical start time.

Now have a look at the list of deliveries waiting to be carried out using the menu *Warehouse* → *Warehouse Management* → *Delivery Orders*. You find a line there for your order representing the items to be sent. Double-click the line to see the detail of the items proposed by OpenERP.

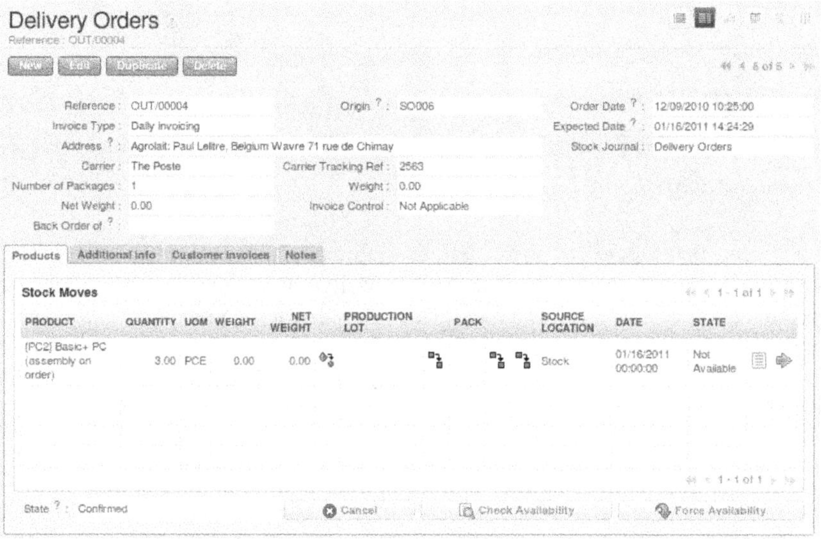

Figure 5.19: *Items on a Customer Order*

> **States**
>
> OpenERP distinguishes between the states **Confirmed** and **Assigned**.
>
> An item is **Confirmed** when it is needed, but the available stock may be insufficient. An item is **Assigned** when it is available in stock and the storesperson reserves it: the necessary products have been reserved for this specific operation.

You can also confirm a customer delivery from a confirmed Sales Order. When you click the *Process* button of *Outgoing Deliveries*, a window opens where you can enter the quantities actually delivered. If you enter a value less than the forecasted one, OpenERP automatically generates a partial delivery note and a new order for the remaining items. For this exercise, just confirm all the products.

However, if you want to look at a partial shipping, an example will be developed at the end of this section.

If you return to the list of current orders, you will see that your order has now been marked as delivered (Done). A progress indicator from 0% to 100% is shown by each order so that the salesperson can follow the progress of his orders at a glance.

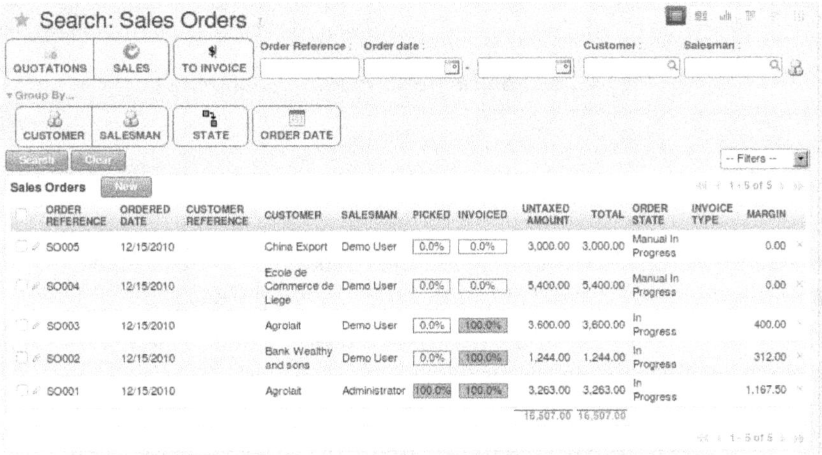

Figure 5.20: *List of Orders with their Delivery State*

---

**Negative Stock**

Stock Management is very flexible to be more effective. For example, if you forget to enter products at goods-in, this will not prevent you from sending them to customers. In OpenERP, you can force all operations manually using the button *Force Availability*. In this case, your stocks risk to become negative. You should monitor all stocks for negative levels and carry out an inventory correction when that happens.

---

## Partial Shipping

Should you have to process a partial delivery, you can go to *Warehouse → Warehouse Management → Delivery Orders*, then select the order to process it. In the new window, change the quantity to ship and then confirm it.

If you go back to the list view, you will now see a new delivery order with a `back order` number equal to the just confirmed order. This is illustrated in the following figure.

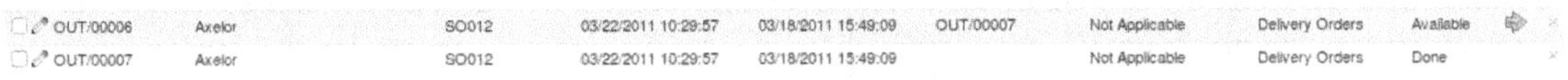

Figure 5.21: *Partial Shipping*

In the stock moves, you will see that there are two moves. The first move is for the remaining quantities to ship and the second one is for the shipped goods. There will be more stock moves if you process

---

partial shipping in more than two times.

Figure 5.22: *Stock Moves in Partial Shipping*

## Return Products from Customers

If a customer returns damaged or wrongly delivered products, you can enter this information in OpenERP via *Warehouse → Warehouse Management → Delivery Orders*.

You have to select the order related to the returned products and click the *Return Products*. A new window will open and will let you choose the invoicing method.

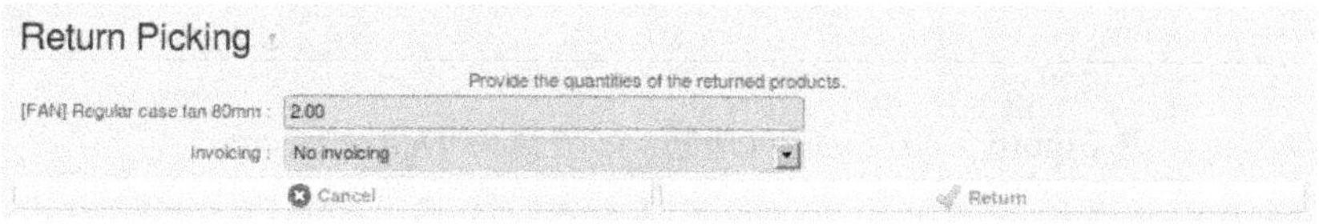

Figure 5.23: *Return Products from Customers*

When the product is returned, it will go back to your stock and you will see a stock move from *Customers –> Shelf 1*.

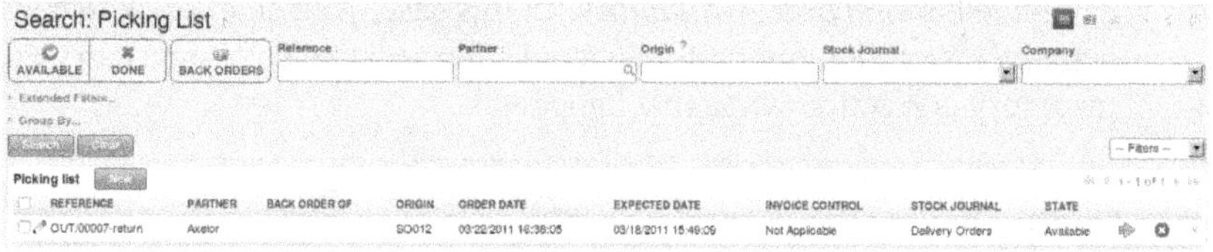

Figure 5.24: *Stock Move for a Returned Product*

## Just In Time

By default, scheduling starts automatically once a day. You should make this scheduling execute overnight to ensure that the system does not slow down under a heavy load of scheduling when you are also trying to use it interactively.

To set the start time for the scheduler, go to the menu *Administration → Configuration → Scheduler → Scheduled Actions*. Select the rule called 'Run mrp scheduler' and modify the date and time of the next execution. Some companies want to plan orders progressively as they are entered, so they do not wait until procurement orders are planned the next day. Install the module `mrp_jit` (*Reconfigure* wizard,

*Just In Time Scheduling*) to handle this. Once the module is installed, each requirement (that could result in a Production or Purchase Order) will be planned in real time as soon as it has been confirmed.

Then if you make a sales order with a product that is `Make To Order`, the quotation request to a supplier will immediately be generated.

> **Delivery from the Supplier or to the Customer**
>
> The `sale_supplier_direct_delivery` module enables you to deliver the product directly from the supplier to the customer. At the time of writing, this module is in `extra-addons`. The logic that the product follows is configured individually for each product and affects only products marked `Make to Order`.

This mode does not always makes sense. Each order is processed immediately when confirmed. So if an order is to be delivered in three months, the scheduler will reserve goods in stock for each order once it has been confirmed. It would have been more sensible to leave these products available for other orders.

If a Purchase Order's *Invoicing Control* is configured `From Order`, the scheduler will immediately create the corresponding supplier quotation request. It might have been better to delay it for several weeks, if you could have used the lead time to group the purchase with other future orders.

So the negative effects of working with the Just in Time module are:

- Poor priority management between orders,

- Additionally stocked products.

## 5.3.4 Logistics Configuration through Advanced Routes

To configure your logistics for advanced push and pull, you need to install `stock_location` module (*Reconfigure* wizard, *Advanced Routes*) as explained before. A complete scenario will be developed at the end of this chapter.

This module supplements the *Warehouse* application by adding support for location paths per product, effectively implementing Push and Pull inventory flows.

Typically this could be used to:

- Manage product manufacturing chains,

- Manage default locations per product,

- Define routes within your warehouse according to business needs, such as:

  - Quality Control
  - After Sales Services
  - Supplier Returns

• Help rental management, by generating automated return moves for rented products.

Once this module is installed, an additional *Logistics Flows* tab appears in the Product form, allowing you to add *Push and Pull* flow specifications.

## Push Flow

Push flows are useful when the arrival of certain products in a given location should always be followed by a corresponding move to another location, optionally after a certain delay.

> **Product**
>
> The core *Warehouse Management* application already supports such Push Flow specifications on the Locations, but these cannot be refined per product.

A push flow specification indicates which location is chained with another location, as well as the parameters used. As soon as a given quantity of products is moved to the source location, a chained move is automatically foreseen according to the parameters set on the flow specification (destination location, delay, type of move, journal, etc.) The new move may be processed automatically, or may require a manual confirmation, according to what you have defined.

Suppose whenever the demo data product CPU3 enters the *Stock* location, it first has to be moved to the *Quality Control* location in order to check the quality.

Look up the product CPU3 using the menu *Warehouse → Product → Products*.

To have OpenERP accomplish this move automatically, you have to configure the *Push* flow as follows:

- *Operation*: Receptions to Quality Control
- *Source Location*: Stock
- *Destination Location*: Quality Control
- *Automatic Move*: Automatic No Step Added
- *Delay (days)*: 1
- *Shipping Type*: Getting Goods
- *Invoice Status*: Not Applicable

A push flow is related to how stock moves should be generated in order to increase or decrease inventory.

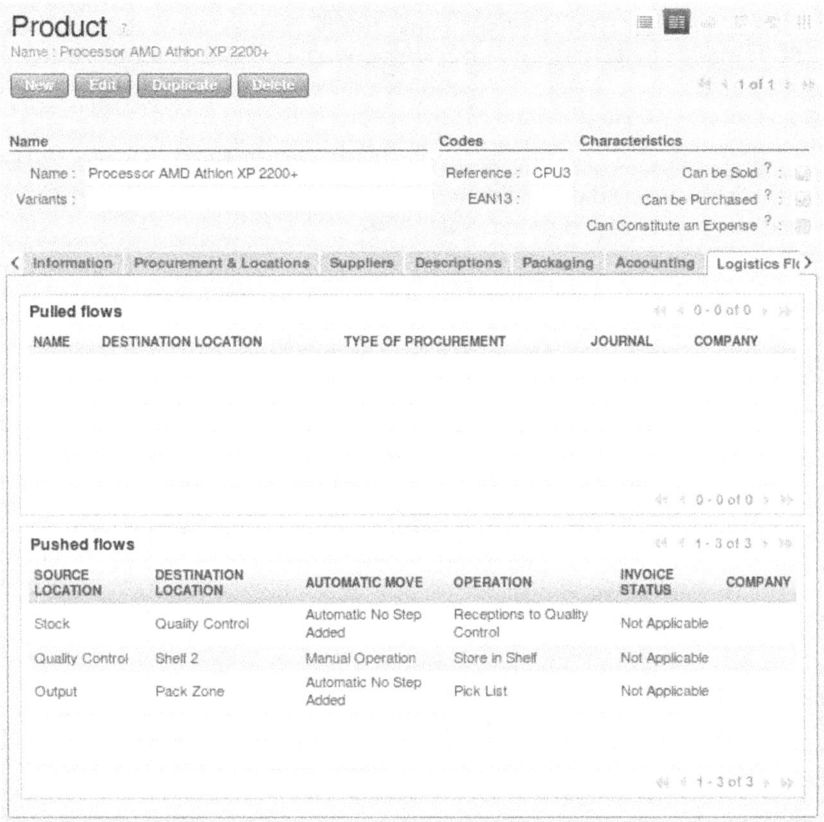

Figure 5.25: *Push Flow Specification for Product CPU3*

## Pull Flow

*Pull* flows are a bit different from Push flows, in the sense that they are not related to the processing of product moves, but rather to the processing of procurement orders. What is being pulled is a *need*, not directly products.

A classical example of a Pull flow is when you have an Outlet company, with a parent Company that is responsible for the supplies of the Outlet.

[ Customer ] <- A - [ Outlet ] <- B - [ Holding ] <- C - [ Supplier ]

> **Demo Data**
>
> In our demo data example, the Outlet Company is Shop 1, while OpenERP SA is the parent company.

When a new procurement order A (resulting from the confirmation of a Sales Order, for example) is created in the Outlet (Shop 1), it is converted into another procurement B (through a Pull flow of the 'move' type) requested from the Holding. When procurement order B is processed by the Holding company (OpenERP SA), and if the product is out of stock, it may be converted into a Purchase Order (C) from the Supplier (Push flow of the 'Buy' type). The result is that the procurement order, the need, is pushed all the way between the Customer and Supplier.

Technically, Pull flows allow to process procurement orders differently, not only depending on the product being considered, but also depending on which location holds the "need" for that product (i.e. the destination location of that procurement order).

To explain a pull flow for the product CPU1, we first have to configure the minimum stock rules of CPU1 for the company OpenERP S.A. and Shop 1 using the menu *Warehouse → Automatic Procurements → Minimum Stock Rules* or by selecting the product concerned and then clicking the Minimum Stock Rules action.

> **Minimum Stock Rules**
>
> If you work with the demo data, these minimum stock rules have already been defined.

For the company *OpenERP S.A.*:

- *Min Quantity* : 10
- *Max Quantity* : 50

For the company *Shop 1*;

- *Min Quantity* : 10
- *Max Quantity* : 20

Look up the product CPU1 using menu *Warehouse → Product → Products* in order to define the configuration of the pulled flow.

There are two specifications of a pull flow for product *CPU1*.

*Specification 1*:

- *Name* : Receive from Warehouse
- *Destination Location* : Shop 1
- *Type of Procurement* : Move
- *Source Location* : Internal Shippings
- *Partner Address* : OpenERP S.A., Belgium Gerompont Chaussee de Namur 40
- *Shipping Type* : Getting Goods
- *Procure Method* : Make to Order

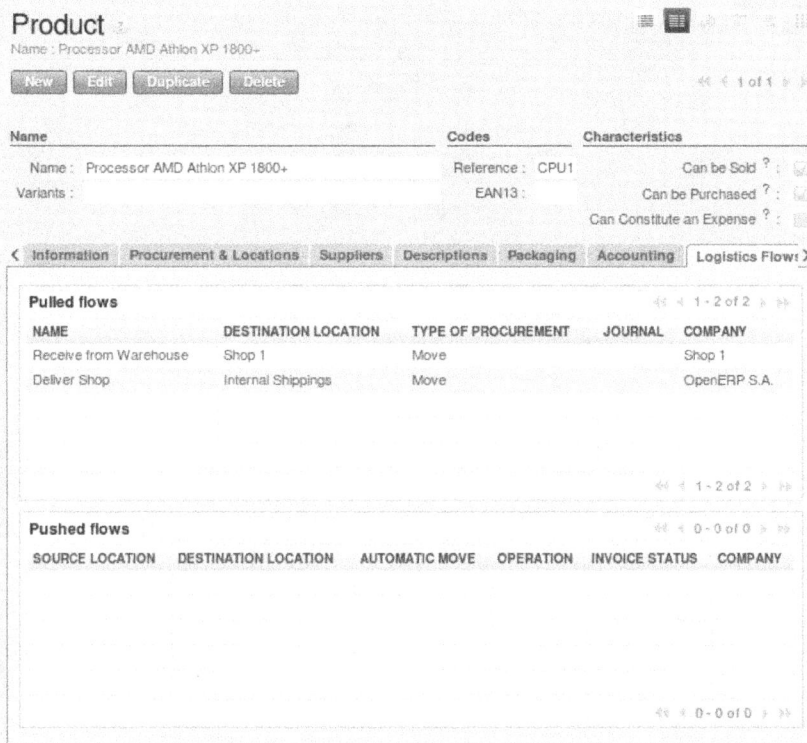

Figure 5.26: *Pull Flow Specification for Product CPU1*

- *Invoice Status*: Not Applicable

*Specification 2*:

- *Name* : Deliver Shop
- *Destination Location* : Internal Shippings
- *Type of Procurement* : Move
- *Source Location* : Stock
- *Partner Address* : Fabien
- *Shipping Type* : Sending Goods
- *Procure Method* : Make to Stock
- *Invoice Status*: Not Applicable

Now sell 1 unit of product CPU1 from the Shop1 (do not forget to confirm your sales order) and run the scheduler using the menu *Warehouse → Schedulers → Compute Schedulers*. Then check the stock moves for product CPU1 from the menu *Warehouse → Traceability → Stock Moves*.

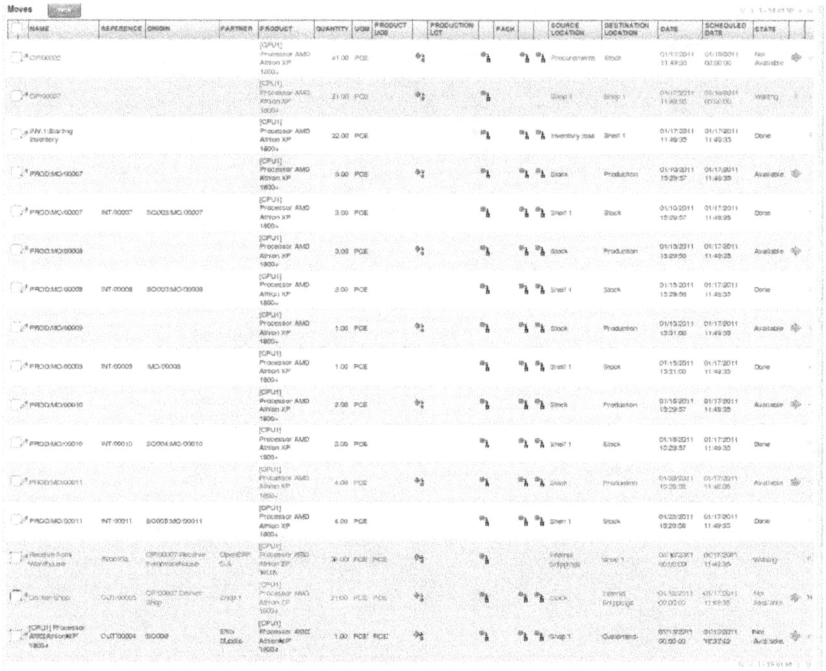

Figure 5.27: *Stock Move of CPU1 related to Pull Flow Specification*

These moves can be explained like this:

[ Customer ] <– [ *Shop 1* ] <– Internal Shippings <– Stock <– [ *OpenERP S.A.* ]

When the company Shop 1 sells one unit of CPU1 to a customer, its stock decreases to 10 units. According to the minimum stock rule of the product CPU1, OpenERP generates a procurement order of 21 units of CPU1 for the company Shop 1 (OP/00007, or another number if you have added extra data). So 21 units of CPU1 move from OpenERP S.A. Stock to Shop 1 according to their internal configuration of Source and Destination Locations.

A pull flow is related to how the procurement process runs in order to find products to increase or decrease inventory.

## 5.3.5 Procurement Methods – Make to Stock and Make to Order

The procurement method determines how the product will be replenished:

- *Make to Stock*: your customers are supplied from available stock. If the quantities in stock are too low to fulfil the order, a Purchase Order (according the minimum stock rules) will be generated in order to get the products required. Example: a classic distributor.

- *Make to Order*: when a customer order is confirmed, you procure or manufacture the products for this order. A customer order 'Make to Order' will not modify stock in the medium term because you restock with the exact amount that was ordered. Example: computers from a large supplier assembled on demand.

You find a mix of these two modes used for the different final and intermediate products in most industries. The procurement method shown on the product form is a default value for the order, enabling the salesperson to choose the best mode for fulfilling a particular order by varying the sales order parameters as needed.

The figures *Change in Stock for a Make to Stock Product* (page 105) and *Change in Stock for a Make to Order Product* (page 105) show the change of stock levels for one product managed as *Make to Order* and another managed as *Make to Stock*. The two figures are taken from OpenERP's *Stock Level Forecast* report, available from the product form.

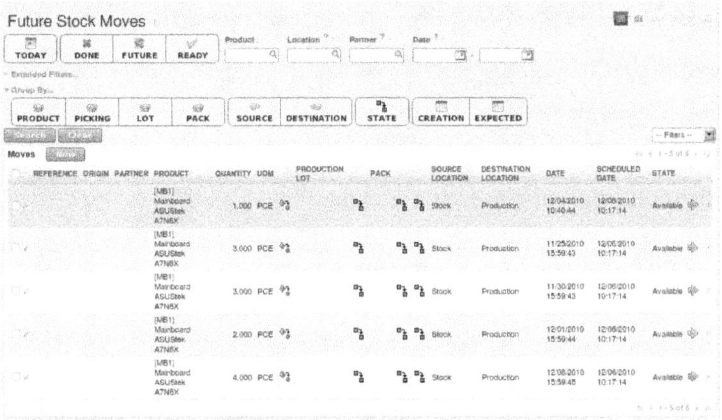

Figure 5.28: *Change in Stock for a Make to Stock Product*

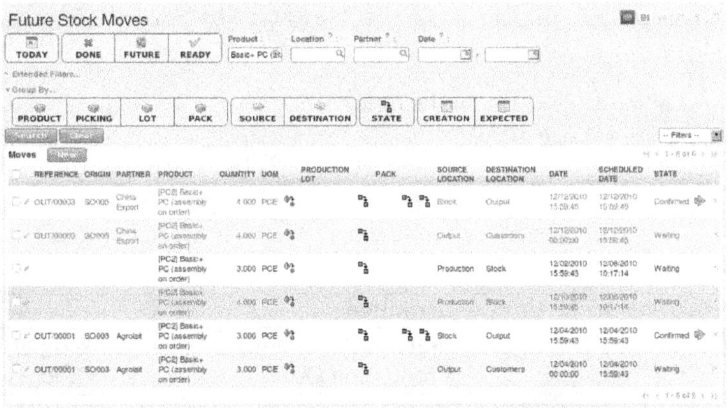

Figure 5.29: *Change in Stock for a Make to Order Product*

## 5.3.6 Choosing Supply Methods

OpenERP supports two supply methods:

- Produce: when the product is manufactured or the service is supplied from internal resources.

- Buy: when the product is bought from a supplier.

These are just the default settings used by the system during automated replenishment. The same product can be either manufactured internally or bought from a supplier.

These three fields (*Supply Method*, *Procurement Method*, *Product Type*) determine the system's behaviour when a product is required. The system will generate different documents depending on the configuration of these three fields when satisfying an order, a price quotation to a supplier or a manufacturing order.

OpenERP manages both stockable products and services. A service bought from a supplier in *Make to Order* mode, will generate a subcontract order from the supplier in question.

Figure *Workflow for Automatic Procurement, depending on the Product Configuration* (page 107) illustrates different cases for automatic procurement.

The table below shows all possible cases for the figure *Workflow for Automatic Procurement, depending on the Product Configuration* (page 107).

Table 5.9: Consequences of Procurement Methods Make to Stock (MTS) and Make To Order (MTO)

| Procurement Method | Produce | Buy |
|---|---|---|
| MTS | Wait for availability | Wait for availability |
| MTO | Production Order | Purchase Order |

Table 5.10: Consequences of Procurement Methods when using Services

| Procurement Method | Produce | Buy |
|---|---|---|
| MTS | / | / |
| MTO | Create task | Subcontract |

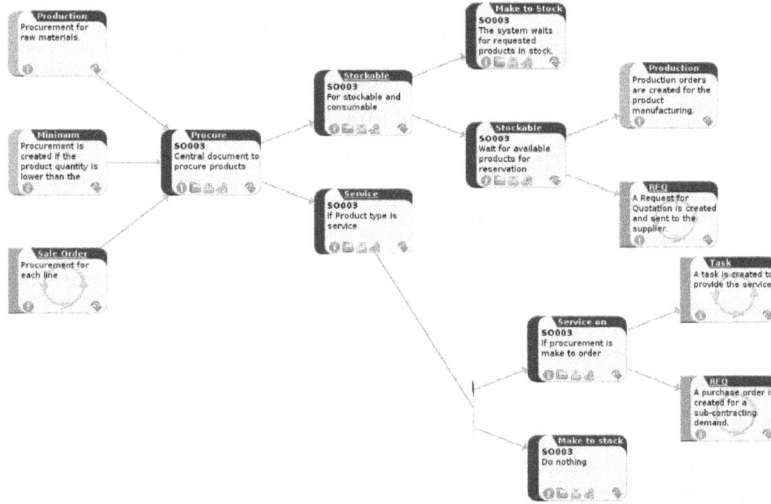

Figure 5.30: *Workflow for Automatic Procurement, depending on the Product Configuration*

## 5.3.7 Packaging with Various Logistics Units of Measure

### Units of Measure

OpenERP supports several units of measure. Quantities of the same product can be expressed in several units of measure at once. For example, you can buy grain by the tonne and resell it by kg. You just have to make sure that all the units of measure used for a product are in the same units of measure category.

> **Categories of Units of Measure**
>
> All units of measure in the same category are convertible from one unit to another.

The table below shows some examples of units of measure and their category. The factor is used to convert from one unit of measure to another as long as they are in the same category.

Table 5.11: Example Units of Measure

| UoM | Category | Ratio | UoM Type |
|---|---|---|---|
| Kg | Weight | 1 | Reference |
| Gram | Weight | 1000 | Smaller |
| Tonne | Weight | 1000 | Bigger |
| Hour | Working time | 8 | Smaller |
| Day | Working time | 1 | Reference |
| Half-day | Working time | 4 | Smaller |
| Item | Unit | 1 | |
| 100 Items | Unit | 0.01 | |

Depending on the table above, you have 1Kg = 1000g = 0.001 Tonnes. A product in the `Weight` category could be expressed in Kg, Tonnes or Grammes. You cannot express it in hours or pieces, for example.

Use the menu *Warehouse → Configuration → Products → Units of Measure → Units of Measure* to define a new unit of measure.

In the definition of a Unit of Measure, you have a *Rounding precision* factor which shows how amounts are rounded after the conversion. A value of 1 gives rounding to the level of one unit. 0.01 gives rounding to one hundredth.

---

**Secondary Units**

OpenERP supports double units of measure. Notice however that the default unit of measure and the purchase unit of measure have to be in the same category. Only the sales unit of measure may be in a different category.

This is very useful in the agro-food industry, for example: you sell ham by the piece, but invoice by the Kg. A weighing operation is needed before invoicing the customer.

---

To activate the management options for double units of measure, assign the group *Useability / Product UoS View* to your user.

In this case, the same product can be expressed in two units of measure belonging to different categories for sales and stock/purchase. You can then distinguish between the unit of stock management (the piece) and the unit of invoicing or sales (kg).

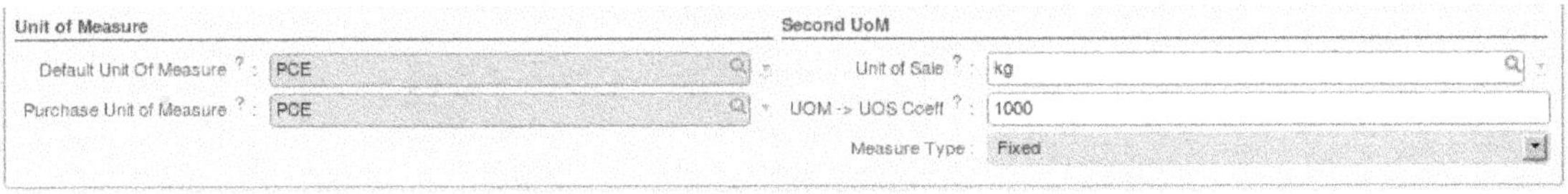

Figure 5.31: *Secondary Unit of Measure*

In the product form you can set one unit of measure for sales and stock management, and one unit of measure for purchases.

For each operation on a product, you can use another unit of measure, as long as it can be found in the same category as the two units already defined. If you use another unit of measure, OpenERP automatically handles the conversion of prices and quantities.

So if you have 430 Kg of carrots at 5.30 EUR/Kg, OpenERP will automatically make the conversion if you want to sell in tonnes – 0.43 tonnes at 5300 EUR / tonne. If you had set a rounding factor of 0.1 for the *tonne* unit of measure, OpenERP will tell you that you have only 0.4 tonnes available.

## Packaging

The packaging allows you to ship products in several ways. For example, you can ship goods by boxes or by pallets.

At first, you have to define possible packaging. To define the packaging, go to :menuselection: *Warehouse –> Configuration –> Product –> Packaging* and click *New*.

Figure 5.32: *Packaging definition*

To complete the creation of a new packaging, you have to give it a name and a type. Different types are available in OpenERP: *Box*, *Pack*, *Pallet* and *Unit*.

Once all packaging is defined, you can attach the packaging to your products through the following menu: *Warehouse → Configuration → Product → Packaging*.

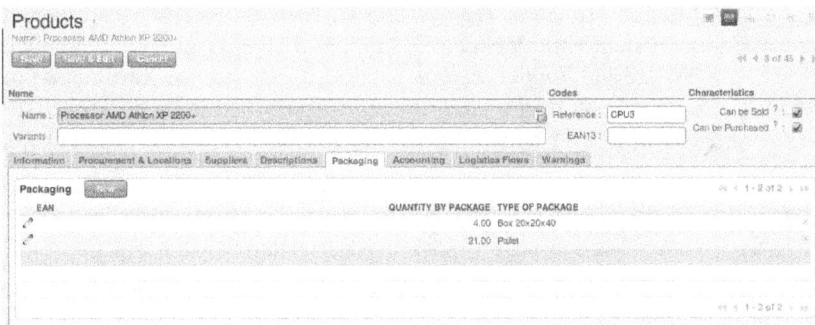

Figure 5.33: *Defining the Packaging for the Product*

# 5.4 Scheduling Procurements

The master production plan, sometimes called the MPS (Master Production Schedule), enables you to generate forecasts for incoming and outgoing material. It is based on forecasts of inputs and outputs by the logistics manager.

To be able to use the production plan, you must install the `stock_planning` module.

> **MPS, Procurement and Production**
>
> OpenERP distinguishes between Production, Purchase and Procurement.
>
> Production is manufacturing, Purchase is the acquisition of goods from another party, and Procurement is either one or both of those. So it would be better to call the MPS the Master Procurement Schedule. Which OpenERP does!

> **Product Trading**
>
> Also called the Production Plan, this tool is also very useful for traded products which are not manufactured. You can use it for stock management with purchased and manufactured products.

## 5.4.1 Processing Exceptions

The set of stock requirements is generated by procurement orders.

In normal system use, you do not need to worry about procurement orders because they are automatically generated by OpenERP and the user will usually work on the results of a procurement: a production order, a purchase order, a sales order and a task.

If there should be configuration problems, the system can remain blocked by a procurement without generating a corresponding document. For example, suppose that you configure a product *Procurement Method* as `Make to Order`, and *Supply Method* as `Produce`, but you have not defined the bill of materials. In that case, procurement of the product will stay blocked in an exception state `No Bill of Materials defined for this product`. You then have to create a bill of materials to solve the problem.

Troubleshooting:

- No bill of materials defined for production: you need to create a BoM or indicate that the product can be purchased instead.

- No supplier available for a purchase: you have to define a supplier in the *Supplier* tab of the product form.

- No address defined on the supplier partner: you have to complete an address for the default supplier for the product concerned.

- No quantity available in stock: you have to create a rule for automatic procurement (for example, a minimum stock rule) and put it in the order, or manually procure it.

Some problems are just those of timing and can be automatically corrected by the system.

Use the menu *Warehouse → Schedulers → Procurement Exceptions* to see all the exceptions.

If a product has to be 'in stock', but is not available in your stores, OpenERP will make the exception as 'temporary' or 'to be corrected'. The exception is temporary if the system can procure it automatically, for example, if a procurement rule is defined for minimum stock.

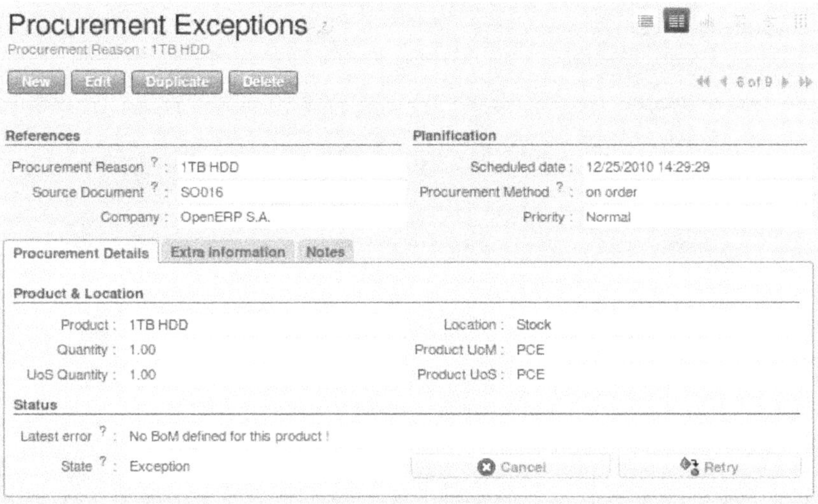

Figure 5.34: *Example of a Procurement in Exception*

If no procurement rule is defined, the exception has to be corrected manually by the user. Once the exception is corrected, you can restart by clicking *Retry*. If you do not do that, OpenERP will automatically recalculate on the next automated requirements calculation.

## 5.4.2 Manual Procurement

To procure internally, you can create a procurement order manually. Use the menu *Warehouse → Schedulers → Procurement Exceptions* and click the *New* button to do this.

The procurement order will then be responsible for calculating a proposal for automatic procurement for the product concerned. This procurement will start a task, a purchase order for the supplier or a production depending on the product configuration.

It is better to encode a procurement order rather than direct purchasing or production. This method has the following advantages:

- The form is simpler because OpenERP calculates the different values from other values and defined rules: purchase date calculated from order date, default supplier, raw materials needs, selection of the most suitable bill of materials, etc.

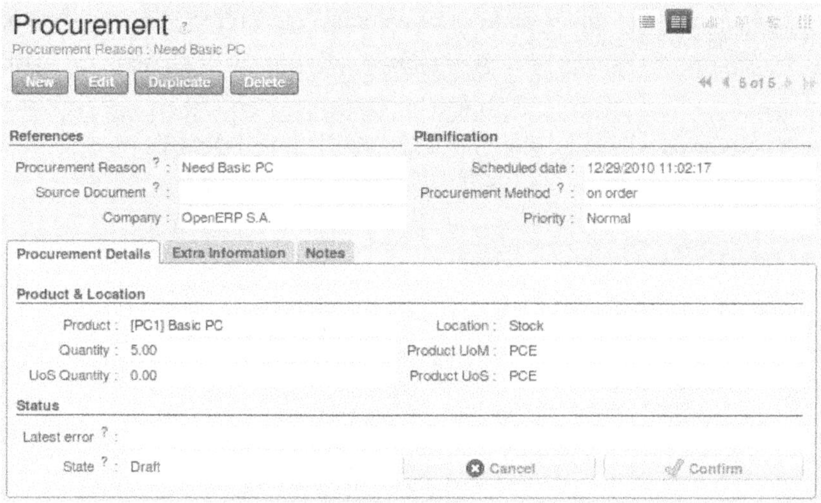

Figure 5.35: *Encoding a New Procurement Order*

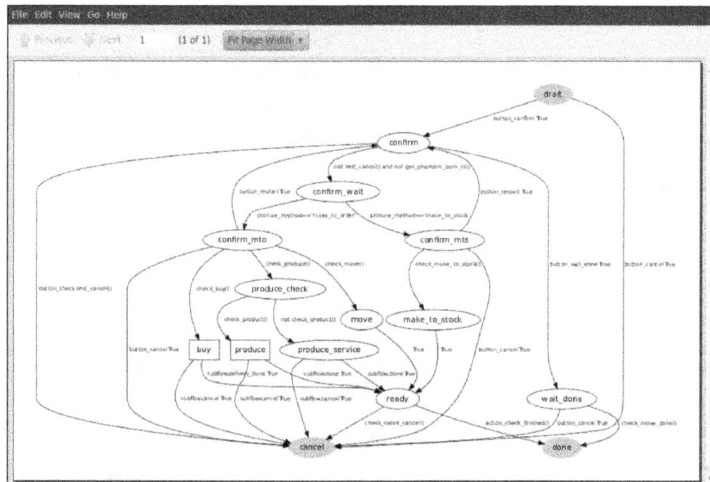

Figure 5.36: *Workflow for Handling a Procurement according to Product Configuration*

- The calculation of requirements prioritises the procurements. If you encode a purchase directly, you short-circuit the planning of different procurements.

---

> **Shortcuts**
>
> On the product form you have an *ACTIONS* shortcut button *Create Procurements* that lets you quickly create a new procurement order.

---

## 5.4.3 Sales Forecasts

The first thing you have to do to work with a production plan is define the periods for stock management. Some companies plan daily, others weekly or monthly.

---

> **Stock Management Interval**
>
> The interval chosen for managing stock in the production plan will depend on the length of your production cycle. You generally work daily, weekly or monthly.
>
> If it takes several days to assemble your products, you most likely will define a weekly plan. If your manufacturing cycles take several months, you can work with a monthly plan.
>
> To predefine these periods you can use the *Stock and Sales Planning Periods* that will automatically generate daily, weekly or monthly periods.

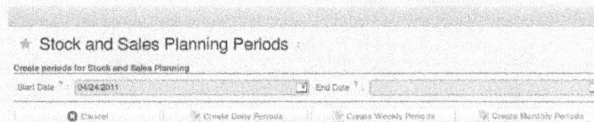

Figure 5.37: *Stock and Sales Planning Periods*

---

Go to the menu *Sales → Configuration → Stock and Sales Periods → Create Stock and Sales Periods*. A window appears enabling you to automatically define the next periods that will be provided for stock management. For this example, create weekly periods.

Salespeople can then enter their sales forecasts by product and by period using the menu *Sales → Sales Forecasts → Sales Forecasts*. The forecasts can be made by quantity or by value. For a forecast by amount, OpenERP automatically calculates the quantity equivalent to the estimated amount. This can be modified manually as needed before completion. A salesperson can create sales forecasts manually, or he can use the *Create Sales Forecasts* wizard in the above menu.

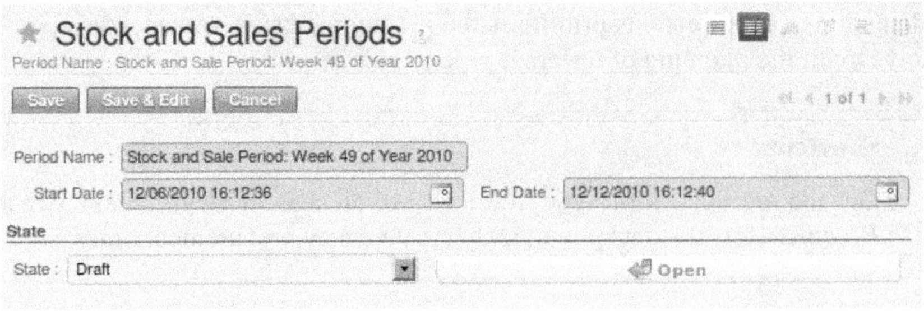

Figure 5.38: *Defining Periods for Stock Management*

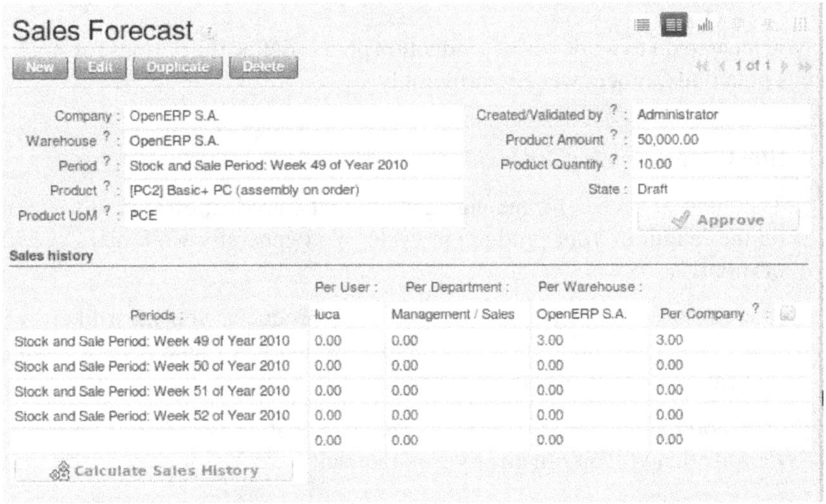

Figure 5.39: *Sales Forecast to Help Create a Master Production Plan*

## 5.4.4 Production Plan

The manager responsible for logistics then plans receipts (manufacturing or purchases) and outgoings (consumption or customer deliveries) by period. From the menu *Warehouse → Stock Planning → Create Stock Planning Lines*, you can create a stock planning per week for a specific product category. Through *Warehouse → Stock Planning → Master Procurement Schedule* you can adjust the planning.

For each period and product, OpenERP gives you the following information:

- Stock estimated at the end of the period, calculated as stock in the following period less the total estimated outgoings plus total estimated inputs,

- Closed entries, coming from production or confirmed purchases,

- Forecast inputs for the period, calculated using the incoming entries less the closing amounts,

- Planned inputs entered manually by the logistics manager,

- Closed outgoings which are the consumption of manufacturing waiting and deliveries to be made to customers,

- Forecast outgoings, calculated from the planned outgoings, less the closing amounts,

- Planned outgoings, manually entered by the logistics manager,

- Sales forecasts, which represent the sum of forecasts made by the salespeople.

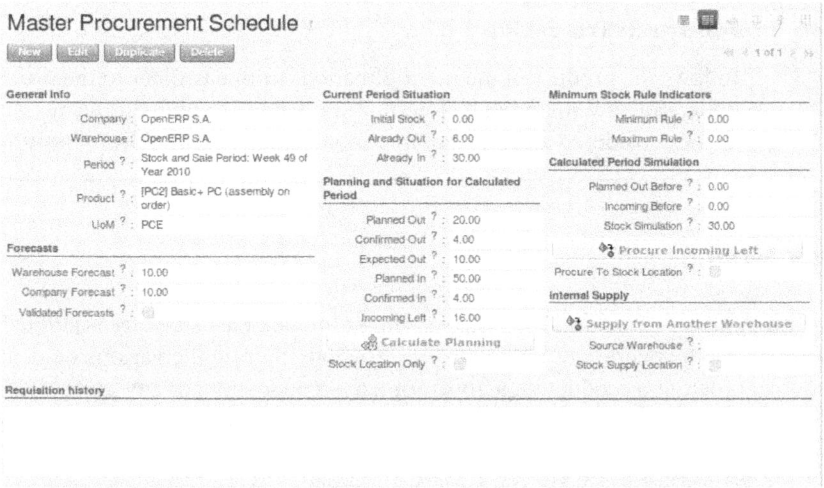

Figure 5.40: *The Master Production Schedule (MPS)*

The production plan enables the logistics manager to play with the forecast receipts and outgoings and test the impact on the future stock for the product concerned. It enables you, for example, to check that the stock does not fall below a certain level for that product.

You can also open the production plan for past periods. In this case, OpenERP shows you the real stock moves, by period for forecast reports.

If you do not have automated procurement rules for a product, you can start procurement at any time based on the estimates of the production plan. To do this, press the button *Procure Incoming Left* (i.e. remaining) on the *Master Procurement Schedule*. OpenERP plans procurement for an amount equal to the entries forecast.

# 5.5 Managing Lots and Traceability

The double-entry management in OpenERP enables you to run very advanced traceability. All operations are formalized in terms of stock moves, so it is very easy to search for the cause of any gaps in stock moves.

> **Upstream Traceability**
>
> It runs from the raw materials received from the supplier and follows the chain to the finished products delivered to customers. (Note that the name is confusing - this would often be considered a downstream direction. Think of it as **Where Used**.)

> **Downstream Traceability**
>
> It follows the product in the other direction, from customer to the different suppliers of raw material. (Note that the name is confusing - this would often be considered an upstream direction. Think of it as **Where Supplied**.)

## 5.5.1 Stock Moves

Use the menu *Warehouse → Traceability → Stock Moves* to track past stock transactions for a product or a given location. All the operations are available. You can filter on the various fields to retrieve the operations about an order, or a production activity, or a source location, or any given destination.

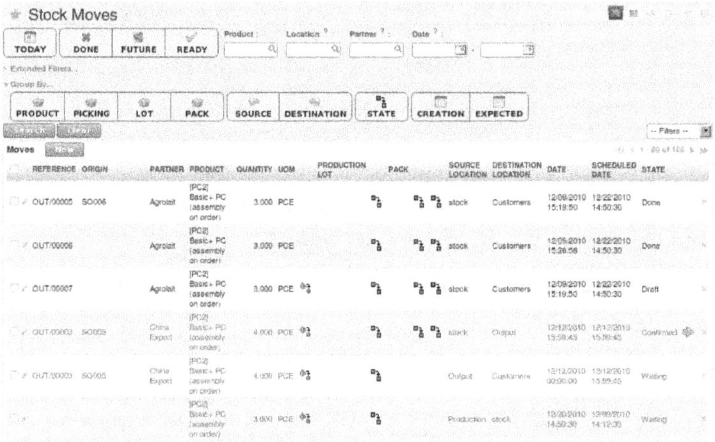

Figure 5.41: *History of Stock Movements*

Each stock move is in a given state. The various states are:

- Draft : the move so far has no effect in the system. The transaction has not yet been confirmed,

- Confirmed : the move will be done, so it will be counted in the calculations of virtual stock. But you do not know whether it will be done without problem because the products have been reserved for the move,

- Validated : the move will be done and the necessary raw materials have been reserved for the transaction,

- `Done` : the stock move has been done, and entered into the calculations of real stock,

- `Waiting` : in the case of transactions `From Order`, this state shows that the stock move is blocked waiting for the end of another move,

- `Cancelled` : the stock move was not carried out, so it is not taken into account in either real stock or virtual stock.

Delivery orders, goods receipts and internal picking lists are just documents that group a set of stock moves. You can also consult the history of these documents using the menu *Warehouse → Traceability → Packs*.

## 5.5.2 Lots

OpenERP can also manage product lots. Two lot types are defined:

- Production lots (batch numbers) are represented by a unique product or an assembly of identical products leaving the same production area. They are usually identified by bar codes stuck on the products. The batch can be marked with a supplier number or your own company numbers.

- Tracking numbers are logistical lots to identify the container for a set of products. This corresponds, for example, to the pallet numbers on which several different products are stocked.

These lots can be encoded onto all stock moves and, specifically, on incoming shipments lines, internal moves and outgoing deliveries.

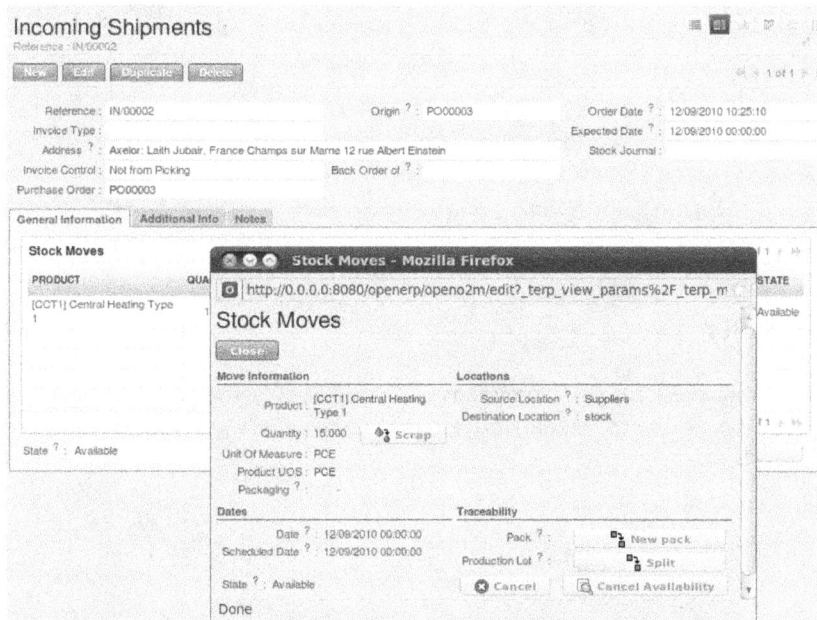

Figure 5.42: *Entering a Line for Production Receipt*

To enter the lot number in an operation, you can use an existing lot number or create a new pack. A production lot (batch number) is used for a single product. A tracking number can be used several times for different products, so you can mix different products on a pallet or in a box.

> **Simplified View**
>
> In the `Simplified` view, the tracking numbers cannot be seen: the field is hidden. To get to `Extended` view mode, assign the group *Useability / Extended View* to the current user, or change the User Preferences.

You can also specify on the product form the operations in which a lot number is required. You can then compel the user to set a lot number for manufacturing operations, goods receipt, or customer packing.

You do not have to encode the lot numbers one by one to assign a unique lot number to a set of several items. You only need to take a stock move for several products line and click the button *Split in Production Lots*. You can then give a lot number prefix (if you want) and OpenERP will complete the prefix in the wizard with a continuing sequence number. This sequence number might correspond to a set of pre-printed barcodes that you stick on each product.

Figure 5.43: *Splitting a Lot into uniquely Identified Parts*

## 5.5.3 Traceability

If you key in the lot numbers for stock moves as described above, you can investigate the traceability of any given lot number. Go to the menu *Warehouse → Traceability → Production Lots* or *Warehouse → Traceability → Packs*.

Search for a particular lot using the filters for the lot number, the date or the product. Once you can see the form about this lot, several actions can be performed:

- *Upstream Traceability*: from supplier through to customers,

- *Downstream Traceability*: from customer back to suppliers,

- Stock in all the physical and virtual locations.

**Upstream Traceability**

| PRODUCT | QUANTITY | UOM | PRODUCTION LOT | PACK | PACKAGING | REFERENCE | SOURCE LOCATION | DESTINATION LOCATION |
|---------|----------|-----|----------------|------|-----------|-----------|-----------------|----------------------|
| Mobile | 2.00 | PCE | 0000001 [Product 10 mobile] | 00000017 [Packing of 10 mobile] | | OUT/00004 | Stock | Customers |
| Mobile | 10.00 | PCE | 0000001 [Product 10 mobile] | 00000017 [Packing of 10 mobile] | | | Stock | Stock |
| Mobile | 7.00 | PCE | 0000001 [Product 10 mobile] | 00000017 [Packing of 10 mobile] | | IN/00002 | Suppliers | Stock |

Figure 5.44: *Tracing Upstream in Make to Order*

**Downstream Traceability**

| PRODUCT | QUANTITY | UOM | PRODUCTION LOT | PACK | PACKAGING | REFERENCE | SOURCE LOCATION | DESTINATION LOCATION |
|---------|----------|-----|----------------|------|-----------|-----------|-----------------|----------------------|
| Mobile | 3.00 | PCE | 0000002 [No production] | 00000031 [20 mob pur form wood] | | | Stock | Shop 1 |
| Mobile | 2.00 | PCE | 0000002 [No production] | 00000031 [20 mob pur form wood] | | | Stock | Shop 2 |
| Mobile | 10.00 | PCE | 0000002 [No production] | 00000031 [20 mob pur form wood] | | | Stock | Quality Control |
| Mobile | 10.00 | PCE | 0000002 [No production] | 00000031 [20 mob pur form wood] | | | Quality Control | Output |
| Mobile | 10.00 | PCE | 0000002 [No production] | 00000031 [20 mob pur form wood] | | | Output | Customers |
| Mobile | 1.00 | PCE | 0000002 [No production] | 00000031 [20 mob pur form wood] | | | Customers | European Customers |
| Mobile | 20.00 | PCE | 0000002 [No production] | 00000031 [20 mob pur form wood] | | IN/00004 | Suppliers | Stock |
| Mobile | 4.00 | PCE | 0000002 [No production] | 00000031 [20 mob pur form wood] | | IN/00006 | Suppliers | Stock |

Figure 5.45: *Tracing Downstream in Make to Stock*

Finally, on a lot, you can enter data on all the operations that have been done for the product. That keeps a useful history of the pre-sales operations.

# 5.6 Scrapping Products

In OpenERP, there are many ways to handle scrap products.

1. *Warehouse → Product Moves → Receive Products*

---

2. *Warehouse → Product Moves → Deliver Products*

3. *Warehouse → Warehouse Management → Incoming Shipments*

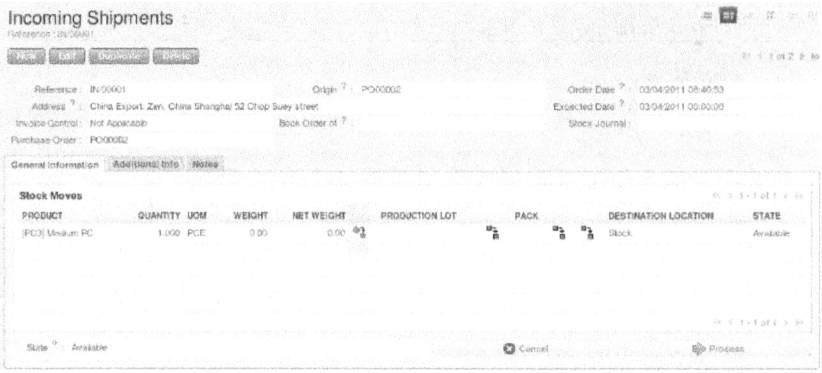

Figure 5.46: *Scrapping from an Incoming Shipment*

4. *Warehouse → Warehouse Management → Internal Moves*

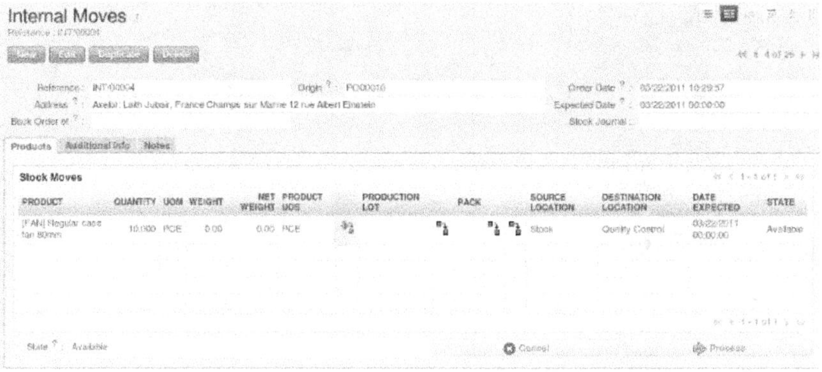

Figure 5.47: *Scrapping from an Internal Move*

5. *Warehouse → Warehouse Management → Delivery Orders*

When you decide to scrap some products, they are transferred to the *Scrap* location. To display the content of this *Virtual Location*, go to :menuselection: *Warehouse –> Inventory Control –> Location Structure*, then select the virtual locations and display the *Scrap* location.

If you want to transfer the products to another location, you can create a new one and check the *Scrap Location* in the additional information.

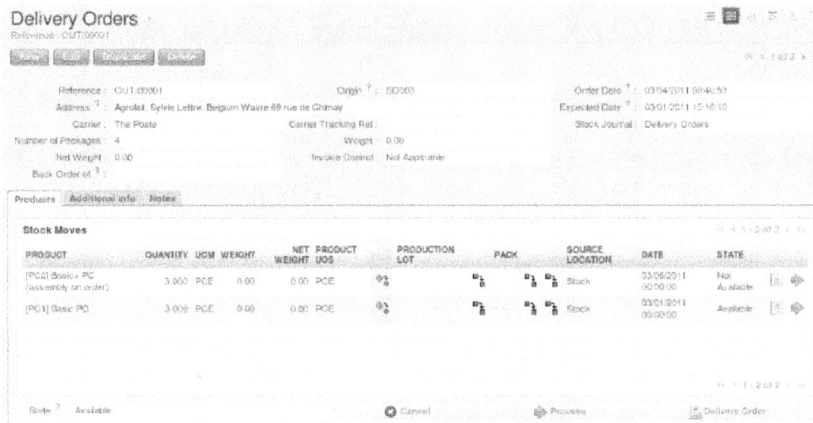

Figure 5.48: *Scrapping from a Delivery Order*

## 5.7 Identifying Products and Locations with Barcodes and RFID Devices

You can the barcode in the product form in the field *EAN13*.

## 5.8 Financial Inventory Management

### 5.8.1 Manual and Real-time Stock Valuation

If you have experience of managing with traditional software, you will know the problem of getting useful indicators. If you ask your accountant for a stock valuation or the value added by production, he will give you a figure.

If you ask for the same figure from your stores manager, you will get an entirely different amount. You have no idea who is right!

In OpenERP, stock management is completely integrated with the accounts, to give strong coherence between the two systems. The double-entry structure of locations enables a very precise correspondence between stocks and accounts.

Each stock movement also generates a corresponding accounting entry in an accounting journal to ensure that the two systems can stay in permanent synchronization.

To do that, set up a general account for each location that should be valued in your accounts. If a product goes to one location or another and the accounts are different in the two locations, OpenERP automatically generates the corresponding accounting entries in the accounts, in the stock journal.

If a stock move will go from a location without an account to a location where an account has been assigned (for example goods receipt from a supplier order), OpenERP generates an accounting entry using the properties defined in the product form for the counterpart. You can use different accounts per location or link several locations to the same account, depending on the level of analysis needed.

You use this system for managing consigned stocks:

- a supplier location that is valued in your own accounts or,
- a location in your own company that is not valued in your accounts.

*How to Configure Accounting Valuation?*

In the Product form, go to the `Accounting` tab and select the `Real Time` (automated) option for Inventory Valuation,

To define your accounts, you have two options. Set them on the product category, or on the product.

1. From the `Accounting Stock Properties` section, for the Product Category, set the `Stock Input Account`, the `Stock Output Account` and the `Stock Variation Account`,

2. From the `Accounting` tab, for the Product, set the `Stock Input Account` and the `Stock Output Account`.

You can also overwrite the accounts from the Product or the Product Category by defining Stock Input Account and Stock Output Account for a Location.

> **account_anglo_saxon**
>
> You can also install the account_anglo_saxon module (Reconfigure wizard, Anglo-Saxon Accounting) to value your stock according to Anglo-saxon principles.

The figure below shows the various accounts that can be used, with and without the account_anglo_saxon module installed.

## 5.8.2 Managing Transportation Costs

In OpenERP, you can handle the delivery methods when installing the `delivery` module.

This module will allow you:

- To select the delivery company

- To define the delivery pricelist according to the price, the weight or the volume.

Now, in each *Delivery Order*, two new fields are available to enter the right value to deliver the products to the customer. You can also find a new field in the *Sales Order* form that enables you to select a delivery method.

---

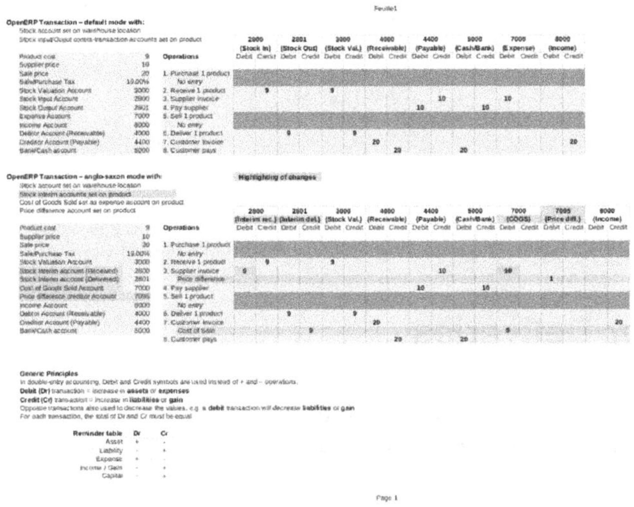
Feuille1

**OpenERP Transaction – default mode with:**
Stock account set on warehouse location
Stock input/Output contra-transaction accounts set on product

| | |
|---|---|
| Product cost | 9 |
| Supplier price | 10 |
| Sale price | 20 |
| Sale/Purchase Tax | 10.00% |
| Stock Valuation Account | 3000 |
| Stock Input Account | 2900 |
| Stock Output Account | 2901 |
| Expense Account | 7000 |
| Income Account | 8000 |
| Debtor Account (Receivable) | 4000 |
| Creditor Account (Payable) | 4400 |
| Bank/Cash account | 5000 |

| Operations | 2900 (Stock In) Debit | Credit | 2901 (Stock Out) Debit | Credit | 3000 (Stock Val.) Debit | Credit | 4000 (Receivable) Debit | Credit | 4400 (Payable) Debit | Credit | 5000 (Cash/Bank) Debit | Credit | 7000 (Expense) Debit | Credit | 8000 (Income) Debit | Credit |
|---|---|---|---|---|---|---|---|---|---|---|---|---|---|---|---|---|
| 1. Purchase 1 product No entry | | | | | | | | | | | | | | | | |
| 2. Receive 1 product | | 9 | | | 9 | | | | | | | | | | | |
| 3. Supplier invoice | | | | | | | | | | 10 | | | 10 | | | |
| 4. Pay supplier | | | | | | | | | 10 | | | 10 | | | | |
| 5. Sell 1 product No entry | | | | | | | | | | | | | | | | |
| 6. Deliver 1 product | | | 9 | | | 9 | | | | | | | | | | |
| 7. Customer invoice | | | | | | | 20 | | | | | | | | | 20 |
| 8. Customer pays | | | | | | | | 20 | | | 20 | | | | | |

**OpenERP Transaction – anglo-saxon mode with:**
Stock account set on warehouse location
Stock interim accounts set on product
Cost of Goods Sold set as expense account on product
Price difference account set on product

Highlighting of changes

| | |
|---|---|
| Product cost | 9 |
| Supplier price | 10 |
| Sale price | 30 |
| Sale/Purchase Tax | 19.00% |
| Stock Valuation Account | 3000 |
| Stock Interim account (Received) | 2900 |
| Stock Interim account (Delivered) | 2801 |
| Cost of Goods Sold Account | 7000 |
| Price difference creditor Account | 7095 |
| Income Account | 8000 |
| Debtor Account (Receivable) | 4000 |
| Creditor Account (Payable) | 4400 |
| Bank/Cash account | 5000 |

| Operations | 2900 (Interim rec.) Debit | Credit | 2801 (Interim del.) Debit | Credit | 3000 (Stock Val.) Debit | Credit | 4000 (Receivable) Debit | Credit | 4400 (Payable) Debit | Credit | 5000 (Cash/Bank) Debit | Credit | 7000 (COGS) Debit | Credit | 7095 (Price diff.) Debit | Credit | 8000 (Income) Debit | Credit |
|---|---|---|---|---|---|---|---|---|---|---|---|---|---|---|---|---|---|---|
| 1. Purchase 1 product No entry | | | | | | | | | | | | | | | | | | |
| 2. Receive 1 product | | 9 | | | 9 | | | | | | | | | | | | | |
| 3. Supplier invoice | 9 | | | | | | | | | 10 | | | 10 | | | | | |
| Price difference | | | | | | | | | | | | | | | 1 | | | |
| 4. Pay supplier | | | | | | | | | 10 | | | 10 | | | | | | |
| 5. Sell 1 product No entry | | | | | | | | | | | | | | | | | | |
| 6. Deliver 1 product | | | 9 | | | 9 | | | | | | | | | | | | |
| 7. Customer invoice | | | | | | | 20 | | | | | | | | | | | 20 |
| Cost of sale | | | | 9 | | | | | | | | | 9 | | | | | |
| 8. Customer pays | | | | | | | | 20 | | | 20 | | | | | | | |

**Generic Principles**
In double-entry accounting, Debit and Credit symbols are used instead of + and – operations.
**Debit (Dr)** transaction = increase in **assets** or **expenses**
**Credit (Cr)** transaction = increase in **liabilities** or **gain**
Opposite transactions also used to decrease the values, e.g. a **debit** transaction will decrease **liabilities** or **gain**
For each transaction, the total of Dr and Cr must be equal

| Reminder table | Dr | Cr |
|---|---|---|
| Asset | + | - |
| Liability | - | + |
| Expense | + | - |
| Income / Gain | - | + |
| Capital | - | + |

Page 1

Figure 5.49: *Setting up Stock Valuation Accounts*

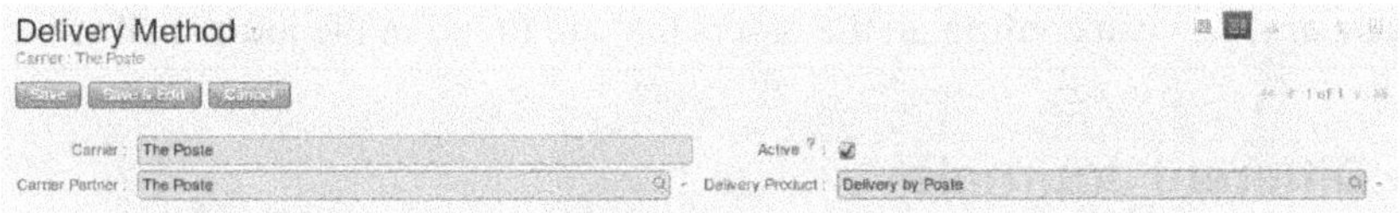


Figure 5.50: *Define the Delivery Method*

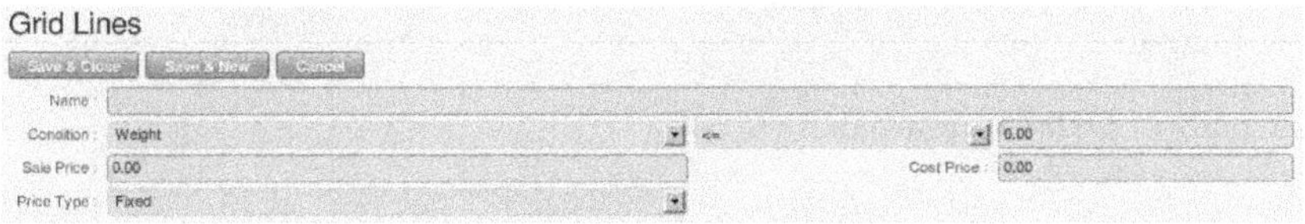


Figure 5.51: *Define the Delivery Costs*

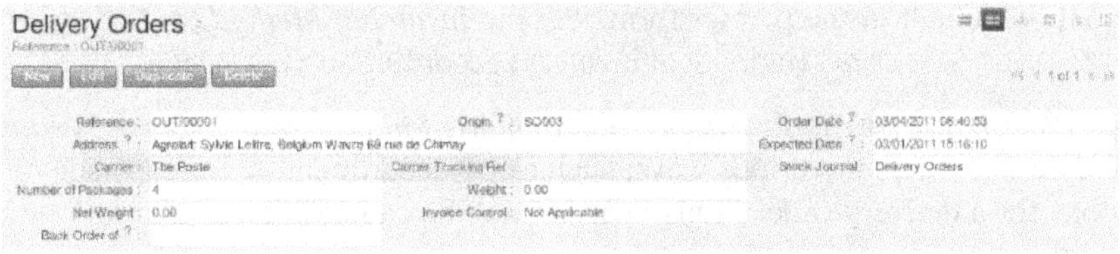


Figure 5.52: *Delivery Cost in the Delivery Orders*

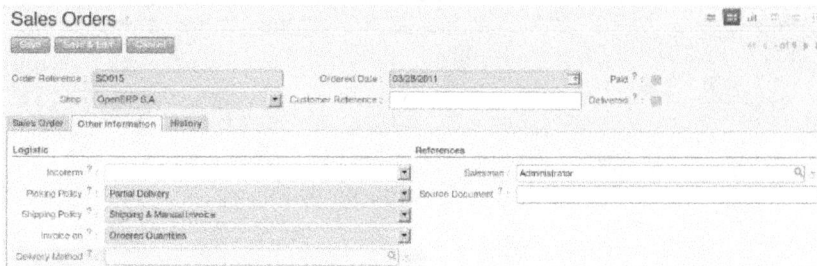

Figure 5.53: *Delivery Method in the Sales Orders*

# 5.9 Organize your Deliveries

You can manage stock through journals in the same way as you can manage your accounts through journals. This approach has the great advantage that you can define journals in various ways to meet your company's needs.

For example, a large company may want to organize deliveries by department or warehouse. You can then create a journal and a manager for each department. The different users can work in a journal as a function of their position in the company. That enables you to better structure your information.

A company doing a lot of transport could organize its journals by delivery vehicle. The different delivery orders will then be assigned to a journal representing a particular vehicle. When the vehicle has left the company, you can confirm all the orders that are found in the journal all at the same time.

## 5.9.1 The Different Journals

Install the Reconfigure option *Invoicing Journals* for Sales Management or the `sale_journal` module to work with different journals. This adds two new concepts to OpenERP:

- Invoicing journals,

- Stock journals or Delivery journals.

**Invoicing journals** (*Sales → Configuration → Sales → Invoice Types*) are used to assign purchase orders and/or delivery orders to a given invoicing journal. Everything in the journal can be invoiced in one go, and you can control the amounts by journal. For example, you can create the following journals: daily invoicing, end-of-week invoicing and monthly invoicing. It is also possible to show the invoicing journal by default in the partner form. Set the *Invoicing Method* to `Grouped` (one invoice per customer) or `Non Grouped` (individual invoices) according to your needs.

**Stock journals** (*Warehouse → Configuration → Warehouse Management → Stock Journals*) allow you to classify the delivery orders in various ways, such as by department, by salesperson or by type. If a salesperson looks for a delivery order in his own journal, he can easily see the work on current items compared with his own orders.

> **Default Values**
>
> To enter all the orders in his own stock journal, a salesperson can use the default values that are entered in the fields when creating orders.

Finally, the stock journals can also be used as **delivery journals** to post each item into a delivery journal. For example, you can create journals dated according to customer delivery dates (such as Monday's deliveries, or afternoon deliveries) or these journals could represent the day's work for delivery vehicles (such as truck1, truck2).

## 5.9.2 Using the Journals

You will now see how to use the journals to organize your stock management in practice. After installing the module `sale_journal` look at the list of partners. In the tab *Sales and Purchases* on any of them you will now see the field *Invoicing Method*.

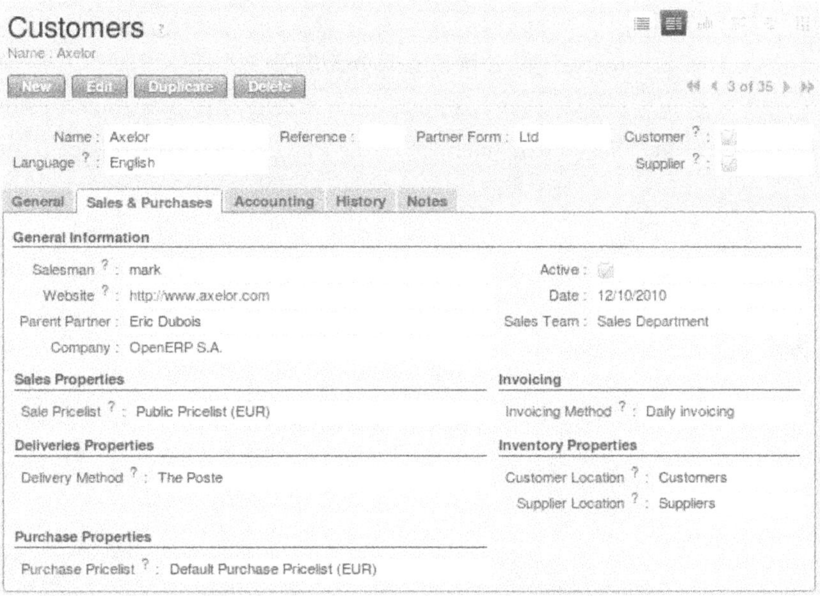

Figure 5.54: *Partner Form in Invoicing Mode*

You can create a new *Invoicing Journal* for a partner through the menu *Sales → Configuration → Sales → Invoice Types*. You can decide if the invoices should be grouped or not when generating them in the journal. Create a second invoicing journal `End-of-Month Invoicing` which you can assign to another partner.

Then enter the data for some sales orders for these two partners. After entering sales order data, the field *Invoicing Mode* in the second tab `Other Information` is completed automatically from the partner settings.

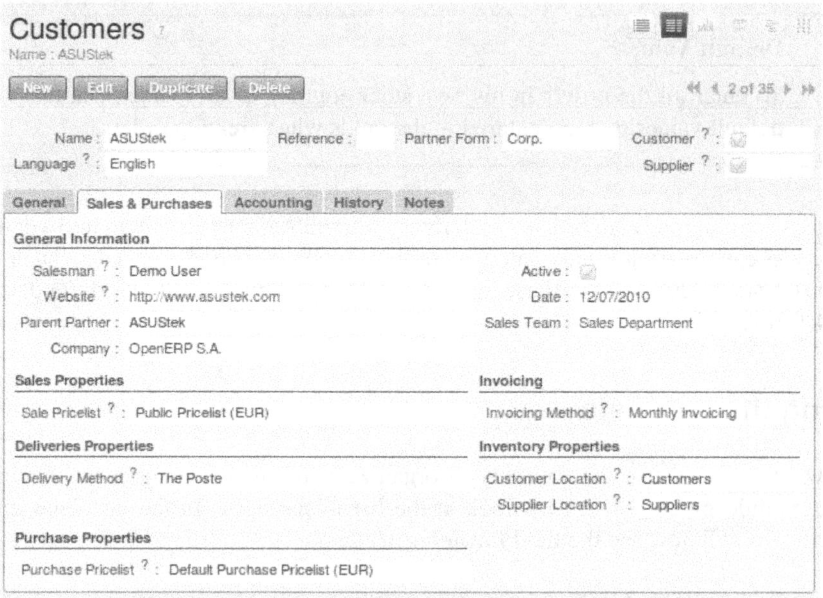

Figure 5.55: *Defining an Invoicing Journal*

Look at the *History* tab of the Sales order, and observe the *Picking List* that has been created. The field *Invoicing Mode* is automatically shown there.

Figure 5.56: *Generated Picking Lists*

At the end of the day, the invoicing supervisor can display the list by journal. Go to the menu *Sales →
Invoicing → Lines to Invoice*. Add a New Filter by selecting *Invoice Type contains Daily*, or any other
part of the invoice journal you are using. Select the different orders in the list. You can automatically

carry out invoicing by clicking the action *Make Invoices* (the gears symbol).

---

💡 **Confirming Invoices**

By default, invoices are generated in the draft state, which enables you to modify them before sending them to the customer. But you can confirm all the invoices in one go by selecting them all from the list and selecting the action *Confirm Draft Invoices*.

---

At the end of the month the invoicing management does the same work, but in the journal 'month-end invoicing'.

You can also enter a journal to confirm / cancel all the orders in one go. Then you can do several quotations, assign them to a journal and confirm or cancel them at once.

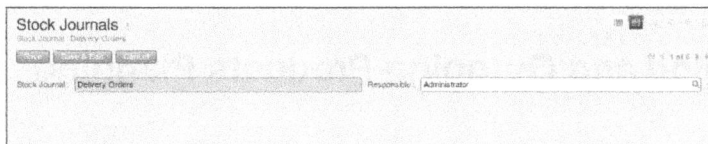

Figure 5.57: *View of an Order Journal*

# 5.10 Estimating Delivery Dates

## 5.10.1 Standard Delivery Time

In order to define the delivery time, you have to know three things:

- Customer Lead Time :

  That is the time you promise to your customer for a delivery. It corresponds to the average delay between the confirmation of the customer order and the delivery of the finished goods. It can be defined in the product form, in the *Procurement and Locations* tab.

  This time will be influenced by the Manufacturing Lead Time and the Delivery Lead Time.

- Manufacturing Lead Time :

  This is the time you need to produce one unit of a product. If this product needs other sub-products, the different manufacturing times will be summed. It can also be defined in the product form, in the *Procurement and Locations* tab.

- Delivery Lead Time :

  This is the time your supplier needs to deliver the goods. This delay can be defined in the product form in the *Suppliers* tab.

For example, if we have to deliver some products to a customer in a month (in 30 days). You promise to deliver the goods to the customer within 10 days, the manufacturing time is equal to 4 days and our suppliers deliver the raw materials within 3 days.

According to those numbers, we will have to start the process in 23 days if we have to order raw materials.

### 5.10.2 Schedule Logistic Flows according to MRP1 Rules

MRP is a software-based production, planning and inventory control system used to manage themanufacturing process.

It is a computer-based system in which the given Master Schedule is exploded with Bills Of Material, into the required amount of raw material, parts and subassemblies needed to produce the final products in each period.

# 5.11 Incoming and Outgoing Products Planning

To be able to plan incoming and outgoing shipments of products, you have to install the module *stock_planning*.

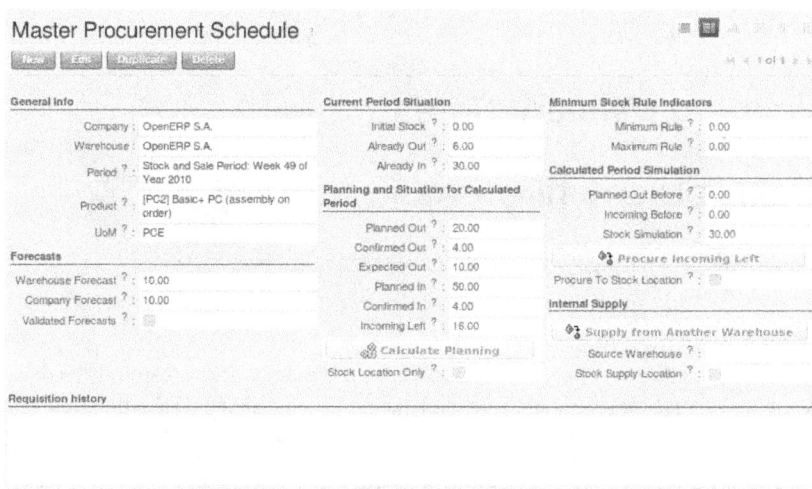

Figure 5.58: *Planning the Deliveries of Customer Products*

Thanks to this module, you will be able to calculate a planning of the stock for a product.

Planned dates on a packing order are put in each stock move line. If you have a packing order containing several products, not all of the lines necessarily need to be delivered the same day. The minimum and maximum dates in a packing order show the earliest and latest dates on the stock move lines for the packing.

If you move a packing order in the calendar view, the planned date in the stock move lines will automatically be moved as a result.

## 5.12 Managing Inventory Reconciliation

Inventory reconciliation involves two steps: physical and accounting.

Physical inventory steps include taking a written inventory record and comparing it to the actual goods in the company's warehouses. Counting obsolete and damaged products is also a reconciliation activity.

Reconciliation steps on the accounting side include verification that all inventory purchases are posted, entering adjustments from the physical count and analysing the dollar differences between months. Inventory reconciliation frequency depends on the size, location, and type of inventory in a company's operations.

## 5.13 Building Reports to Track Activity

With OpenERP, you can build your own reports in order to track the different activities in your warehouses. To create your own reports, you have to install the *base_report_creator*. It will add a submenu in *Administration → Customization → Reporting*.

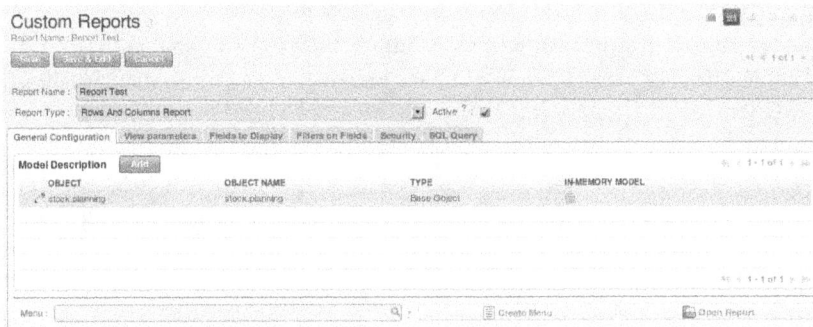

Figure 5.59: *Create your Own Reports*

This newly added section allows you to define for your new report:

- The general configuration:

  The aim of this tab is to choose the models your report will rely on.

- The view parameters

  This tab will define the display of your report. You can choose between the traditional available views (Tree/List, Form, Graph and Calendar) and you can define three different ways to display your report.

- The fields to display

The fields available to display will depend on the models you choose in the *General Configuration* tab.

When you add a new field to your report, different fields have to be specified:

– Sequence - defines the order in which the fields will be displayed in the report

– Field - the information you want to display in your report

– Grouping method - affects the way the field is displayed. You can choose between *Grouped*, *Sum*, *Minimum*, *Count*, *Maximum* and *Average*

– Graph mode - defines which axe of the graph the field will represent

– Calendar mode - defines the meaning of the field for the calendar (*Starting or Ending date*, *Delay*, *End Date*, *Unique Colours*)

• The filters on fields

  This tab will let you choose which data to display according to the value of a field. It is possible to manually modify or add new filters according to your needs.

• The security

  The security tab is used to select the groups that are able to display the report.

---

**Create Report with OpenOffice**

You can also create or edit reports with OpenOffice using the *base_report_designer* module.

In order to add the extension to OpenOffice, load this module and start the configuration. A new window will ask you to *Save As* a file that contains the extension.

Once you have saved the file, start OpenOffice and go to *Tools →
Extension Manager*, then click Add and select the previously saved file. Restart OpenOffice.org and now you have the extension installed.

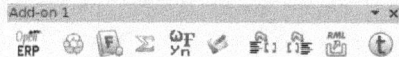

Figure 5.60: *Extension to Create a Report in OpenOffice*

---

# 5.14 Import / Export

Managing import / export with foreign companies can sometimes be very complex. Between a departure port and the destination company, products can get stopped for several weeks at sea or somewhere in the numerous transportation stages and customs. To manage such deliveries efficiently it is important to:

• know where your products are,

---

- know when they are likely to arrive at their destination,

- know your value in transit,

- follow the development of the different steps.

Linked locations in OpenERP enable you to manage all this rather elegantly. You can use a structure like this:

- Suppliers

    - European Suppliers
    - Chinese Suppliers

- In transit

    - Shanghai Port
    - Pacific Ocean
    - San Francisco Port
    - San Francisco Customs

## 5.14.1 Stock

The transit locations are linked between themselves with a manual confirmation step. The internal stock move is validated at each port and customs arrival. OpenERP prepares all the linked moves automatically.

> **Intrastat**
>
> Companies that do import / export should install the module `report_intrastat`. This enables them to prepare the reports needed to declare product exports.

You can use the lead times between different locations to account for real delays. Your lead times and stock forecasts are calculated by OpenERP to estimate the arrival of incoming products, so that you can respond to a customer's needs as precisely as possible.

You can also value the products in transit in your account depending on the chosen stock location configuration.

## 5.14.2 Rental Locations

You can manage rental locations in OpenERP very simply using the same system of linked locations. Using the `stock_location` module you can set a return date for rental items sent to a customer location after a certain rental period.

Then the set of real and virtual stocks is maintained daily in real time. The different operations such as delivery and receipt after a few days are automatically suggested by OpenERP which simplifies the work of data entry.

You then have the product list found in the customer locations and your own stock in your stock location. The list of waiting goods receipts is automatically generated by OpenERP using the location links.

Suppose you want to rent a product (*PC3*) to your customer (*Axelor*) for 30 days. Two stock movement entries are needed to manage this scenario:

1. Product goes from *Stock* (your company's location) to *Axelor - Rental Location* (your customer location).

2. Product will be returned into *Stock* (your company's location) from *Axelor - Rental Location* (your customer location) after 30 days.

To manage rental products by linking locations, configure a rental location (*Axelor - Rental Location*) as shown in the following figure using the menu *Warehouse → Configuration → Warehouse Management → Locations*.

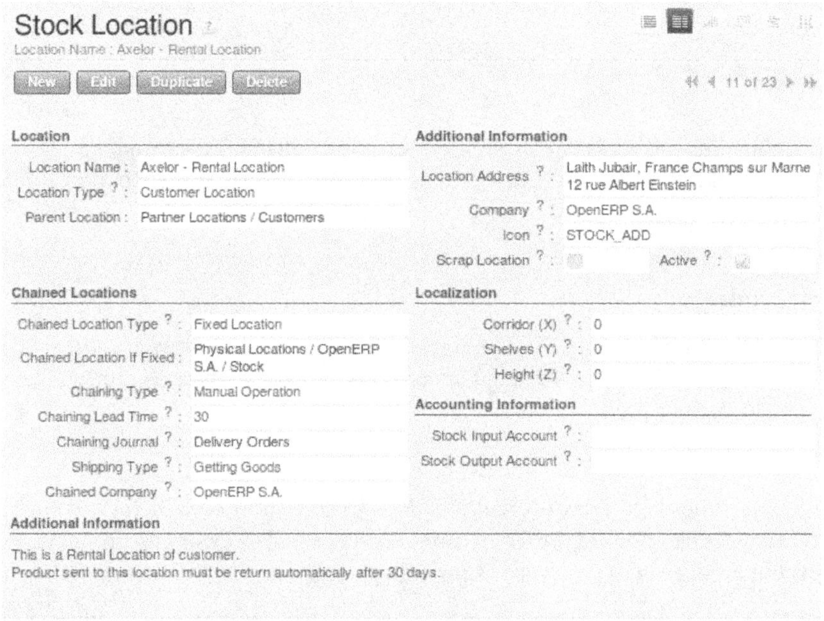

Figure 5.61: *Configuration of a Rental Location 'Axelor - Rental Location'*

Through the menu *Warehouse → Traceability → Stock Moves*, you can create a stock movement entry from *Stock* to *Customer Location* (*Axelor - Rental Location*) in OpenERP for a rental product (*PC3*).

The stock movement entry from *Customer Location* (*Axelor - Rental Location*) to *Stock* is generated automatically on the proper *Scheduled Date* by OpenERP when you have confirmed the previous stock movement entry by clicking the *Process Now* button.

Figure 5.62: *Stock Movement Entry to Send the Product 'PC3' to the Customer Location*

The same principle is used for internal stock to generate quality control for certain products.

### 5.14.3 Consigned Products

The principle of linked locations is used to manage consigned products. You can specify that certain products should be returned to you a certain number of days after they have been delivered to customers.

When the products have been delivered, OpenERP automatically creates goods receipts for the consigned product. The specified date is obviously approximate but enables you to forecast returns.

## 5.15 Stock Location Example

In this section, we will develop a more detailed example that includes different concepts seen in the previous sections.

The following example will use the *Stock Location types*, the *Logistic Flows* and the *Bill Of Materials*.

We have two companies: OpenERP SA and OpenERP US.

We have three products: Product A, Product B and Product C. For each product, we will have to define the Stock Location to determine where to take these products.

To make one unit of Product A, we need the Product B and the Product C. So we will have to define a *Bill of Material*.

Table 5.12: Bill of Materials

| Field | Value |
|-------|-------|
| Product | Product A |
| Product Qty | 1 |
| Name | Product A |
| BoM Type | Normal |
| Company | OpenERP US |

The different components to produce one unit of Product A are one unit of Product B and one unit of Product C.

Table 5.13: Companies and Products

| Company | What |
|---------|------|
| OpenERP SA | Sell the Product A |
| OpenERP SA | Store the Product C |
| OpenERP US | Produce the Product A |
| OpenERP US | Store the Product B |

Table 5.14: Logistics Flows

| Name | Type | Product | Goal of the flow |
|------|------|---------|------------------|
| Ask for Production | Pull | Product A | OpenERP SA asks OpenERP US to produce the Product A |
| Launch Production | Pull | Product A | OpenERP US launches the production of the Product A |
| Send Product to Transit | Pull | Product C | OpenERP US asks for the Product C to OpenERP SA |
| Get Product from Transit | Pull | Product C | OpenERP US receives the Product C |

Here are the details of the different flows:

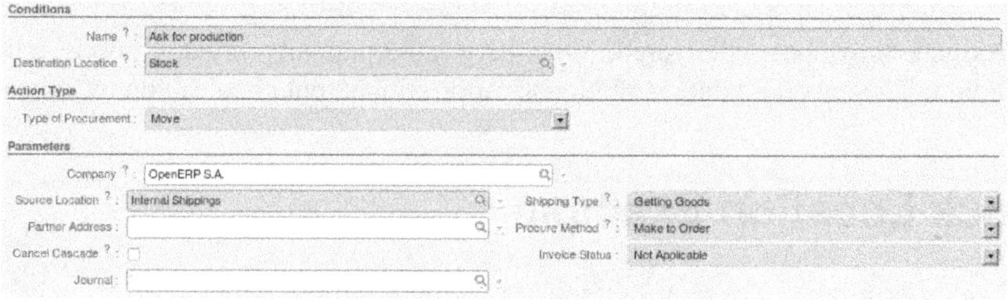

Figure 5.63: *Ask for Production*

With this configuration, when a Sales Order for 3 units of Product A is confirmed and the scheduler has been launched, you will have the following procurements:

And the following stock moves have been generated:

Because we are working in two different companies, different stock moves have been generated. The products have to move from OpenERP SA to OpenERP US for the products C. After the manufacturing process, the products A have to move from OpenERP US to OpenERP SA to be sold to the customer.

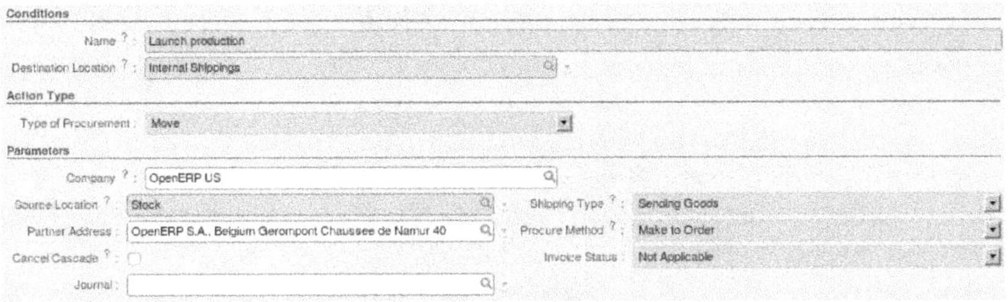

Figure 5.64: *Launch Production*

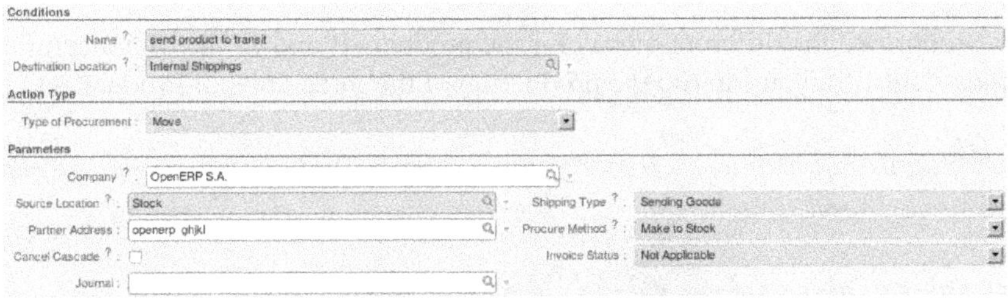

Figure 5.65: *Send Product to Transit*

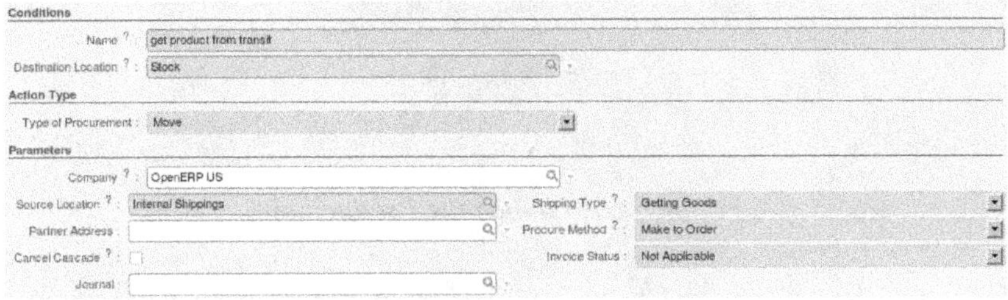

Figure 5.66: *Get Product from Transit*

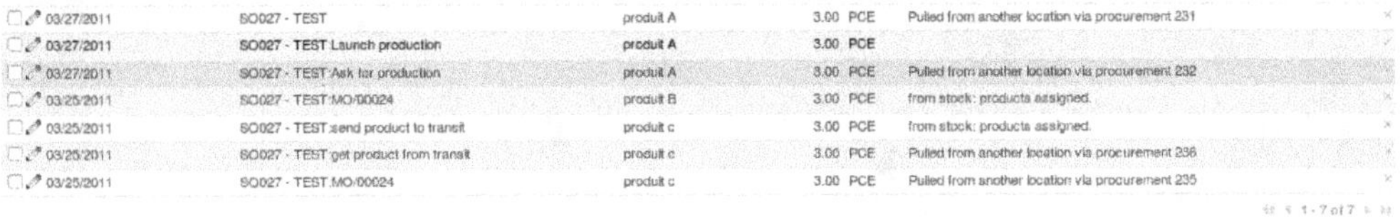

Figure 5.67: *Procurements View*

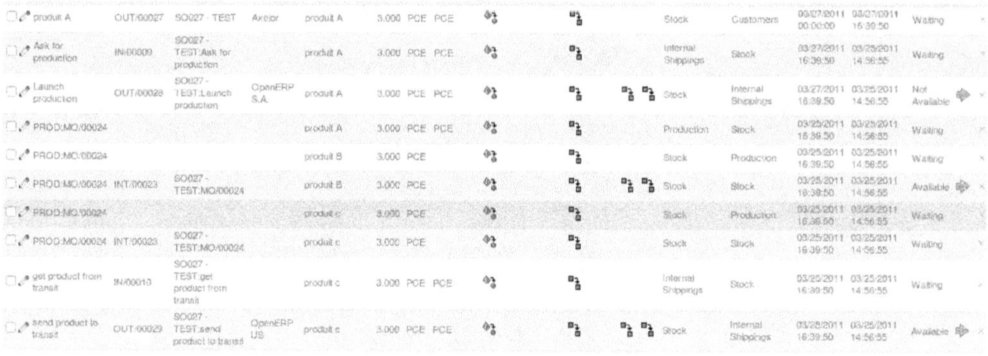

Figure 5.68: *Stock Moves*

Once you have confirmed the different moves for the products B and C, the Manufacturing Order is in *ready to produce* status. So you can run the production of the three units of Product A.

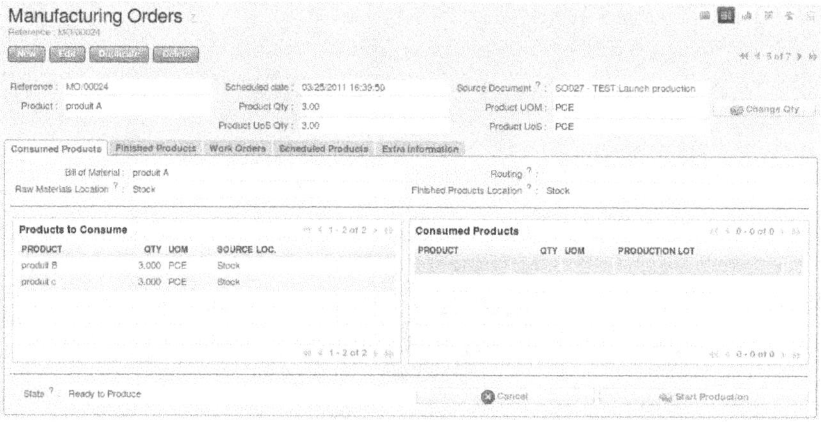

Figure 5.69: *Launch the Production*

Once again due to the use of two companies, you have to confirm different deliveries. One to deliver the product from OpenERP US to OpenERP SA and another to deliver the product from OpenERP SA to the customer. Now you have to confirm the delivery of the three units from OpenERP US to OpenERP SA, then to confirm the reception of the products in OpenERP SA and finally, deliver the products to you final customer.

# Part IV

# Streamlining your Manufacturing

# Defining your Master Data 6

*The management of manufacturing described in this chapter covers planning, ordering, stocks and the manufacturing or assembly of products from raw materials and components. It also discusses consumption and production of products, as well as the necessary operations on machinery, tools or human resources.*

Manufacturing management in OpenERP is based on its stock management and equally very flexible in both its operations and its financial control. It particularly benefits from the use of double-entry stock management for production orders. Manufacturing management is implemented by the `mrp` module. It is used to transform all kinds of products:

- Assemblies of parts: composite products, soldered or welded products, assemblies, packs,

- Machined parts: machining, cutting, planing,

- Foundries: clamping, heating,

- Mixtures: mixing, chemical processes, distillation.

You will work in two areas: with products in the first part of this chapter, and with operations in the second part. The management of products depends on the concept of classifications while operations management is related to routing and workcenters.

> **Bills of Materials**
>
> Bills of Materials, or manufacturing specifications, go by different names depending on their application area, for example:
>
> - Food: Recipes,
>
> - Chemicals: Equations,
>
> - Building: Plans.

For this chapter you should start with a fresh database that includes demo data, with `mrp` (`Manufacturing`) and its dependencies installed and a generic chart of accounts configured. As you will notice, when you select `Manufacturing` to be installed, OpenERP will install the linked applications automatically.

## 6.1 Bill of Materials and Components

### 6.1.1 Using Bills of Materials

Bills of Materials are documents that describe the list of raw materials used to make a finished product. To illustrate the concept of specification, you will work on a shelf (or cabinet) where the manufacturing plan is given by the figure *Plan of Construction of a Shelf* (page 140).

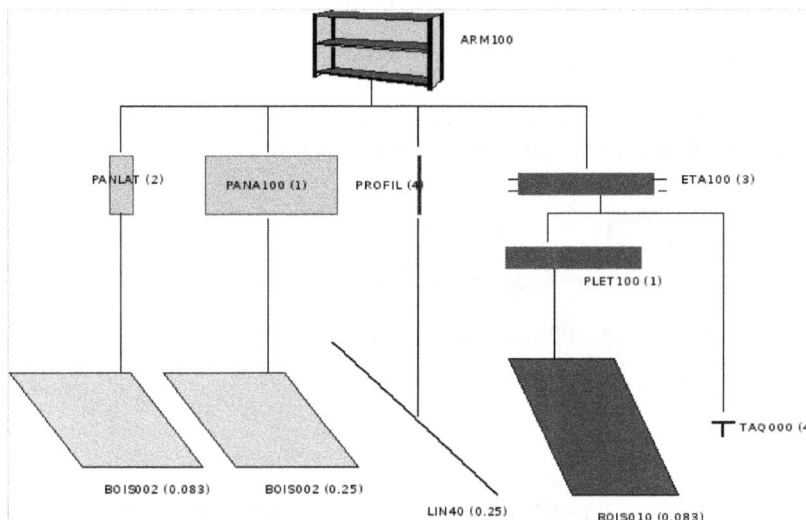

Figure 6.1: *Plan of Construction of a Shelf*

The shelf is assembled from raw materials and intermediate assemblies. The Image Code refers to the picture, the Product Reference is the corresponding code in OpenERP.

Change the unit of the Wood Lintel 4m (LIN40) product to m instead of PCE.

Table 6.1: Product Definitions before defining Bills of Materials (already defined)

| Image Code | Product Reference | Description |
|------------|-------------------|-------------|
| ARM100 | SHE100 | Shelf 100 cm |
| PANLAT | SIDEPAN | Side Panel |
| PANA100 | RPAN100 | Rear Panel SHE100 |
| PROFIL | PROFIL | Assembly Section |
| ETA100 | RCK100 | Rack 100cm |
| BOIS002 | WOOD002 | Wood 2mm |
| TAQ000 | METC000 | Metal Cleats |
| LIN40 | LIN40 | Wood Lintel 4m |

Table 6.2: New Products to be created before defining Bill
of Materials

| Image Code | Product Reference | Description |
|---|---|---|
| PLET100 | SPAN100 | Shelf Panel |
| BOIS010 | WOOD010 | Wood 10mm |

**Copy**

To create the above products, duplicate existing ones, such as Side Panel
and Wood 2mm, from the Purchase or Sales menu *Purchases → Products
→ Products.*

To describe how this shelf should be assembled, you define a bill of materials for each intermediate
product and for the final shelf assembly. These are shown in the tables below. You can start from the
demo data and complete them according to the specifications. To create or change a bill of materials,
go to *Manufacturing → Master Data → Bill of Materials.*

Table 6.3: Bill of Materials for 1 SHE100 Unit
(already defined)

| Product Ref. | Quantity | Unit of Measure |
|---|---|---|
| PROFIL | 4 | PCE |
| SIDEPAN | 2 | PCE |
| METC000 | 12 | PCE |
| RPAN100 | 1 | PCE |
| RCK100 | 3 | PCE |

Table 6.4: Bill of Materials for 1 RCK100 PCE

| Product Code | Quantity | Unit of Measure |
|---|---|---|
| SPAN100 | 1 | PCE |
| METC000 | 4 | PCE |

Table 6.5: Bill of Materials for 1 SPAN100 PCE

| Product Code | Quantity | Unit of Measure |
|---|---|---|
| WOOD010 | 0.083 | m |

Table 6.6: Bill of Materials for 1 PROFIL PCE

| Product Code | Quantity | Unit of Measure |
|---|---|---|
| LIN40 | 0.25 | m |

Table 6.7: Bill of Materials for 1 RPAN100 PCE

| Product Code | Quantity | Unit of Measure |
|---|---|---|
| WOOD002 | 0.25 | m |

Table 6.8: Bill of Materials for 1 SIDEPAN PCE

| Product Code | Quantity | Unit of Measure |
|---|---|---|
| WOOD002 | 0.083 | m |

The bills of materials are then used by the software to calculate the raw material needs based on the requirements of the finished products. So if you want to manufacture 10 shelves, the system can calculate the actual products that will be consumed:

Table 6.9: Total Quantities per Shelf

| Product Code | Quantity | Unit of Measure |
|---|---|---|
| WOOD002 | 0.416 (2 * 0.083 + 0.25) | m |
| LIN40 | 1 (4 * 0.25) | m |
| WOOD010 | 0.249 (0.083 * 3) | m |
| METC000 | 132 ((3 * 4) + (10 * 12)) | PCE |

---

**Bill of Materials**

To see the bill of materials in tree view, use the menu *Manufacturing* → *Master Data* → *Bill of Materials* then select the product and click the action *BOM Structure*.

---

**BOM Structure**

Page 1 of 1

| BOM Name | Product Name | Quantity | BOM Ref |
|---|---|---|---|
| Default BOM for Shelf of 100cm | [ SHE100 ] Shelf of 100cm | 1.00 PCE | SHE100 |
| - Assembly Section | [ PROFIL ] Assembly Section | 4.00 PCE | |
| - Wood Lintel 4m | [ LIN40 ] Wood Lintel 4m | 1.00 m | |
| - Side Panel | [ SIDEPAN ] Side Panel | 2.00 PCE | |
| - Metal Cleats | [ METC000 ] Metal Cleats | 12.00 PCE | |
| - Rear panel SHE100 | [ RPAN100 ] Rear Panel SHE100 | 1.00 PCE | |
| - Shelf 100 | [ RCK100 ] Rack 100cm | 3.00 PCE | |

Figure 6.2: *Bill of Materials structure*

Use the menu *Manufacturing* → *Master Data* → *Bill of Materials* and click the *New* button to define a new bill of materials.

---

**The Different Views**

To change the view in the bill of materials you can:

- From the list, select a bill of materials name and then click *Form View*,

- From a product form, use the menu *Product BoM Structure* to the right.

---

**Bill of Materials**
Name : Default BOM for Shelf of 100cm

New | Edit | Duplicate | Delete

Product : [SHE100] Shelf of 100cm     Name : Default BOM for Shelf of 100cm     Reference : SHE100
Product Qty : 1.00     Product UOM ? : PCE     Routing ? :
BoM Type ? : Normal BoM

Components | Revisions | Properties

**Components**

| PRODUCT | PRODUCT QTY | PRODUCT UOM | VALID FROM |
|---|---|---|---|
| [PROFIL] Assembly Section | 4.00 | PCE | |
| [SIDEPAN] Side Panel | 2.00 | PCE | |
| [METC000] Metal Cleats | 12.00 | PCE | |
| [RPAN100] Rear Panel SHE100 | 1.00 | PCE | |
| [RCK100] Rack 100cm | 3.00 | PCE | |

Figure 6.3: *Defining a Bill of Materials (Extended view)*

In the `Product` field of the bill of materials, you should set the finished product, which will be manufactured or assembled. Once the product has been selected, OpenERP automatically completes the name of the bill of materials and the default Unit of Measure for this product.

The type of BoM (*BoM Type* : `Sets/Phantom` or `Normal BoM`) and the *Routing* field will be described in more detail later in the chapter.

Now you can select the raw materials (`Components`) that are used to manufacture the finished product. The quantities are set out based on the quantities of finished product and the quantities needed to produce them from the bill of materials. The second tab, *Revisions*, is used to register all the changes made to the bill of materials. On each change, you can specify a revision number and some notes on the modifications you carried out.

> **Simplified View**
>
> The *Revisions* tab is only visible if the user works in the `Extended` view mode (which means that the user should belong to the group `Useability / Extended View`.

**Bill of Materials**
Name : Default BOM for Shelf of 100cm

Save | Save & Edit | Cancel

Product : [SHE100] Shelf of 100cm     Name : Default BOM for Shelf of 100cm     Reference : SHE100
Product Qty : 1.00     Product UOM ? : PCE     Routing ? :
BoM Type ? : Normal BoM

Components | Revisions | Properties

**BoM Revisions** New

| REVISION | AUTHOR | MODIFICATION DATE | MODIFICATION NAME |
|---|---|---|---|
| 1 | Administrator | 06/20/2011 | Change of colour |

Figure 6.4: *Revisions of a Bill of Materials (Extended view)*

In the third tab, *Properties*, you can put a free text reference to a plan, a sequence number that is used to determine the priorities between bills of materials, dates between which a bill of materials is valid, and values for rounding and production efficiency.

*Rounding* is used to set the smallest *Unit of Measure* in which the quantities of the selected product can be expressed. So if you set the rounding to 1.00, you will not be able to manufacture half a piece. The *Efficiency* of the product lets you indicate the percentage you lose during manufacturing. This loss

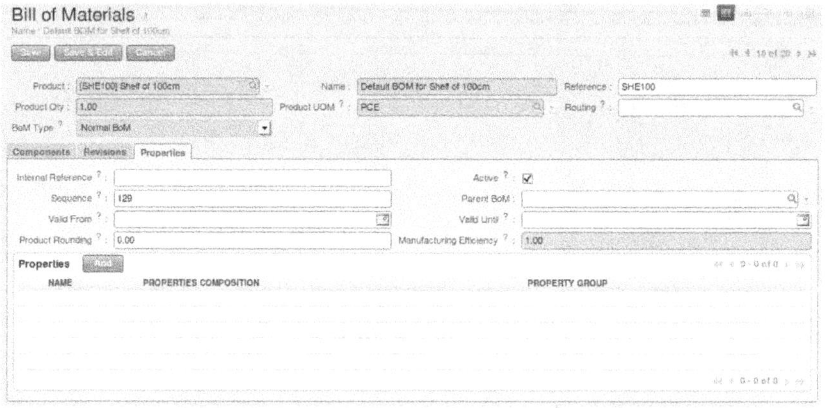

Figure 6.5: *Properties of a Bill of Materials*

can be defined for the finished product or for each raw materials (components) line. The impact of this efficiency figure is that OpenERP will reserve more raw materials for manufacturing than you would otherwise use just from the Bill of Materials calculations.

The final part of the third tab lets you set some properties for the product's manufacturing processes. These will be detailed further on in the chapter in the section about configurable products.

## 6.1.2 Multi-level Bills of Materials

In OpenERP, each line of a bill of materials may itself be a bill of materials. This allows you to define BoMs with several levels. Instead of defining several BoMs for the shelf in the figure *Plan of Construction of a Shelf* (page 140), you could define the single bill of materials below:

Table 6.10: Single Bill of Materials for 1 SHE100 Unit

| Product Ref. | Quantity | Unit of Measure |
|---|---|---|
| SHE100 | 1 | PCE |
| SIDEPAN | 2 | PCE |
| WOOD002 | 0.166 | m |
| RPAN100 | 1 | PCE |
| WOOD002 | 0.25 | m |
| PROFIL | 4 | PCE |
| LIN40 | 1 | m |
| RCK100 | 3 | PCE |
| SPAN100 | 3 | PCE |
| WOOD010 | 0.249 | m |
| METC000 | 132 | PCE |

OpenERP behaves differently depending on whether the bill of materials is defined in several small BoMs each on a single level or in one BoM tree-structured on several levels.

If you select a BoM using intermediate products that automatically generates production orders based on calculated requirements, OpenERP will propose to manufacture an intermediate product. To manufacture a shelf according to the different bills of materials defined, you would create 6 production orders:

Table 6.11: Production Order

| Product Ref. | Quantity | Unit of Measure |
|---|---|---|
| SPAN100 | 3 | PCE |
| WOOD010 | 0.249 | m |

Table 6.12: Production Order

| Product Ref. | Quantity | Unit of Measure |
|---|---|---|
| RCK100 | 3 | PCE |
| SPAN100 | 3 | PCE |
| METC000 | 12 | PCE |

Table 6.13: Production Order

| Product Ref. | Quantity | Unit of Measure |
|---|---|---|
| PROFIL | 4 | PCE |
| LIN40 | 1 | m |

Table 6.14: Production Order

| Product Ref. | Quantity | Unit of Measure |
|---|---|---|
| RPAN100 | 1 | PCE |
| WOOD002 | 0.25 | m |

Table 6.15: Production Order

| Product Ref. | Quantity | Unit of Measure |
|---|---|---|
| SIDEPAN | 2 | PCE |
| WOOD002 | 0.17 | m |

Table 6.16: Production Order

| Product Ref. | Quantity | Unit of Measure |
|---|---|---|
| SHE100 | 1 | PCE |
| SIDEPAN | 2 | PCE |
| RPAN100 | 1 | PCE |
| PROFIL | 4 | PCE |
| RCK100 | 3 | PCE |
| METC000 | 12 | PCE |

In the case where a single bill of materials is defined in multiple levels, a single manufacturing order will be generated for each shelf, including all of the sub BoMs. You would then get the following production order:

Table 6.17: Single Production from a tree-structured BoM

| Product Ref. | Quantity | Unit of Measure |
|---|---|---|
| SHE100 | 1 | PCE |
| WOOD002 | 0.17 | m |
| WOOD002 | 0.25 | m |
| LIN40 | 1 | m |
| WOOD010 | 0.249 | m |
| METC000 | 132 | PCE |

## 6.1.3 Phantom Bills of Materials

If a finished product is defined using intermediate products that are themselves defined using other BoMs, OpenERP will propose to manufacture each intermediate product. This will result in several production orders. If you only want a single production order, you can define a single BoM with several levels.

Sometimes, however, it may be useful to define the intermediate product separately and not as part of a multi-level assembly, even if you do not want separate production orders for intermediate products.

In the example, the intermediate product RCK100 is used in the manufacturing of different shelves (SHE100, SHE200, ...). So you would prefer to define a unique BoM for it, even though you do not want any instances of this product to be built, nor would you want to rewrite these elements in a series of different multi-level BoMs.

If you only want a single production order for the complete shelf, and not one for the BoM itself, you can define the BoM line corresponding to product RCK100 in the shelf's BoM as type *Sets/Phantom*. Then OpenERP will automatically put RCK100's BoM contents into the shelf's production order, even though it has been defined as multi-level.

This way of representing the assembly is very useful, because it allows you to define reusable assembly elements and keep them isolated.

If you define the BoM for the SHE100 shelf in the way shown by the table below, you will get two production orders on confirmation of a sales order, as also shown in the tables.

Table 6.18: Defining and Using Phantom BoMs

| Product Ref. | Quantity | Unit of Measure | Type of BoM |
|---|---|---|---|
| SHE100 | 1 | PCE | normal |
| SIDEPAN | 2 | PCE | normal |
| RPAN100 | 1 | PCE | phantom |
| PROFIL | 4 | PCE | phantom |
| RCK100 | 3 | PCE | phantom |

Table 6.19: Production Order from Phantom BoMs

| Product Ref. | Quantity | Unit of Measure |
|---|---|---|
| SHE100 | 1 | PCE |
| SIDEPAN | 2 | PCE |
| WOOD002 | 0.25 | m |
| LIN40 | 1 | m |
| WOOD010 | 0.249 | m |
| METC000 | 12 | PCE |

Table 6.20: Production Order from Normal BoM

| Product Ref. | Quantity | Unit of Measure |
|---|---|---|
| SIDEPAN | 2 | PCE |
| WOOD002 | 0.17 | m |

## 6.1.4 Bills of Materials for Kits/Sets

> **Sales Bills of Materials**
>
> In other software, this is sometimes called a Sales Bill of Materials. In OpenERP, the term Kits/Sets is used, because the effect of the bill of materials is visible not only in sales, but also elsewhere, for example, in the intermediate manufactured products.

Kits/Sets bills of materials enable you to define assemblies that will be sold directly. These could also be used in deliveries and stock management rather than just sold separately. For example, if you deliver the shelf in pieces for self-assembly, set the SHE100 BoM to type Sets / Phantom.

When a salesperson creates an order for a SHE100 product, OpenERP automatically changes the SHE100 from a set of components into an identifiable package for sending to a customer. Then it asks the storesperson to pack 2 SIDEPAN, 1 RPAN100, 4 PROFIL, 3 RCK100. This is described as a SHE100, not just the individual products delivered.

# 6.2 Work Centers

Work centers represent units of product, capable of doing material transformation operations. You can distinguish two types of work centers: machines and human resources.

> **Work Center**
>
> Work centers are units of production consisting of one or several people and/or machines that can be considered as a unit for the purpose of forecasting capacity and planning.

Use the menu *Manufacturing* → *Configuration* → *Resources* → *Work Centers* to define a new work center. You get a form as shown in the figure *Defining a Work Center* (page 148).

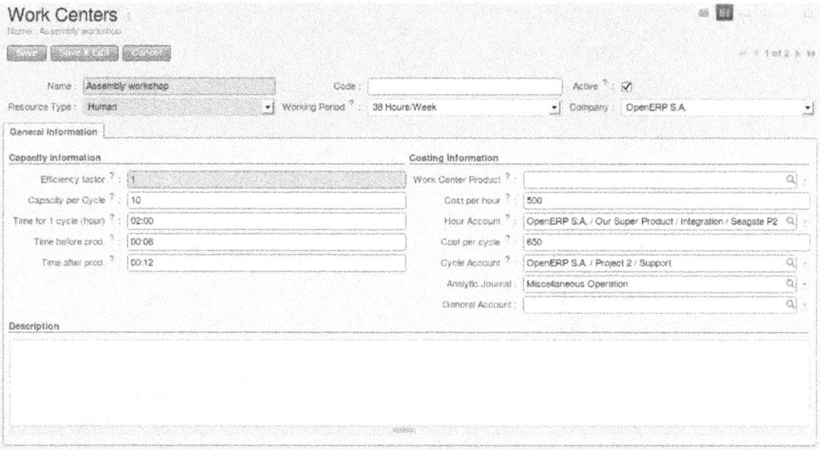

Figure 6.6: *Defining a Work Center*

> **Missing fields**
>
> If some fields such as *Analytic Journal, General Account* in the view are missing, you have to add the user group Useability / Analytic Accounting.

A work center should have a name. You then assign a type: Machine or Human, a code and the operating hours, i.e. Working Period. The Working Time(s) can be defined through the menu *Manufacturing* → *Configuration* → *Resources* → *Working Time*. The figure *Defining a Work Center* (page 148) represents the hours from Monday to Friday, from 08:00 to 18:00 with a break of an hour from 12:00.

You can also add a description of the work center and its operations.

Once the work center is defined, you should enter data about its production capacity. Depending on whether you have a machine or a person, a work center will be defined in cycles or hours. If it represents a set of machines and people you can use cycles and hours at the same time.

> **A Cycle**
>
> A cycle corresponds to the time required to carry out an assembly operation. The user is free to determine which is the reference operation for a given work center. It should be represented by the cost and elapsed manufacturing time.
>
> For example, for a printing work center, a cycle might be the printing of 1 page or of 1000 pages depending on the printer.

To define the capacity properly, it is necessary to know, for each work center, what will be the reference operation which determines the cycle. You can then define the data relative to the capacity.

*Capacity per Cycle* (CA): the number of operations that can be done in parallel during a cycle. Generally, the number defines the number of identical machines or people defined by the work center.

*Time for 1 cycle (hour)* (TC): the duration in hours for one cycle or the operations defined by a cycle.

*Time before production* (TS): the time in hours required to initialize production operations. Generally, this represents the machine setup time.

*Time after production* (TN): the delay in hours after the end of a production operation. Generally, this represents the cleaning time necessary after an operation.

*Efficiency factor* (ET): the factor that is applied to the TC, TS and TN times to determine the real production time. This factor enables you to readjust the different times progressively and as a measure of machine utilization. You cannot re-adjust the other times, because generally they are taken from the machine's data sheet. By default, the efficiency is set to 1, representing a load of 100%. When you set the efficiency to 2 (i.e. 200%), the load will be 50%.

The total time for carrying out X operations is then given by the following formula:

$$((X / CA) * TC + TS + TN ) * ET$$

In this formula the result of the division is rounded upwards. Then, if the capacity per cycle is 6, it takes 3 cycles to realize 15 operations (15/6 = 2.5, rounded upwards = 3).

With the *Hour Account* and *Cycle Account* you define the links to analytical accounting, to report the costs of the work center operations. If you leave the different fields empty, it will not have any effect on the analytic accounts.

# 6.3 Routings

Routings define the manufacturing operations to be done in work centers to produce a certain product. A routing is usually attached to bills of materials, which will define the assembly of products required for manufacturing or to produce finished products.

A routing can be defined directly in a bill of materials or through the menu *Manufacturing* → *Configuration* → *Master Bill of Materials* → *Routings*. A routing has a name, and a code. You can also add a description. Later in this chapter you will see that a routing can also be associated with a stock location. This enables you to indicate where an assembly takes place.

> **Subcontracting Assembly**
>
> You will see further on in this chapter that you can also link a routing to a stock location for the customer or the supplier. You can use this functionality when you have subcontracted the assembly of a product to a supplier, for instance.

In the routing, you have to enter the list of operations that has to be executed. Each operation has to be done at a specific work center and includes a number of hours and/or cycles.

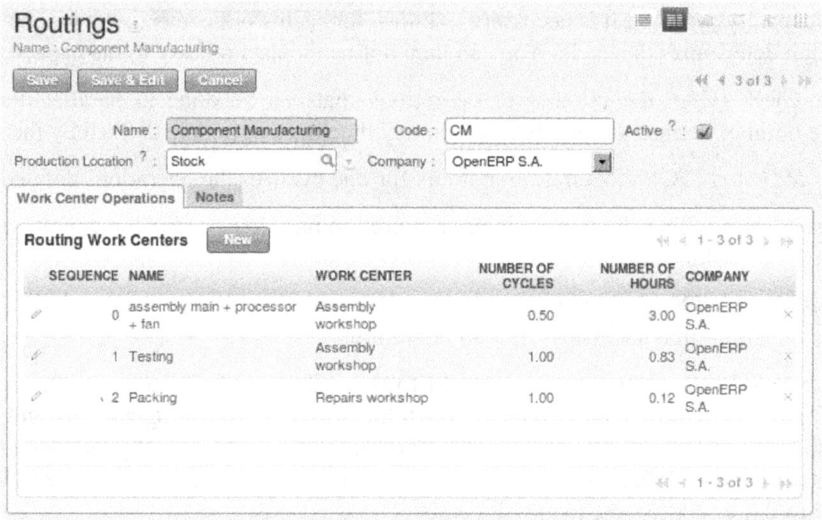

Figure 6.7: *Defining a routing with Three Operations*

> 💡 **Multi-level Routing**
>
> It is possible to define routing on several levels to support multi-level bills of materials. You can select the routing on each level of a bill of materials ( BoM in a BoM can have a different routing). The levels are then linked to hierarchies of bills of materials.

# 6.4 Manufacturing Orders

Once the bills of materials have been defined, OpenERP is capable of automatically deciding on the manufacturing route according to the needs of the company.

Production orders can be proposed automatically by the system depending on several criteria described in the preceding chapter:

- Using the `Make to Order` rules,
- Using the `Order Point` (Minimum Stock) rules,
- Using the Production plan.

Of course, you can also start production manually by clicking the button *New* in the menu *Manufacturing* → *Manufacturing* → *Manufacturing Orders*.

If you have not installed the Just-in-Time planning module `mrp_jit`, you should start using OpenERP to schedule the Production Orders automatically using the various system rules. To do this, use the menu *Warehouse* → *Schedulers* → *Compute Schedulers*.

Figure 6.8: *Manufacturing Order*

> **Procurement Exceptions**
>
> Pay attention to the fact that you have to define *minimum stock rules* for each product set as `Make to Stock`.

## 6.5 Complete Production Workflow

To understand the usefulness and the functioning of the system you should test a complete workflow on the database installed with the demonstration data. We will show you:

- How to create a sales order,

- The manufacturing workflow for an intermediate product,

- The manufacturing of an ordered product,

- The delivery of products to a customer,

- Invoicing at the end of the month,

- Traceability for after-sales service.

> **Demonstration data**
>
> To exactly follow the workflow as shown below, you should keep the same quantities as in the example and start from a new database. Then you will not run into exceptions resulting from a lack of stock.

This more advanced case of handling problems in procurement will be sorted out later in the chapter.

To be able to do the following step, add `Sales Management` through the Reconfigure wizard.

## 6.5.1 The Sales Order

Begin by encoding a sales (or customer) order through the menu *Sales Management* → *Sales Orders* -> *New Quotation*. Enter the following information:

- *Customer* : Agrolait,

- *Shipping Policy* : Invoice from the picking (Other Information tab),

- *Sales Order Lines*, click *New*:

  - *Product* : PC2 – Basic PC (assembly on order),

  - *Quantity (UoM)* : 1,

  - *Product UoM* : PCE,

  - *Procurement Method* : on order.

Once the quotation has been entered, you can confirm it immediately by clicking the button *Confirm Order* at the bottom to the right. Keep note of the order reference because this follows all through the process. Usually, in a new database, this will be SO007 . At this stage, you can look at the process linked to your order using the *Question Mark* button next to the Sales Orders title.

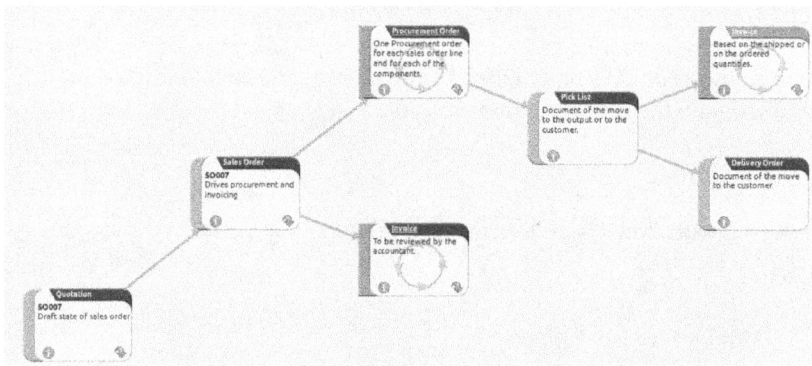

Figure 6.9: *Process for Handling Sales Order SO007*

Start the requirements calculation using the menu *Manufacturing* → *Compute All Schedulers*.

## 6.5.2 Producing an Intermediate Product

To understand the implications of requirements calculation, you should know the configuration of the sold product. To do this, go to the form for product PC2 and click the link *Product BoM Structure* to the right. You get the scheme shown in *Composition of PC2* (page 153) which is the composition of the selected product.

The PC2 computer has to be manufactured in two steps:

1: The intermediate product: CPU_GEN

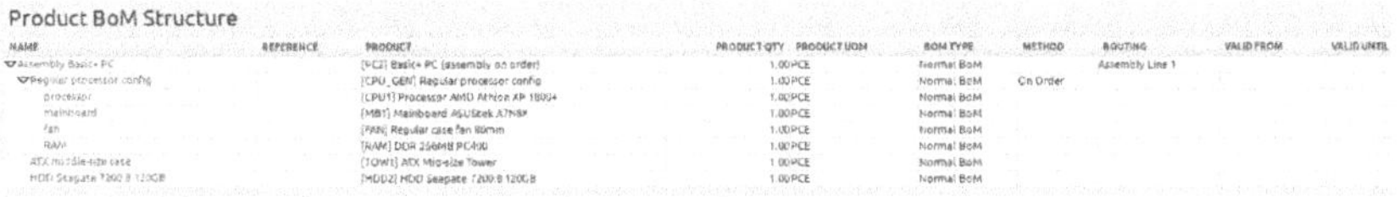

**Product BoM Structure**

| NAME | REFERENCE | PRODUCT | PRODUCT QTY | PRODUCTION UOM | BOM TYPE | METHOD | ROUTING | VALID FROM | VALID UNTIL |
|------|-----------|---------|-------------|----------------|----------|--------|---------|------------|-------------|
| ▼ Assembly Basic PC | | [PC2] Basic+ PC (assembly on order) | 1.00 | PCE | Normal BoM | | Assembly Line 1 | | |
| ▼ Regular processor config | | [CPU_GEN] Regular processor config | 1.00 | PCE | Normal BoM | On Order | | | |
| processor | | [CPU1] Processor AMD Athlon XP 1800+ | 1.00 | PCE | Normal BoM | | | | |
| Mainboard | | [MB1] Mainboard ASUStek A7N8P | 1.00 | PCE | Normal BoM | | | | |
| fan | | [FAN] Regular case fan 80mm | 1.00 | PCE | Normal BoM | | | | |
| RAM | | [RAM] DDR 256MB PC400 | 1.00 | PCE | Normal BoM | | | | |
| ATX midi-tide case | | [CQM1] ATX Midi-size Tower | 1.00 | PCE | Normal BoM | | | | |
| HDD Seagate 7200.9 120GB | | [HDD2] HDD Seagate 7200.9 120GB | 1.00 | PCE | Normal BoM | | | | |

Figure 6.10: *Composition of PC2*

2: The finished product using that intermediate product: PC2

The manufacturing supervisor can then consult the production orders using the menu *Manufacturing → Manufacturing → Manufacturing Orders*. You then get a list of orders to start (Ready to Produce) and the estimated start date (Scheduled Date) to meet the customer delivery date.

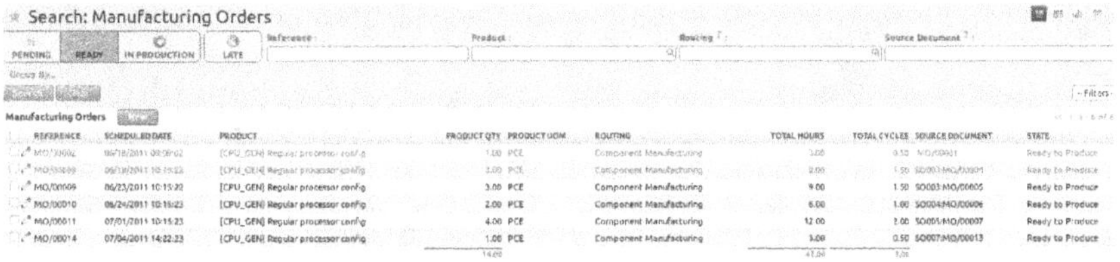

Figure 6.11: *List of Manufacturing Orders*

You will see the production order for CPU_GEN, but not the one for PC2 because it depends on an intermediate product that has to be produced first. Return to the production order for CPU_GEN and click it. If there are several of them, select the one corresponding to your order using the source document that contains your order number (in this example SO007 ).

Figure 6.12: *Details of a Production Order*

The system shows you that you have to manufacture product CPU_GEN using the components: MB1, CPU1, FAN, RAM. You can then confirm the production twice:

Start production: consumption of raw materials,

Produce: manufacturing of finished product.

Click the Start Production button, then click the Edit button, and edit the line for the product MB1. Enter a lot number for it by putting the cursor in the field *Production Lot* and pressing <F1> to create a new lot. Enter an internal reference, for example: `MB1345678`. The system may then show you a warning because this lot is not in stock, but you can ignore this message.

Click the `Produce` button to manufacture the finished product.

The production order has to be in the closed state as shown in the figure *Production Order after the Different Stages* (page 154).

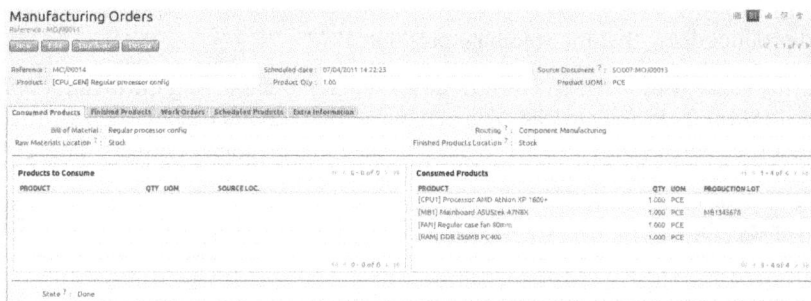

Figure 6.13: *Production Order after the Different Stages*

## 6.5.3 Finished Product Manufacturing

Having manufactured the intermediate product CPU_GEN, OpenERP automatically proposes the manufacturing of the computer PC2 using the order created earlier. Return to the Manufacturing Orders menu and look at the orders Ready to Produce through *Manufacturing → Manufacturing → Manufacturing Orders*.

You will find computer PC2 which has been sold to the customer (source document SO007), as shown in the figure hereafter.

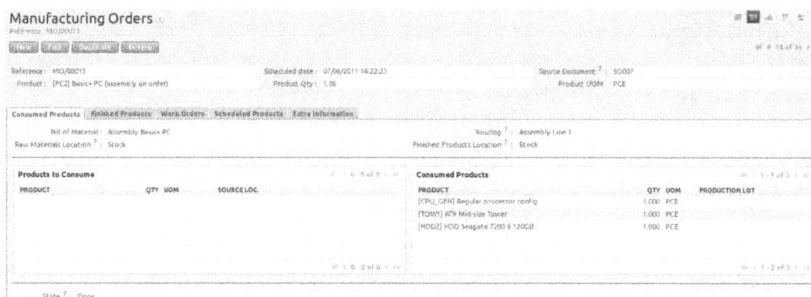

Figure 6.14: *Completed Production for PC2*

Now that the production has been completed, the product sold to the customer has been manufactured and the raw materials have been consumed and taken out of stock.

## 6.5.4 Subproduct Production

If you need to manage subproducts, you should install the module `mrp_subproduct` (Reconfigure wizard, MRP Sub- products). The normal behaviour of manufacturing in OpenERP enables you to manufacture several units of the same finished product from raw materials (A + B > C). With Subproduct management, the manufacturing result can be to have both finished products and secondary products (A + B > C + D).

If the module `mrp_subproduct` has been installed, you get a new tab Sub products in the Bill of Material that lets you set secondary products resulting from the manufacturing of the finished product.

When OpenERP generates a production order based on a bill of materials that uses a secondary product, you pick up the list of all products in the the second tab of the production order `Finished Products`.

Secondary products enable you to generate several types of products from the same raw materials and manufacturing methods - only these are not used in the calculation of requirements. Then, if you need the secondary products, OpenERP will not ask you to manufacture another product to use the waste products and secondary products of this production. In this case, you should enter another production order for the secondary product.

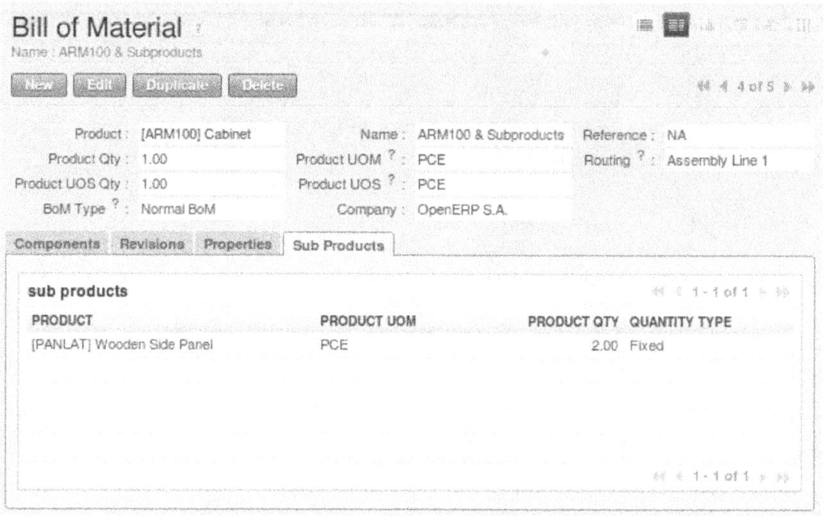

Figure 6.15: *Definition of Subproducts*

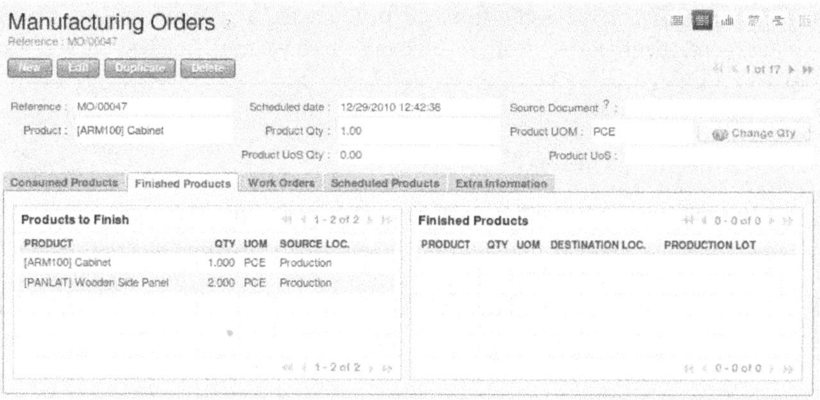

Figure 6.16: *Production Order producing Several Finished Products*

---

**Services in Manufacturing**

Unlike most software for production management, OpenERP manages services as well as stockable products. So it is possible to put products of type Service in a bill of materials. These do not appear in the production order, but their requirements will be taken into account.

If they are defined as Make to Order, OpenERP will generate a task for the manufacturing or a subcontract order for the operations. The behaviour will depend on the Supply Method configured in the product form: Buy or Produce.

---

## 6.5.5 Scrapping

If you have to scrap the final product before it is finished, you will have to scrap every component allowed for this product.

Figure 6.17: *Scrapping a Product to Finish*

If you scrap a Product to Finish, you will get the situation illustrated in the previous figure. A finished product will be *created* and put in the scrapped virtual location. A new Product to Finish has been added to the manufacturing order.

> **Scrap a product**
>
> To scrap a product, you have to edit the manufacturing order and then select the product to be scrapped by clicking the little pencil at the left of the item.

This new product has been added for the following reason: when you have to manufacture a product and if this product has to be scrapped, you have to produce another product to replace the scrapped one. The reason why you have to scrap each component manually is that the production problem can come from one component.

If the production process is finished and you see that you have to scrap the finished product, you will not have to scrap the different components. They are already *consumed*. They are not available anymore for further manufacturing orders; they have been moved to the production Stock Location.

## 6.5.6 Production Orders

To open a Production Order, use the menu *Manufacturing → Manufacturing → Manufacturing Orders* and click the *New* button. You get a blank form to enter a new production order as shown in the figure *New Production Order* (page 158).

The production order follows the process given by the figure *Process for Handling a Production Order* (page 158).

The *Scheduled date* , *Product Qty* and *Reference*, are automatically completed when the form is first opened. Enter the product that you want to produce, and the quantity required. The *Product UOM* by default is completed automatically by OpenERP when the product is first selected.

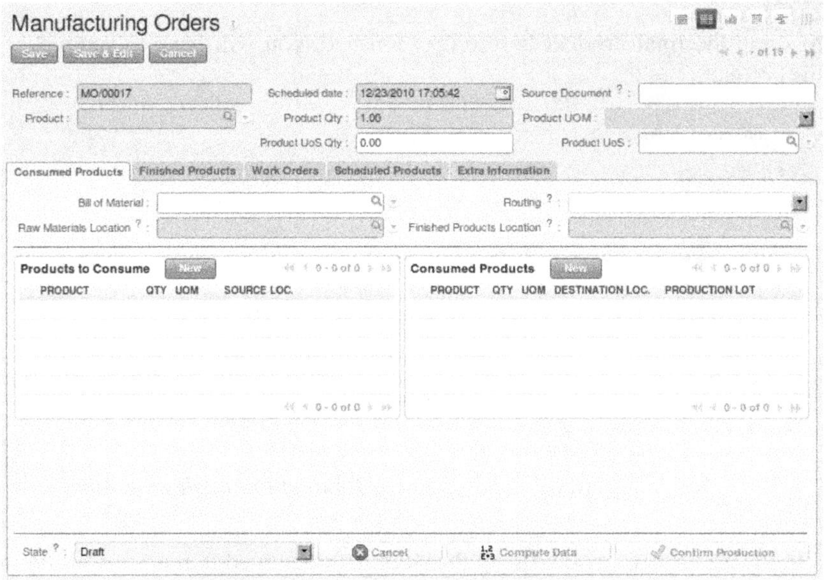

Figure 6.18: *New Production Order*

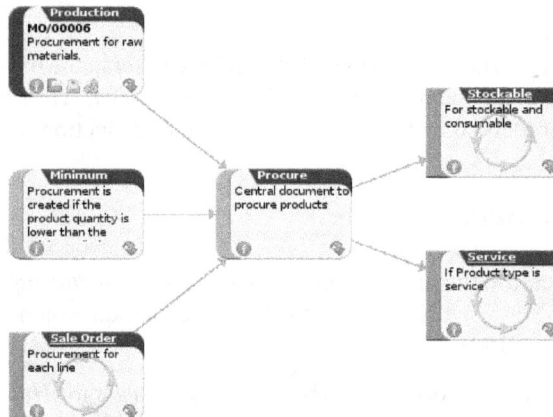

Figure 6.19: *Process for Handling a Production Order*

You then have to set two locations:

- The location from which the required raw materials should be found, and

- The location for depositing the finished products.

For simplicity, put the `Stock` location in both places. The field *Bill of Materials* will automatically be completed by OpenERP when you select the product. You can then overwrite it with another BoM to specify something else to use for this specific manufacturing, then click the button *Compute Data*.

The tabs *Scheduled Products* and *Work Orders* are also completed automatically when you click *Compute Data* (in the *Work Orders* or *Scheduled Products* tabs). You will find the raw materials there that are required for the production and the operations needed by the assembly staff.

If you want to start production, click the button *Confirm Production*, and OpenERP automatically completes the *Products to Consume* field in the *Consumed Products* tab and *Products to Finish* field in *Finished Products* tab.

The information in the *Consumed Products* tab can be changed if:

- you want to enter a serial number for raw materials,

- you want to change the quantities consumed (lost during production).

For traceability, you can set lot numbers on the raw materials used, or on the finished products. Note the *Production Lot* and *Pack* numbers.

Once the order is confirmed, you should force the reservation of materials using the *Force Reservation* button. This means that you do not have to wait for the scheduler to assign and reserve the raw materials from your stock for this production run. This shortens the procurement process.

If you do not want to change the priorities, just leave the production order in this state and the scheduler will create a plan based on the priority and your planned date.

To start the production of products, click *Start Production*. The raw materials are then consumed automatically from stock, which means that the draft ( `Waiting` ) movements become `Done`.

Once the production is complete, click *Produce*. The finished products are now moved into stock.

# 6.6 Logistics and Manufacturing

## 6.6.1 Manufacturing Stock Locations

OpenERP allows you to define a specific location to keep track of your manufacturing moves.

To get an overview of all stock moves, go to *Warehouse* → *Traceability* → *Stock Moves*. You can enter your Production location in the `Location` search field and then group by Source or Destination according to the moves you would like to check.

## 6.6.2 Traceability

With traceability you can easily track your production lots in the software. With this functionality you can quickly find where your products are in your warehouse. In counterpart, you will be forced to mention a number of lot to each product to be able to track it in the system.

To enable traceability in the manufacturing process, go to *Warehouse* → *Product* → *Products*. In the `Product` form, you have to select the box *Track Manufacturing Lots* in the *Lots* section on the `Information` tab.

In the manufacturing order, you have to mention a production lot number in order to continue the process. You can select the production lot in the *Manufacturing Order* form on the second tab, called *Finished Products*. You have to click the Products to Finish you want to trace, a new window will open. In the *Production Lot* field, click to link the manufacturing order to a production lot.

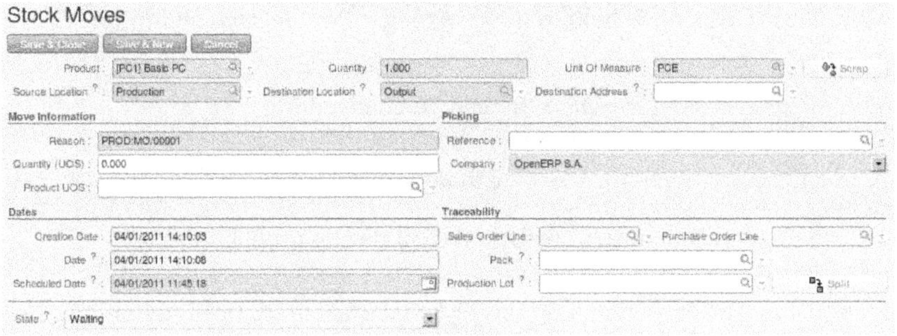

Figure 6.20: *Tracking a Manufacturing Order*

When you have linked some manufacturing orders to production lots, you can trace them from the menu *Warehouse* → *Traceability* → *Production Lots*. In this view, you see the different production lots linked to a product. If you select one lot, you will have the possibility to choose between *Upstream Traceability* or *Downstream Traceability*.

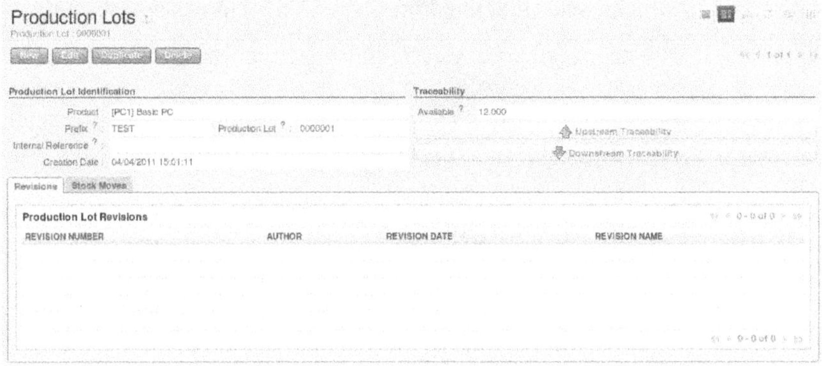

Figure 6.21: *Choosing between Upstream and Downstream Traceability*

> **Traceability**
>
> **Upstream Traceability**: It starts from the raw materials received from the supplier and follows the chain to the finished products delivered to customers. Note that the name is confusing - this would often be considered a downstream direction. Think of it as **Where Used**.
>
> **Downstream Traceability**: It follows the product in the other direction, from customer to the different suppliers of raw material. Note that the name is confusing - this would often be considered an upstream direction. Think of it as **Where Supplied**.

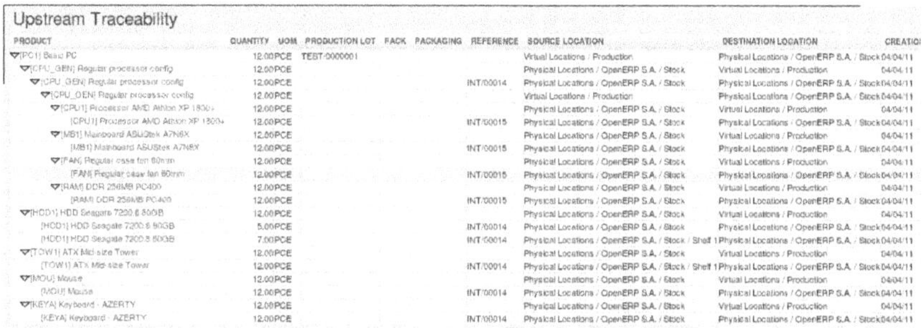


Figure 6.22: *Upstream Traceability*

The different lines show the stock moves attached to the production of the product. There are several stock moves that are traced due to the Bill of Materials attached to the product *[PC1] Basic PC*.

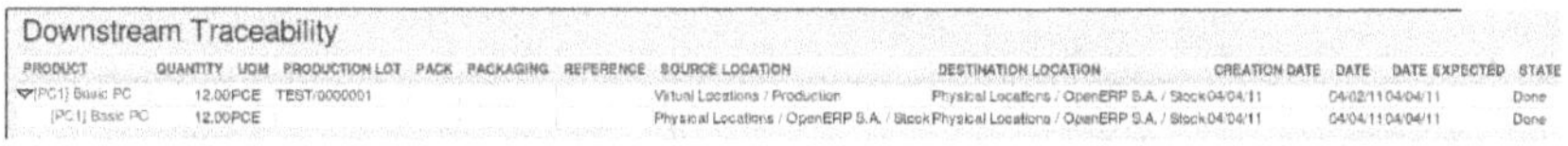


Figure 6.23: *Downstream Traceability*

In this window, you only see the move for the finished product. This is related to the definition of the concept of Downstream Traceability, which only shows the flow from the customer to the supplier of raw materials.

## 6.7 Managing Repairs: from Repair to Invoicing and Stock Movements

The management of repairs is carried out through the module `mrp_repair`. Once installed, this module adds a new *Manufacturing → Manufacturing → Repair Orders* menu under the `Manufacturing` menu to create repair jobs and review repairs in progress.

> **Repairs**
>
> To install this module, you can also use the `Reconfigure` wizard. In the *MRP Application Configuration* screen, check the `Repairs` option.

In OpenERP, a repair will have the following effects:

- Use of materials: items for replacement,
- Production of products: items replaced from reserved stock,
- Quality control: tracking the reasons for repair,
- Accounting entries: following stock moves,
- Receipt and delivery of product from and to the end user,
- Adding operations that can be seen in the product's traceability,
- Invoicing items used and/or free for repairs.

## 6.7.1 Entering Data for a New Repair

Use the menu *Manufacturing* → *Manufacturing* → *Repair Orders* to enter a new repair into the system. You will see a blank form for the repair data, as shown in the figure *Entering a New Repair* (page 162) below.

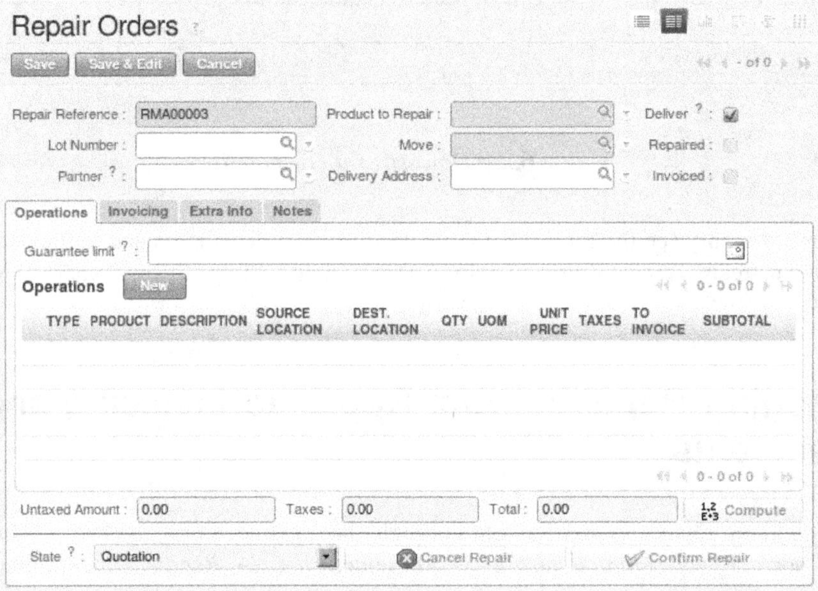


Figure 6.24: *Entering a New Repair*

First enter the product to repair, then identify the product that will be repaired using the *product lot number*. OpenERP then automatically completes fields from the selected lot – the partner fields, address, delivery location and stock move.

If a warranty period has been defined in the product description, in months, OpenERP completes the field *Guarantee limit* with the correct warranty date.

Now you have to specify the components that you will be adding, replacing or removing in the *Operations* part. On each line, you should specify the following:

Add or remove a component of the finished product:

- *Product,*
- *Qty,*
- *UoM,*
- *Unit Price,*
- *To Invoice* or not.

Once the component has been selected, OpenERP automatically completes most of the fields:

- *Qty*: 1,
- *UoM*: unit for managing stock defined in the product form,
- *Unit Price*: calculated from the customer list price,
- *Source Location*: given by the stock management,
- *To Invoice*: depends on the actual date and the guarantee period.

This information is automatically proposed by the system, but you can modify it all yourself.

On the second tab of the `Repair` form, `Invoicing`, you can select whether the repair has to be invoiced or not, and if invoiced whether it should be before or after the repair. You can also select the applicable list price, a specific address and encode additional charges that need to be added to the repair invoice.

The third tab, `Extra Info` shows information about linked invoice and picking. You receive information about the current location, and you can change the `Delivery Location`. The `Notes` tab allows you to register internal notes and information that should be written on the Quotation.

## 6.7.2 Repair Workflow

A defined process handles a repair order – both the repair itself and the customer invoicing. The figure *Process to Handle a Repair* (page 164) shows this repair process.

Once a repair has been entered in the system, it is in the `Quotation` state. In this state, a repair order has no impact on the rest of the system. You can print a quotation through the action *Quotation / Order*.

On the second tab, you can specify the *Invoice Method*:

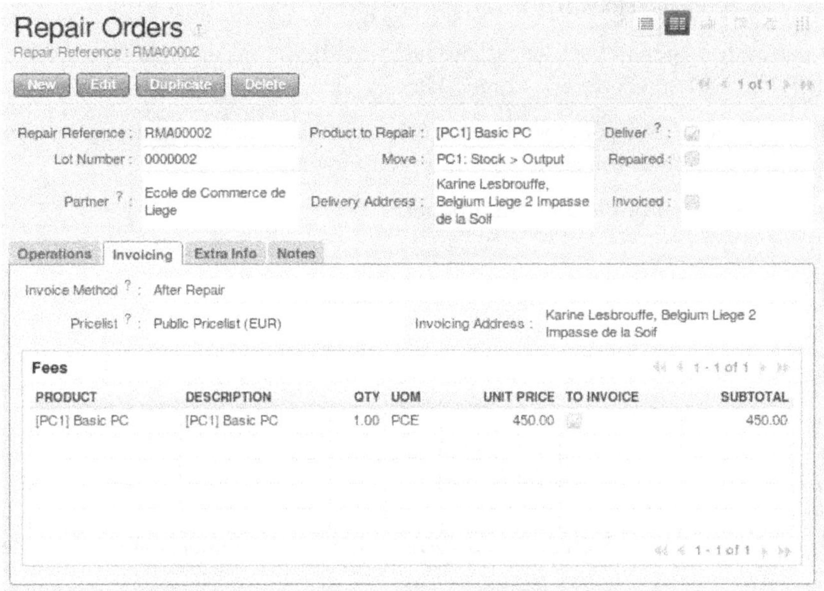

Figure 6.25: *Repair Form, Invoicing Tab*

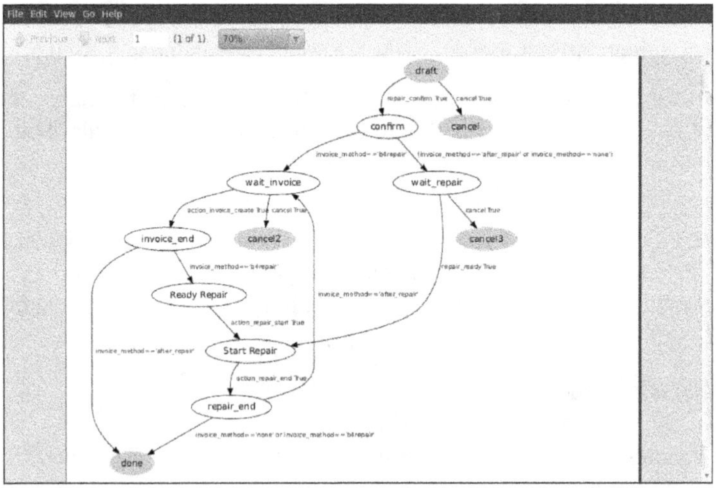

Figure 6.26: *Process to Handle a Repair*

- No Invoice,

- Before Repair,

- After Repair.

You can then confirm the repair operation or create an invoice for the customer depending on the Invoice Method.

The repair quotation can now be sent to the customer. Once the customer approves the repair, click the *Confirm Repair* button. From the menu *Manufacturing → Manufacturing → Repair Orders* you can easily find the confirmed repair orders by selecting the Confirmed button. Click *Start Repair* to indicate that you can start working on the repair. The Repair order will now be in the Under Repair state. When you finish the repair, click the End Repair button.

## 6.7.3 Invoicing the Repair

When the repair is to be invoiced, a draft invoice is generated by the system. For an After Repair invoice, you can click the Make Invoice button. OpenERP will then show the draft invoice created at the top of the repair order (red text). You can easily go to that invoice simply by clicking the corresponding red text. This invoice contains the raw materials used (replaced components) and any other costs such as the time used for the repair. These other costs are entered on the second tab of the *Repair* form. Any information you entered for the quotation on the Notes tab will also be displayed on the invoice.

If the product to be repaired is still under guarantee, OpenERP automatically suggests that the components themselves are not invoiced, but will still use any other defined costs. You can override any of these default values while entering the data.

> **Extra Info**
>
> The link to the generated invoice is shown on the Extra Info``tab of the repair document. To open the invoice, simply click the ``Invoice field.

## 6.7.4 Stock Movements and Repairs

When the repair has been carried out, OpenERP automatically carries out stock movements for components that have been removed, added or replaced on the finished product. From the menu *Warehouse → Traceability → Stock Moves*, you can for instance enter the production lot to see all moves for the repaired product.

The move operations are carried out using the locations shown in the first tab of the Repair form. If a destination location has been specified, OpenERP automatically handles the final customer delivery order when the repair has been completed. This also lets you manage the delivery of the repaired products.

For example, take the case of the shelf that was produced at the start of this chapter. If you have to replace the shelf SIDEPAN, you should enter data for the repair as shown in figure *Repair for a Side Panel* (page 166).

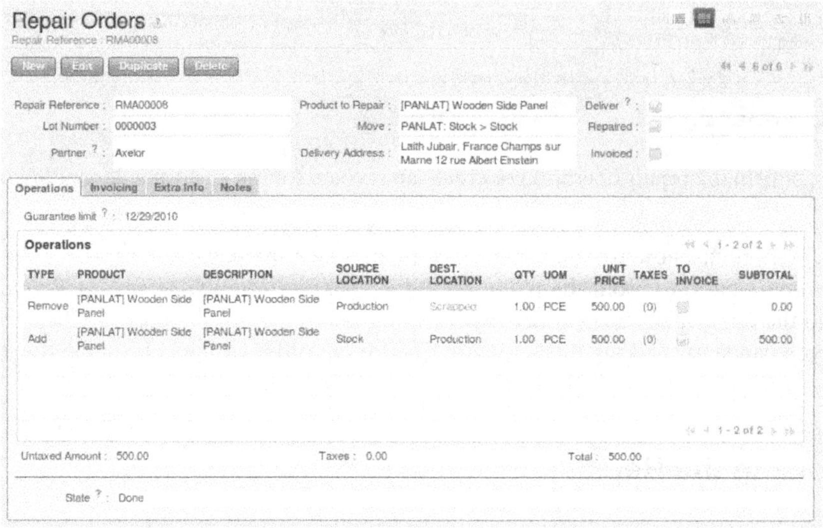

Figure 6.27: *Repair for a Side Panel*

In this example, you would carry out the following operations:

- Remove a SIDEPAN shelf in the cabinet and put the faulty shelf in the *Scrapped* location,

- Place a new SIDEPAN shelf that has been taken from stock.

When the repair is ready to be confirmed, OpenERP will generate the following stock moves:

- Put faulty SIDEPAN into suitable stock location *Default Production > Scrapped*,

- Consume SIDEPAN: *Stock > Production*.

If you analyze the traceability of this lot number, you will see all the repair operations in the upstream and downstream traceability lists of the products concerned.

# 6.8 Forecasting and Supplying

## 6.8.1 Scheduler

The requirements scheduler is the calculation engine which plans and prioritises production and purchasing automatically according to the rules defined on products. By default, the scheduler is set to run once a day (OpenERP automatically creates a *Scheduled Action* for this). You can also start the scheduler manually from the menu *Warehouse* → *Schedulers* → *Compute Schedulers*. The scheduler uses all the relevant parameters defined for products, suppliers and the company to determine the priorities between the different production orders, deliveries and supplier purchases.

**Starting Time**

You can set the starting time of the scheduler by modifying the corresponding action in the menu *Administration* → *Configuration* → *Scheduler* → *Scheduled Actions*. Modify the `Run mrp Scheduler` configuration document.

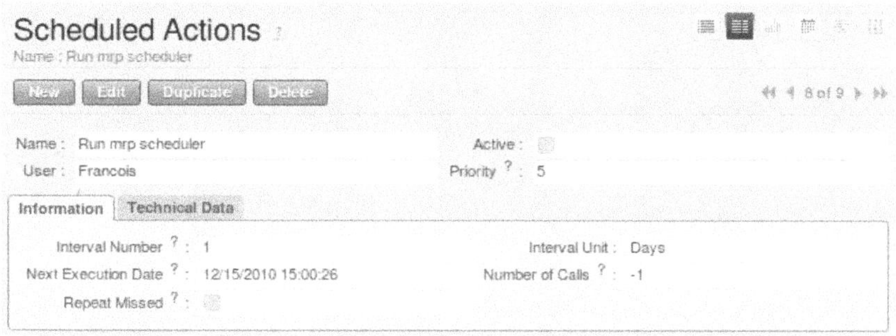


Figure 6.28: *Configuring the Start Time to Calculate Requirements*

**Calculating Requirements / Scheduling**

Scheduling only validates procurements that are confirmed but not yet started. These procurement reservations will themselves start production, tasks or purchases depending on the configuration of the requested product.

You take into account the priority of operations when starting reservations and procurements. Urgent requests, those with a date in the past, or requests with a date earlier than the others will be started first. In case there are not enough products in stock to satisfy all the requests, you can be sure that the most urgent requests will be produced first.

### 6.8.2 Planning

In OpenERP, you can plan the production in an easy way. Simply by going to *Manufacturing* → *Planning*, you can plan manufacturing orders, work orders and/or work centers.

By clicking `Manufacturing Orders` in the *Planning* menu, a calendar view will open in which you can select a day to create the order whenever you want. You will also see the already planned orders. By dragging and dropping a manufacturing order in Calendar view, you can change the starting date of the order.

When you click in a day in the Calendar view, an empty manufacturing order window will open and let you choose which product you want to produce.

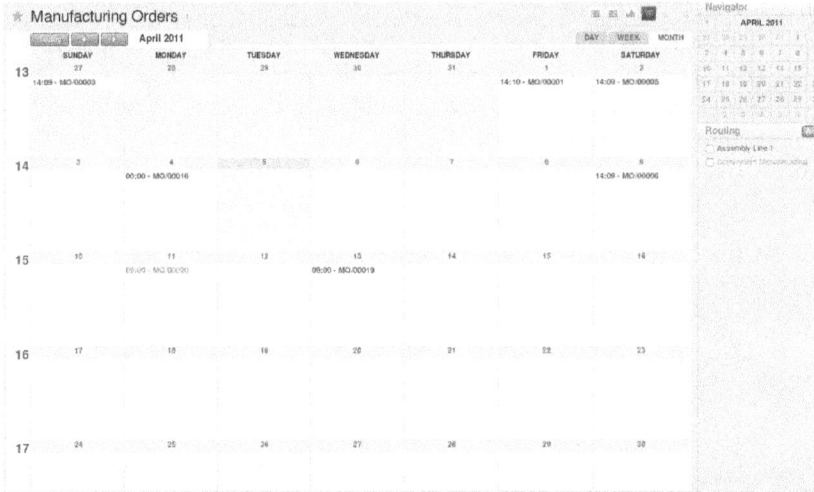

Figure 6.29: *Planning Manufacturing Orders*

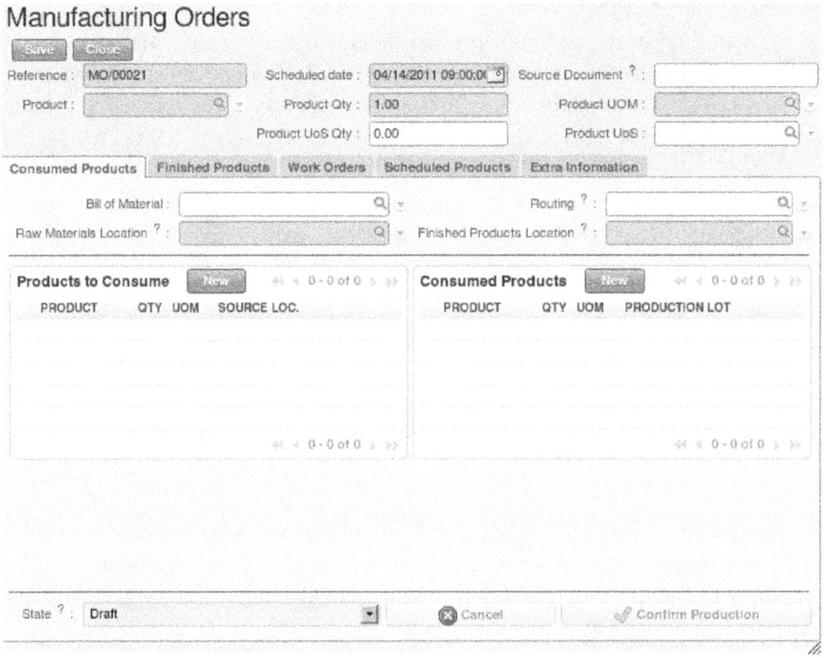

Figure 6.30: *New Manufacturing Order*

## Scheduler and Just in Time

When you want to work according to the *Just in Time* way, you should install the module `mrp_jit`.

If you install this module, you will not have to run the regular procurement scheduler anymore (but you still need to run the minimum order point rule scheduler, or for example let it run daily.)

All procurement orders will be processed immediately, which could in some cases entail a small performance impact.

It may also increase your stock size because products are reserved as soon as possible and the scheduler time range is not taken into account anymore. In that case, you can no longer use priorities for the different picking orders.

## Lead times

All procurement operations (that is, the requirement for both production orders and purchase orders) are automatically calculated by the scheduler. But more than just creating each order, OpenERP plans the timing of each step. A planned date calculated by the system can be found on each order document.

To organize the whole chain of manufacturing and procurement, OpenERP bases everything on the delivery date promised to the customer. This is given by the date of the confirmation in the order and the lead times shown in each product line of the order. This lead time is itself proposed automatically in the field *Customer Lead Time* shown in the product form. This Customer Lead Time is the difference between the time on an order and that of the delivery.

To see a calculation of the lead times, take the example of the cabinet above. Suppose that the cabinet is assembled in two steps, using the two following bills of materials.

Table 6.21: Bill of Materials for 1 SHE100 Unit

| Product Code | Quantity | Unit of Measure |
| --- | --- | --- |
| SIDEPAN | 2 | PCE |
| WOOD002 | 0.25 | m |
| LIN040 | 1 | m |
| WOOD010 | 0.249 | m |
| METC000 | 12 | PCE |

Table 6.22: Bill of Materials for 2 SIDEPAN Units

| Product Code | Quantity | Unit of Measure |
| --- | --- | --- |
| WOOD002 | 0.17 | m |

The SIDEPAN is made from an order using the workflow shown. The WOOD002 is purchased on order and the other products are all found in stock. An order for the product SHE100 will then generate two production orders (SHE100 and SIDEPAN) then produce two purchase orders for the product WOOD002. Product WOOD002 is used in the production of both SHE100 and SIDEPAN. Set the lead times on the product forms to the following:

Table 6.23: Lead Times

| Product Code | Customer Lead Time | Manufacturing Lead Time | Supplier Lead Time |
|---|---|---|---|
| SHE100 | 30 days | 5 days | |
| SIDEPAN | | 10 days | |
| WOOD002 | | | 5 days |

A customer order placed on the 1st January will set up the following operations and lead times:

- Delivery SHE100: 31 January (=1st January + 30 days),

- Manufacture SHE100: 26 January (=31 January – 5 days),

- Manufacture SIDEPAN: 16 January (=26 January – 10 days),

- Purchase WOOD002 (for SHE100): 21 January (=26 January – 5 days),

- Purchase WOOD002 (for SIDEPAN): 11 January (=16 January – 5 days).

In this example, OpenERP will propose placing two orders with the supplier of product WOOD002. Each of these orders can be for a different planned date. Before confirming these orders, the purchasing manager could group (merge) these orders into a single order.

### Security Days

The scheduler will plan all operations as a function of the time configured on the products. But it is also possible to configure these factors in the company. These factors are then global to the company, whatever the product concerned may be. In the description of the company, on the *Configuration* tab, you find the following parameters:

- *Scheduler Range Days*: all the procurement requests that are not between today and today plus the number of days specified here are not taken into account by the scheduler.

- *Manufacturing Lead Time*: number of additional days needed for manufacturing,

- *Purchase Lead Time*: additional days to include for all purchase orders with this supplier,

- *Security Days*: number of days to deduct from a system order to cope with any problems of procurement,

> **Purchase Lead Time**
>
> The security delay for purchases is the average time between the order generated by OpenERP and the real purchase time from the supplier by your purchasing department. This delay takes into account the order process in your company, including order negotiation time.

Take for instance the following configuration:

- *Manufacturing Lead Time* : 1,

- *Purchase Lead Time* : 3,

- *Security Days* : 2.

The example above will then be given the following lead times:

- Delivery SHE100: 29 January (= 1st January + 30 days – 2 days),

- Manufacture SHE100: 23 January (= 29 January – 5 days – 1 day),

- Manufacture SIDEPAN: 12 January (= 26 January – 10 days – 1 day),

- Purchase WOOD002 (for SHE100): 15 January (= 26 January – 5 days – 3 days),

- Purchase WOOD002 (for SIDEPAN): 4 January (= 12 January – 5 days – 3 days).

## 6.8.3 Procurement

In normal system use, you do not need to worry about procurement orders, because they are automatically generated by OpenERP and the user will usually work on the results of a procurement: a production order, a purchase order, a sales order and a task.

But if there are configuration problems, the system can remain blocked by a procurement without generating a corresponding document. Exception management allows you to solve possible issues.

### Automating Purchasing and Replenishment

In the Product form view, you can choose between two procurement methods:

- Make to Stock (MTS)

- Make to Order (MTO)

These two methods will impact the way you have to configure your automatic purchasing and replenishment. For the MTS method, you will have to define Minimum Stock Rules to order products when the minimum treshold has been reached, as well as a supplier to define where to order the products. For the MTO method, you have to define a supplier for the product in order to buy new products when a sales order or a manufacturing order is confirmed.

### Managing Scheduler Exceptions

In OpenERP, you can have different procurement exceptions. An exception appears in the Procurement Exception view when the system does not know what to do with an object, such as a Manufacturing Order or a Purchase Order.

There are four types of exceptions:

- No bill of materials defined for production: in this case you have got to create a BoM or indicate that the product can be purchased instead (change the `Supply Method`).

- No supplier available for a purchase: you have to define a supplier in the `Supplier` tab of the product form.

- No address defined on the supplier partner: you have to complete an address for the supplier for the product in consideration.

- Not enough stock: you have to create a rule for automatic procurement (for example, a minimum stock rule), or manually procure it.

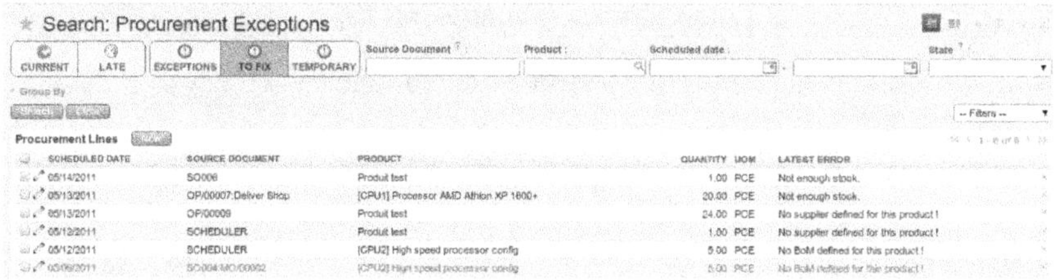

Figure 6.31: *Procurement Exceptions*

Some problems are just timing issues and can be automatically corrected by the system (this will be temporary exceptions).

If a product has to be 'in stock' but is not available in your stores, OpenERP will make the exception as 'temporary' or 'to be corrected'. The exception is temporary if the system can procure it automatically, for example, when a procurement rule has been defined for minimum stock.

When an exception is raised, you can check the configuration of your product in order to correct the misconfiguration. Then you can choose to relaunch the scheduler or you can retry to execute the action by selecting the line, and clicking the *Retry* button, then click *Run procurement*.

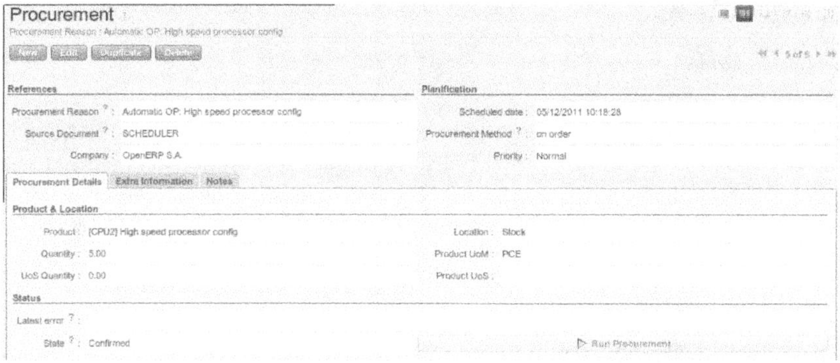

Figure 6.32: *Correct a Procurement Exception*

The exception related to the BoM definition comes from the fact that a product with a supply method set to *Produce* has no Bill of Materials. The system does not know how to produce this product and then raises an exception.

## Manual Procurement

To procure internally, you can create a procurement order manually. Use the menu *Warehouse* → *Schedulers* → *Procurement Exceptions* and click the New button to do this.

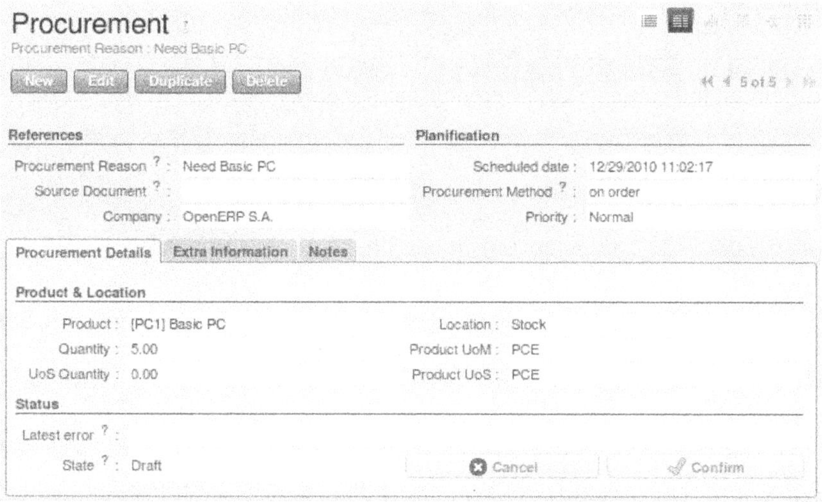

Figure 6.33: *Manual Procurement*

The procurement order will then be responsible for calculating a proposal for automatic procurement for the product concerned. This procurement will start a task, a purchase order for the supplier or a production depending on the product configuration.

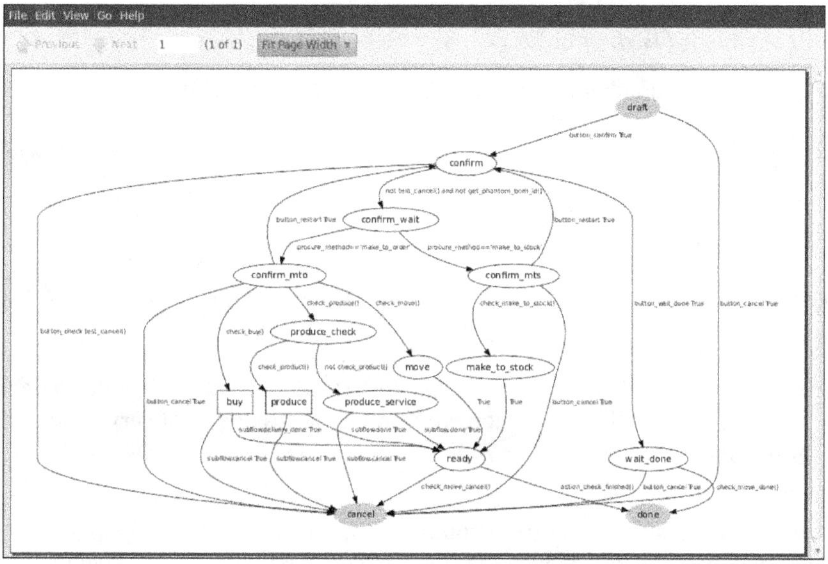

Figure 6.34: *Procurement Flow*

It is better to encode a procurement order rather than direct purchasing or production. The procurement method has the following advantages:

1. The form is simpler, because OpenERP calculates the different values according to other values and defined rules: purchase date calculated from order date, default supplier, raw materials needs, selection of the most suitable bill of materials, etc.

2. The calculation of requirements prioritises the procurements. If you encode a purchase directly, you short-circuit the planning of different procurements.

> **Shortcuts**
>
> On the Product form you have an **action** shortcut button *Procurement Request* that lets you quickly create a new procurement order.

## 6.9 Working with Subcontractors

In OpenERP, you can also subcontract production operations (for example, painting and item assembly) at a supplier's. To do this, you should indicate on the relevant routing document a supplier location for stock management.

Configure a location dedicated to this supplier with the following data:

- *Location Type*: Supplier,
- *Location Address*: Select an address of the subcontracting partner,
- *Chained Location Type*: Fixed,
- *Chained Location if Fixed*: your Stock,
- *Chaining Lead Time*: number of days before receipt of the finished product.

Then once the manufacturing has been planned for the product concerned, OpenERP will generate the following steps:

- Delivery of raw materials to the stores for the supplier,
- Production order for the products at the supplier's and receipt of the finished products in the stores.

Once the production order has been confirmed, OpenERP automatically generates a delivery order to send to the raw materials supplier. The storesperson can access this delivery order from the menu *Warehouse → Warehouse Management → Internal Moves*. The raw materials will then be placed in stock at the supplier's stores.

Once the delivery of raw materials has been confirmed, OpenERP activates the production order. The supplier uses the raw materials to produce the finished goods which will automatically be put in your own stores. This manufacturing is confirmed when you receive the products from your supplier. Then you will indicate the quantities consumed by your supplier.

> **Subcontract without Routing**
>
> If you do not use routing, you can always subcontract work orders by creating an empty routing in the subcontracting bill of materials.

Production orders can be found in the menu *Manufacturing → Manufacturing → Manufacturing Orders*. A production order is always carried out in two stages:

1. Consumption of raw materials,

2. Production of finished products.

Depending on the company's needs, you can specify that the first step is confirmed at the acknowledgement of the manufacturing supplier, and the second at the receipt of finished goods in the warehouse.

# 6.10 Matching Sales Orders and Bills of Materials

In OpenERP, you can define several bills of materials for the same product. In fact, you can have several manufacturing methods or several approved raw materials for a given product. You will see in the following section that the manufacturing procedure (the routing) is attached to the Bill of Materials, so the choice of bill of materials implicitly includes the operations to make it.

Once several bills of materials have been defined for a particular product, you need to have a system to enable OpenERP to select one of them for use. By default, the bill of materials with the lowest sequence number is selected by the system.

To gain more control over the process during selling or procuring, you can use **Properties**. The menu *Manufacturing → Configuration → Master Bill of Materials → Properties* enables you to define properties, which can be set up arbitrarily to help you select a bill of materials when you have a choice of BoMs.

> **Properties**
>
> Properties is a concept that enables the selection of a method to manufacture a product. Properties define a common language between salespeople and technical people, letting the salespeople have an influence on the manufacturing of the products using non-technical language and the choices decided on by the technicians who define Bills of Materials.

For example, you can define the following property groups and properties:

Table 6.24: Properties

| Property Group | Property |
|---|---|
| Warranty | 3 years |
| Warranty | 1 year |
| Method of Manufacture | Serial |
| Method of Manufacture | Batch |

Once the bills of materials have been defined, you could associate the corresponding properties with them. Then when the salesperson enters a sales order line, he can attach the properties required (Extra Info tab). If the product has to be manufactured, OpenERP will automatically choose the bill of materials that matches the defined properties in the order most closely.

> **Extended View**
>
> Note that the properties are only visible in the Bills of Materials and Sales Management if you are working in the Extended view mode. If you cannot see it on your screen, add the group Useability /Extended View to your user.

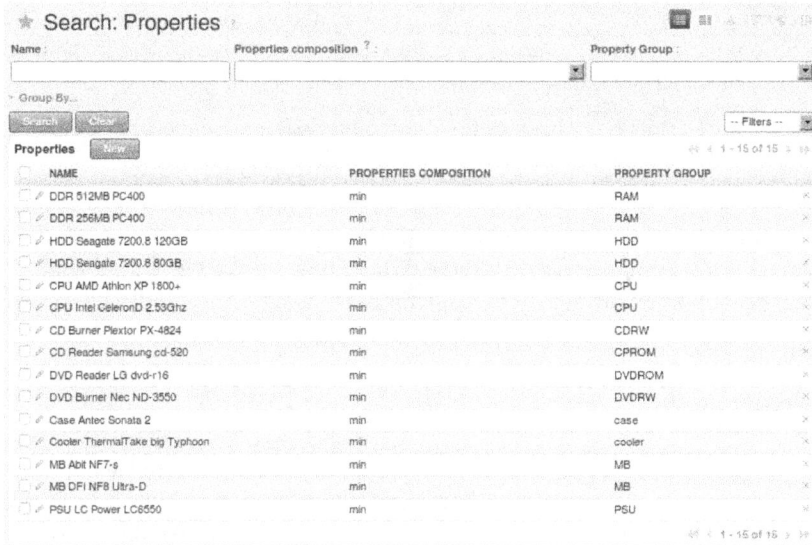

Figure 6.35: *Properties in a Customer Order Line*

*Example: Manufacturing in a Batch or on a Production Line*

As an example, take the manufacturing of the shelf presented above. You can imagine that the company has two methods of manufacturing for this cabinet:

- Manually: the staff assembles the shelves one by one and cuts the wood plank by plank. This approach is usually used to assemble prototypes. It gets you very rapid production, but at a high cost and only in small quantities.

- On a production line: the staff uses machines that are capable of cutting wood by bandsaw. This method is used for production runs of at least 50 items because the lead times using this method are quite lengthy. The delay to start the production is much longer, yet the cost per unit is considerably lower in this volume.

You define two bills of materials for the same cabinet. To distinguish between them, you will define two properties in the same group: `manual assembly` and `production line assembly`. In the quotation, the salesperson can set the method of manufacture he wants on each order line, depending on the quantities and the lead time requested by the customer.

---

**Bills of Materials and Substitute Products**

In some software, you use the term `substitute` for this principle of configurable properties in a bill of materials.

---

By putting a bill of materials on its own line, you can also implement substitute products. You set the bill of materials to type `Sets/Phantom` to make the substitution transparent and to prevent OpenERP from proposing an intermediate production order.

# 6.11 Production and Services

In OpenERP, you can handle three types of goods: two types of products (Stockable or Consumable products) and one type of services.

For this last category, OpenERP can react in two different ways. Once a manufacturing order is generated for a product and this product contains a *Service*, a task can be automatically generated or not.

---

**Tasks**

In order to automatically generate a task, you have to install the module `project_mrp` which requires the installation of the module `project`.

---

By default, the generated task is not linked to any project. You can change this behaviour by creating a project and link the service to this project. This can be done in the `Product` form, on the tab *Procurement & Locations* in the *Miscellaneous* section. Select the project to be linked in the `Project` field.

To illustrate this process, follow the next example:

First, you have to create a project to which you want to link the service. We will call this project *Consulting*. After creating the project, we have to create a new product. Here are the characteristics of this product:

---

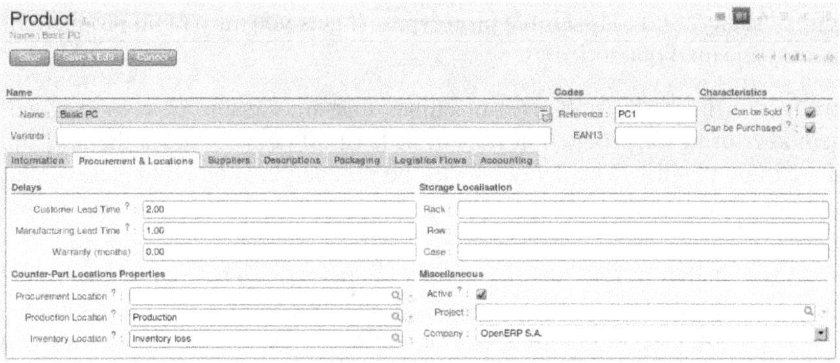

Figure 6.36: *Link a Service Product to a Project*

Table 6.25: Configure a New Service

| Field | Value |
|---|---|
| Name | Consulting |
| Reference | CSLT |
| Product Type | Service |
| Procurement Method | Make to Order |
| Supply Method | Produce |
| Default UoM | Hour |
| **Project** | **Consulting** |

Once you have configured your project and your product, you can create a Sales Order to order hours of consultancy. When you confirm the Sales Order, a task will be created.

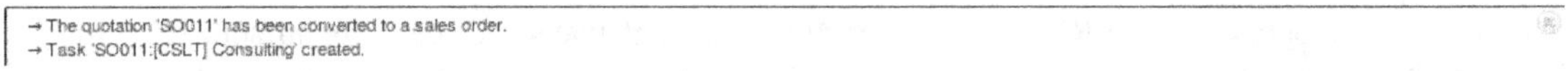

→ The quotation 'SO011' has been converted to a sales order.
→ Task 'SO011:[CSLT] Consulting' created.

If you go to *Project → Project → Tasks*, you will find a new task called: *SO011:[CSLT] Consulting*. This task is linked to the project :guilabel'Consulting'. Note that the Sales Order number may be different in your database.

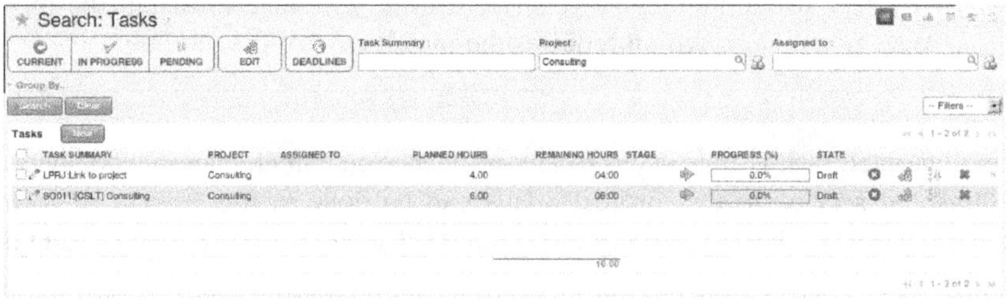

Figure 6.37: *A Product linked to a Task and a Project*

# Part V

# On Site installation

# OpenERP Installation on Linux $7$

The installation procedure of OpenERP V6.0 is explained in this chapter. This procedure is well tested on Ubuntu version 10.04.

There are four main procedures that you have to follow in order to run OpenERP V6.0 smoothly:

- PostgreSQL Server Installation and Configuration
- OpenERP Server Installation
- OpenERP Client Installation
- OpenERP Web Installation

## 7.1 PostgreSQL Server Installation and Configuration

> **Methods**
>
> The PostgreSQL download page lists the available installation methods. Choose the one that best suits your needs.

### 7.1.1 Example on Ubuntu

Use the following command at your system's command prompt to install the **postgresql** package:

```
sudo apt-get install postgresql
```

For example:

```
openerp@openerp-desktop:/$ sudo apt-get install postgresql
```

For a graphical user interface of **postgresql**, use the following command:

```
sudo apt-get install pgadmin3
```

For example:

```
openerp@openerp-desktop:/$ sudo apt-get install pgadmin3
```

You can find the new menu item **pgAdmin III** in your Ubuntu system menu from *Applications* → *Programming* → *pgAdmin III*.

## 7.1.2 Setup a PostgreSQL user for OpenERP

When the installations of the required software are done, you must create a PostgreSQL user. This user must be the same as your system user. OpenERP will use this user to connect to PostgreSQL.

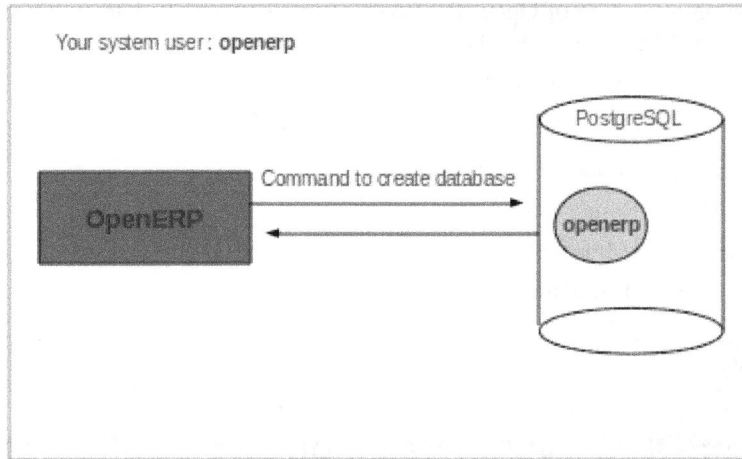

Figure 7.1: *Figure demonstrating how OpenERP uses the PostgreSQL user to interact with it*

> **Database**
> Without creating and configuring a PostgreSQL user for OpenERP as described below, you cannot create a database using OpenERP Client.

### First Method

The default superuser for PostgreSQL is called **postgres**. You may need to login as this user first.

```
openerp@openerp-desktop:/$ sudo su postgres
password: XXXXXXXXXX
```

Now create PostgreSQL user **openerp** using the following command:

```
postgres@openerp-desktop:/$ createuser openerp
Shall the new role be a superuser? (y/n) y
```

Make this new user a superuser. Only then you can create a database using OpenERP Client. In short, **openerp** is the new user created in PostgreSQL for OpenERP. This user is the owner of all the tables created by OpenERP Client.

Now check the list of tables created in PostgreSQL using following command:

```
postgres@openerp-desktop:/$ psql -l
```

You can find the table **template1**, run the following command to use this table:

```
postgres@openerp-desktop:/$ psql template1
```

To apply access rights to the role **openerp** for the database which will be created from OpenERP Client, use the following command:

```
template1=# alter role openerp with password 'postgres';
ALTER ROLE
```

## Second Method

Another option to create and configure a PostgreSQL user for OpenERP is shown below:

```
postgres@openerp-desktop:/$ createuser --createdb --username postgres --no-createrole
--pwprompt openerp
Enter password for new role: XXXXXXXXXX
Enter it again: XXXXXXXXXX
Shall the new role be a superuser? (y/n) y
CREATE ROLE
```

> **Password**
>
> Note that the password is *postgres*.

Option explanations:

- `--createdb` : the new user will be able to create new databases
- `--username postgres` : *createuser* will use the *postgres* user (superuser)
- `--no-createrole` : the new user will not be able to create new users
- `--pwprompt` : *createuser* will ask you the new user's password
- `openerp` : the new user's name

To access your database using **pgAdmin III**, you must configure the database connection as shown in the following figure:

You can now start OpenERP Server. You will probably need to modify the OpenERP configuration file according to your needs which is normally located in ~/.openerprc.

---

| Properties | |
|---|---|
| Name | localhost |
| Host | localhost |
| Port | 5432 |
| SSL | ▼ |
| Maintenance DB | postgres ▼ |
| Username | openerp |
| Password | ●●●●●●●● |
| Store password | ☑ |
| Restore env? | ☑ |
| DB restriction | |
| Service | |
| Connect now | ☑ |
| Colour | ... |

Help          OK          Cancel

---

**Developer Book**

You can find information on configuration files in the Developer Book, section *Configuration*

---

## 7.2 OpenERP Server Installation

### 7.2.1 Installing the required packages

You need to have Python (at least 2.5 for OpenERP v6.0) in your Ubuntu system, which is in-built in Ubuntu version 10.04 and above.

You also need to install the following Python libraries, because OpenERP Server uses these packages.

To install the required libraries on your Ubuntu system, you can do the following in your favourite shell:

- *lxml* : lxml is the most feature-rich and easy-to-use library for working with XML and HTML in the Python language.

---

```
sudo apt-get install python-lxml
```

- *mako* : Hyperfast and lightweight templating for the Python platform.

```
sudo apt-get install python-mako
```

- *mxdatetime* : Provides the most natural and robust way of dealing with date/time values in Python.

```
sudo apt-get install python-egenix-mxdatetime
```

- *python-dateutil* : The dateutil module provides powerful extensions to the standard datetime module, available in Python 2.3+.

```
sudo apt-get install python-dateutil
```

- *psycopg2* : Psycopg is the most popular PostgreSQL adapter for the Python programming language.

```
sudo apt-get install python-psycopg2
```

- *pychart* : PyChart is a Python library for creating high quality Encapsulated Postscript, PDF, PNG, or SVG charts.

```
sudo apt-get install python-pychart
```

- *pydot* : This module provides a full interface to create, handle, modify and process graphs in Graphviz's dot language.

```
sudo apt-get install python-pydot
```

- *pytz* : World Timezone Definitions for Python.

```
sudo apt-get install python-tz
```

- *reportlab* : The ReportLab Toolkit is the time-proven, ultra-robust, open-source engine for programmatically creating PDF documents and forms the foundation of RML. It also contains a library for creating platform-independent vector graphics. It is a fast, flexible, cross-platform solution written in Python.

```
sudo apt-get install python-reportlab
```

- *pyyaml* : PyYAML is a YAML parser and emitter for Python.

```
sudo apt-get install python-yaml
```

- *vobject* : VObject simplifies the process of parsing and creating iCalendar and vCard objects.

```
sudo apt-get install python-vobject
```

## 7.2.2  Downloading the OpenERP Server

The OpenERP server can be downloaded from the OpenERP website's download page

## 7.2.3  Testing the OpenERP Server

If you only want to test the server, you do not need to install it. Just unpack the archive and start the openerp-server executable:

```
tar -xzf openerp-server-6.0.2.tar.gz
cd openerp-server-6.0.2/bin
python openerp-server.py
```

The list of available command line parameters can be obtained with the −h command-line switch:

```
python openerp-server.py -h
```

## 7.2.4  Installing the OpenERP Server

The OpenERP Server can be installed very easily using the *setup.py* file:

```
tar -xzf openerp-server-6.0.2.tar.gz
cd openerp-server-6.0.2
sudo python setup.py install
```

If your PostgreSQL server is up and running, you can now run the server using the following command:

```
openerp-server
```

If you do not already have a PostgreSQL server up and running, you can read *PostgreSQL Server Installation and Configuration* (page 181).

You can find the OpenERP server configuration file at ~/openerp-server-6.0.2/doc/openerp-server

# 7.3  OpenERP Client Installation

## 7.3.1  Installing the required packages

You need to have Python (at least 2.5 for OpenERP v6.0) in your Ubuntu system, which is in-built in Ubuntu version 10.04 and above.

You also need to install the following Python libraries, because OpenERP Client uses these packages.

To install the required libraries on your Ubuntu system, you can do the following in your favourite shell:

- *gtk* : GTK+ is a highly usable, feature-rich toolkit for creating graphical user interfaces which boosts cross-platform compatibility and an easy-to-use API.

  ```
  sudo apt-get install python-gtk2
  ```

- *glade* : Glade is a RAD tool to enable quick & easy development of user interfaces for the GTK+ toolkit and the GNOME desktop environment.

  ```
  sudo apt-get install python-glade2
  ```

- *matplotlib* : matplotlib is a Python 2D plotting library which produces publication quality figures in a variety of hard-copy formats and interactive environments across platforms.

  ```
  sudo apt-get install python-matplotlib
  ```

- *mxdatetime* : Provides the most natural and robust way of dealing with date/time values in Python.

  ```
  sudo apt-get install python-egenix-mxdatetime
  ```

- *xml* : XML support for Python platform.

  ```
  sudo apt-get install python-xml
  ```

- *tz* : World Timezone definitions for Python.

  ```
  sudo apt-get install python-tz
  ```

- *hippocanvas* : The Hippo Canvas is a Cairo/GObject/GTK+ based canvas, written in C with support for flexible layout, CSS styling, and initial work on animations.

  ```
  sudo apt-get install python-hippocanvas
  ```

- *pydot* : Python interface to Graphviz's Dot language.

  ```
  sudo apt-get install python-pydot
  ```

> **PDF Viewer**
>
> You will also need a PDF viewer (e.g. xpdf, acroread, kpdf).
>
> See the *Configuring a PDF Viewer* (page 188) section.

### 7.3.2  Downloading the OpenERP Client

The OpenERP client can be downloaded from the OpenERP website's download page

### 7.3.3  Testing the OpenERP Client

If you only want to test the client, you do not need to install it. Just unpack the archive and start the openerp-client executable:

```
tar -xzf openerp-client-6.0.2.tar.gz
cd openerp-client-6.0.2/bin
python openerp-client.py
```

The list of available command line parameters can be obtained with the −h command-line switch:

```
python openerp-client.py -h
```

### 7.3.4  Installing the OpenERP Client

The client can be installed very easily using the *setup.py* file:

```
tar -xzf openerp-client-6.0.2.tar.gz
cd openerp-client-6.0.2
sudo python setup.py install
```

You can now run the client using the following command:

```
openerp-client
```

### 7.3.5  Configuring a PDF Viewer

To preview PDF files, OpenERP Client by default supports:

1. evince

2. xpdf

3. gpdf

4. kpdf

5. epdfview

6. acroread

The client will try to find one of these executables (in this order) in your system and open the PDF document with it.

> **PDF**
>
> For example, if *xpdf*, *kpdf* and *acroread* are the only PDF viewers installed on your system, the OpenERP client will use *xpdf* for previewing PDF documents.

If you want to use another PDF viewer or if you do not want to use the first one the client will find, you have to edit the OpenERP configuration file, normally located in `~/.openerprc`. Find the `[printer]` section and edit the `softpath` parameter. For example:

```
[printer]
softpath = kpdf
```

# 7.4 OpenERP Web Installation

## 7.4.1 Downloading & Installing the OpenERP Web Client

The OpenERP Web Client can be downloaded from the OpenERP website's download page

You need to install the following Python libraries, because OpenERP Web Client uses these packages:

1. Python >= 2.4

2. CherryPy >= 3.1.2

3. Mako >= 0.2.4

4. Babel >= 0.9.4

5. FormEncode >= 1.2.2

6. simplejson >= 2.0.9

7. pyparsing >= 1.5.0

There is no need to install the above packages one by one. You can just run the following commands in your favourite shell:

```
$ sudo apt-get install python python-dev build-essential
$ sudo apt-get install python-setuptools
```

This will install dependencies required for the following:

```
$ cd /path/to/openerp-web-6.0.2/lib
$ ./populate.sh
$ cd ..
```

This will install all required dependencies in private lib directory, and you do not need to install anything.

## 7.4.2 Testing the OpenERP Web Client

If you only want to test the web client, you do not need to install it. Just unpack the archive and start the openerp-web executable:

```
tar -xzf openerp-web-6.0.2.tar.gz
cd openerp-web-6.0.2/
python openerp-web.py
```

The list of available command line parameters can be obtained with the −h command line switch:

```
python openerp-web.py -h
```

## 7.4.3 Installing the OpenERP Web Client

The OpenERP Web Client can be installed very easily using the *setup.py* file:

```
tar -xzf openerp-web-6.0.2.tar.gz
cd openerp-web-6.0.2
sudo python setup.py install
```

You can now run the OpenERP Web Client using the following command:

```
openerp-web
```

you can find the OpenERP Web Client configuration file at ~/openerp-web-6.0.2/doc/openerp-web.conf.

## 7.4.4 Web Browser Compatibilities

### Supported Browsers

*OpenERP Web Client* is known to work best with *Mozilla* based web browsers. Here is a list of supported browsers:

1. Firefox >= 3.6

2. Internet Explorer >= 7.0

3. Safari >= 4.1

4. Google Chrome >= 9.0

5. Opera >= 10.0

## Flash Plugin

Your browser should have the Flash plugin installed because *OpenERP Web Client* uses some Flash components.

Apply the following command in order to install the Flash plugin on an Ubuntu system:

```
$ sudo apt-get install flashplugin-nonfree
```

# OpenERP Installation on Windows    8

In this chapter, you will see the installation of OpenERP v6.0 on a Windows system. This procedure is well-tested on Windows 7.

You have two options for the installation of OpenERP on a Windows system:

- **All-In-One Installation** This is the easiest and quickest way to install OpenERP. It installs all components (OpenERP Server, Client, Web and PostgreSQL database) pre-configured on one computer. This installation is recommended if you do not have any major customizations.

- **Independent Installation** If you choose this mode of installation, all the components required to run OpenERP will have to be downloaded and installed separately. You will have to opt for an independent installation if you plan to install the components on separate machines. This mode is also practical if you are already working with or plan to use a different version of PostgreSQL than the one provided with the All-In-One installer.

## 8.1 OpenERP All-In-One Installation

Each time a new release of OpenERP is made, OpenERP supplies a complete Windows auto-installer for it. This contains all of the components you need – the PostgreSQL database server, the OpenERP application server, the GTK application client and the Web client.

This auto-installer enables you to install the whole system in just a few mouse clicks. The initial configuration is set up during installation, making it possible to start using it very quickly, as long as you do not want to change the underlying code. It is aimed at the installation of everything on a single PC, but you can later connect GTK clients from other PCs, Macs and Linux boxes to it as well.

### 8.1.1 Downloading OpenERP All-In-One

The first step is to download the OpenERP All-In-One installer. At this stage, you must choose which version to install – the stable version or the development version. If you are planning to put it straight into production we strongly advise you to choose the stable version.

To download OpenERP for Windows, follow these steps:

1. Navigate to the site http://www.openerp.com.

2. Click the *Downloads* button at the right, then, under *Windows Auto-Installer*, select **All-In-One**.

3. Before you can proceed with the download, you will be asked to fill an online form with your contact and company details and information regarding your interest in OpenERP.

4. Once you submit the online form, the All-In-One Windows installer (currently **openerp-allinone-setup-6.0.2.exe**) becomes available for download.

5. Save the file on your PC - it is quite a substantial size because it downloads everything including the PostgreSQL database system (version 8.3, at the time of writing), so it will take some time.

## 8.1.2 Installing the OpenERP All-In-One

To install OpenERP and its database, you must be signed in as an Administrator on your PC.

If you have previously tried to install the All-In-One version of OpenERP, you will have to uninstall that first, because various elements of a previous installation could interfere with your new installation. Make sure that all Tiny ERP, OpenERP and PostgreSQL applications are removed: you are likely to have to restart your PC to finish removing all traces of them.

Double-click the installer file to install OpenERP and accept the default parameters on each dialog box as you go. The All-In-One installer is the simplest mode of installation and has the following steps:

- 1. **Select installation language** The default is English. The other option is French.

- 2. **Welcome message** Carefully follow the recommendations given in this step.

- 3. **Licence Agreement** It is important that you accept the GNU General Public License to proceed with installation.

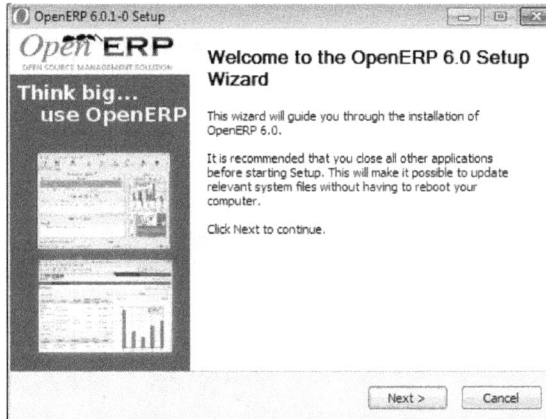

Figure 8.1: *Welcome to OpenERP*

- **4. Select components to install** You can proceed with the default install type `All In One`, which will install the OpenERP Server, GTK Desktop Client, Web Client and PostgreSQL Database (version 8.3, at the time of writing). Or, you may customize your installation by selecting only the components you require.

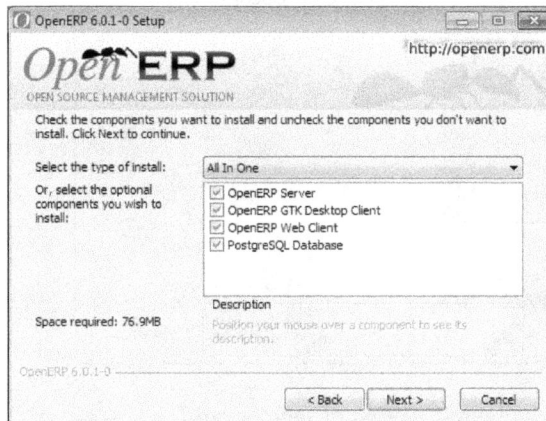

Figure 8.2: *Customize component installation*

- **5. Configure PostgreSQL connection** The installer will suggest default parameters to complete your PostgreSQL connection configuration. You may accept the defaults, or change it according to your requirement.

- **6. Select folder for installation** By default, OpenERP is installed in `C:\Program Files\OpenERP 6.0`. To install in a different folder, browse for a different location(folder) in this step.

- **7. Install** The automatic installation of OpenERP begins and you can view its progress.

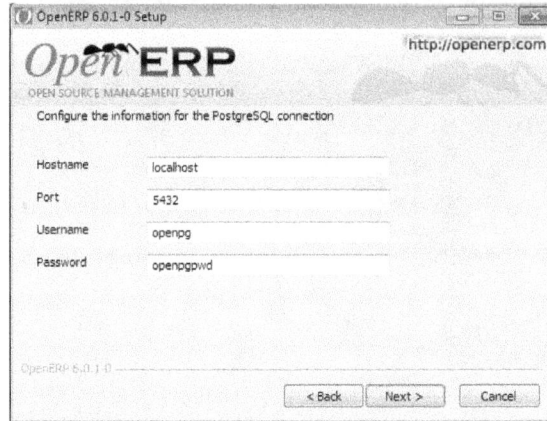

Figure 8.3: *PostgreSQL configuration*

- 8. **Finish** On successful installation of OpenERP, you will get an appropriate confirmation. You can click *Finish* to close the setup wizard.

Figure 8.4: *End of setup wizard*

## 8.1.3 Starting the OpenERP Client

You do not need to manually start the OpenERP Server, because it is installed as a Windows service. But you may trigger various actions from the shortcuts created in the *Start* menu for *OpenERP GTK Client 6.0*, *OpenERP Server 6.0* and *PostgreSQL 8.3*. The OpenERP Client can be opened, ready to use the OpenERP system, once you have completed the All-In-One installation.

You will find the *OpenERP Client* icon on your desktop, which you double-click to access the OpenERP client interface. Use the menu *File → Connect...* to connect to a database. As this would be the first time you are using OpenERP since its installation, your database will be empty. You can create a new database through *File → Databases → New database*.

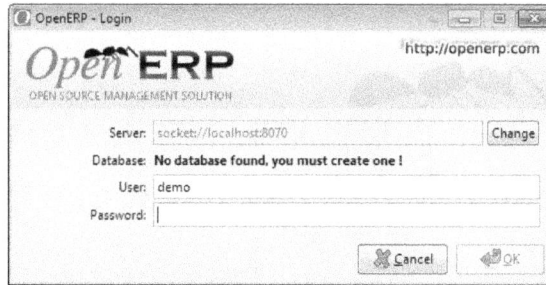

Figure 8.5: *Database on first run*

## 8.2 PostgreSQL Server Installation and Configuration

In this chapter, you will see how to configure PostgreSQL for its use with OpenERP. The following procedure is well-tested on PostgreSQL v9.0.

### 8.2.1 Installing PostgreSQL Server

You can download the Windows installer from the PostgreSQL download page

Depending on your need, choose either the *One Click Installer* or the *pgInstaller* and run the executable you have just downloaded.

### 8.2.2 Setup a PostgreSQL User

When the required software installations are complete, you must create a PostgreSQL user. OpenERP will use this user to connect to PostgreSQL.

#### Add a User

Start a Windows console (run the cmd command in the *Search programs and files* text box of the *Start* menu).

Change the directory to the *PostgreSQL* bin directory (e.g. C:\Program Files\PostgreSQL\9.0\bin) or add this directory to your *PATH* environment variable.

The default superuser for PostgreSQL is called *postgres*. The password was chosen during the PostgreSQL installation.

In your Windows console, type:

```
C:\Program Files\PostgreSQL\9.0\bin>createuser.exe --createdb --username postgres --
Enter password for new role: openpgpwd
Enter it again: openpgpwd
Shall the new role be a superuser? (y/n) y
Password: XXXXXXXXXX
```

---

```
* line 1 is the command itself
* line 2 asks you the new user's password
* line 3 asks you to confirm the new user's password
* line 4 new role is superuser or not?
* line 5 asks you the *postgres* user's password
```

Option explanations:

- `--createdb` : the new user will be able to create new databases

- `--username postgres` : *createuser* will use the *postgres* user (superuser)

- `--no-createrole` : the new user will not be able to create new users

- `--pwprompt` : *createuser* will ask you the new user's password

- `openpg` : the new user's name. Alternatively, you may specify a different username.

- `openpgpwd` : the new user's password. Alternatively, you may specify a different password.

> **Password**
>
> In OpenERP v6, `openpg` and `openpgpwd` are the default username and password used during the OpenERP Server installation. If you plan to change these defaults for the server, or have already installed the server with different values, you have to use those user configuration values when you create a PostgreSQL user for OpenERP.

Now use *pgAdmin III* to create database "openerpdemo" with owner "openpg":

```
CREATE DATABASE openerpdemo WITH OWNER = openpg ENCODING = 'UTF8';
COMMENT ON DATABASE openerpdemo IS 'OpenERP Demo DB';
```

If you have installed the OpenERP Server, you can start it now. If needed, you can override the server configuration by starting the server at a Windows console and specifying command-line options. For more on this, refer the section *Customized Configuration* (page 201).

To change a user's password in any Windows version, execute the following:

```
net user <accountname> <newpassword>
e.g. net user postgres postgres
```

If it is a domain account, just add "/DOMAIN" at the end.

If you want to delete it, just execute:

```
net user <accountname> /delete
```

**Case-Insensitive Search Issue**

For an installation which needs full UTF8 character support, consider using postgres >= 8.2.x. Using versions prior to this, OpenERP search will not return the expected results for case-insensitive searches, which are used for searching partners, products etc.

Example:

```
SELECT 'x' FROM my_table WHERE 'bét' ilike 'BÉT'
--matches only in 8.2.x
```

# 8.3 OpenERP Server Installation

The OpenERP Server 6.0 installation works with disks formatted in NTFS (not a FAT or FAT32 partition). The following installation procedure has been well-tested on Windows 7.

> **Windows Versions**
>
> OpenERP Server does not work on Windows 98 or ME; for obvious reasons – these cannot be formatted using NTFS.

You will need a PostgreSQL server up and running. If it is not the case, you can read the *PostgreSQL Server Installation and Configuration* (page 197) section.

## 8.3.1 Downloading the OpenERP Server

The OpenERP Server can be downloaded from OpenERP website's download page.

Under *Windows Auto-Installer*, choose **Server** to download the OpenERP Server standalone.

## 8.3.2 Installing the OpenERP Server

Execute the installer you have just downloaded. It has the following stages:

- 1. **Select installation language** The default is English. The other option is French.

- 2. **Welcome message** Carefully follow the recommendations given in this step.

- 3. **Licence Agreement** It is important that you accept the GNU General Public License to proceed with installation.

- 4. **Select folder for installation** By default, OpenERP Server is installed in C:\Program Files\OpenERP 6.0\Server. To install in a different folder, browse for a different location(folder) in this step.

---

- 5. **Configure PostgreSQL connection** The installer will suggest default parameters to complete your PostgreSQL connection configuration. You may accept the defaults, or change it according to your requirement.

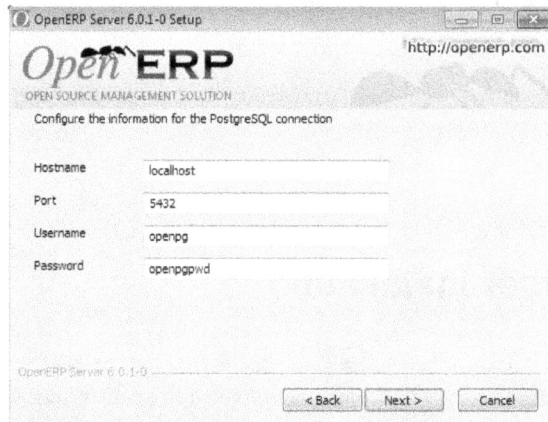

*PostgreSQL configuration*

- 6. **Create shortcuts** Select a folder in the *Start* menu where you would like to create the program's shortcuts.

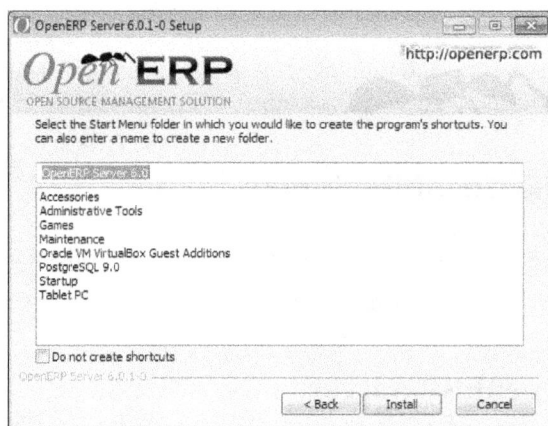

*Create Start menu shortcuts*

- 7. **Install** The automatic installation of OpenERP Server begins and you can view its progress.

- 8. **Finish** On successful installation of OpenERP Server, you will get an appropriate confirmation. You can click *Finish* to close the setup wizard.

*End of setup wizard*

The OpenERP Server installs as a Windows service. This means you do not have to start the server each time you start the computer and it runs without the need of an open user session.

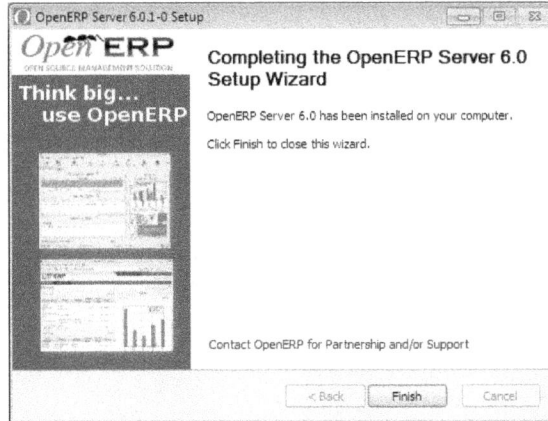

## 8.3.3 Customized Configuration

To initialize the server with configurations of your choice, you have to invoke it at the Windows Command prompt with the options you wish to override.

Navigate to the installation directory in `C:\Program Files\OpenERP 6.0\Server\` and type this command but do not execute it yet:

```
openerp-server.exe -d <db_name> -r <db_user> -w <db_password>
--db_host=<postgresql_server_address>
--db_port=<port_no> --logfile="<logfile>"
```

The initialization of OpenERP Server provides necessary information for connection to the PostgreSQL database and the choice of data to load. Here is the explanation of used options:

- `-d <db_name>` : Name of the database created for OpenERP Server.

- `-r <db_user>` : Name of the PostgreSQL user (role).

- `-w <db_password>` : Password of the PostgreSQL user.

- `--db_host=<postgresql_server_address>` :  Address of the server where PostgreSQL is. If you have installed PostgreSQL on the same computer as OpenERP Server, you can enter `localhost`, else, the IP address or the name of the distant server.

- `--db_port=<port_no>` : Port number where PostgreSQL listens. The default is 5432.

- `--stop-after-init` : This option stops the server after initialization.

- `--logfile="<logfile>"` :  specify an alternate logfile where all the output of server will be saved.  The default is `C:\Program Files\OpenERP 6.0\Server\openerp-server.log`.

Before the execution of this command you have to decide the purpose of the database created in OpenERP.

Sample command:

```
openerp-server.exe -d openerpdemo -r openpg -w openpgpwd
--db_host=localhost --logfile="C:\Users\tiny\Desktop\demo_db.log"
--db_port=5430 --stop-after-init
```

Here you have to enter the username and password specified in the PostgreSQL connection configuration during server installation.

When you execute the initialization command, if you specify a logfile, the server runtime output is written to that file, and you will not see any server output in the prompt window. You have only to wait until the prompt comes back.

### Deciding about the purpose of the database

You can initialize the database with OpenERP Server to:

1. Take a look at the system with modules installed and demo data loaded

2. Install a new clean database system (without demo data)

3. Upgrade an existing version

## With modules and demo data

If you execute the sample command above, you will get a database with only base modules installed and loaded with demo data. To initialize OpenERP Server with additional modules and its demo data, you need to add this option to the above command:

```
-i <module name>
```

Sample command:

```
openerp-server.exe -d openerpdemo --stop-after-init -i sale
```

This command will initialize the OpenERP Server with the module `sale` and its dependencies, and fill its PostgreSQL database with their related demo data. As can be seen, you must specify the target database for the module installation.

To install more than one module, specify a comma-separated module list at the command-line.

## Without demo data (or new clean version)

Execute the command with an option excluding the demo data:

```
--without-demo=all
```

This will load base modules (and other modules if -i option is used), but will not load its demo data.

Sample command usage:

```
openerp-server.exe -d openerpdemo --stop-after-init --without-demo=all
```

If you have already initialized the database with demo data loaded, you can create a new database and execute the above command on it.

## Update the database

Execute the command with an option that updates the data structures:

```
--update=all
```

Sample command usage:

```
openerp-server.exe -d openerpdemo --stop-after-init --update=all
```

## 8.3.4 Monitoring the OpenERP Server

The service and some runtime information is accessible through the Computer Management console in Administrative Tools.

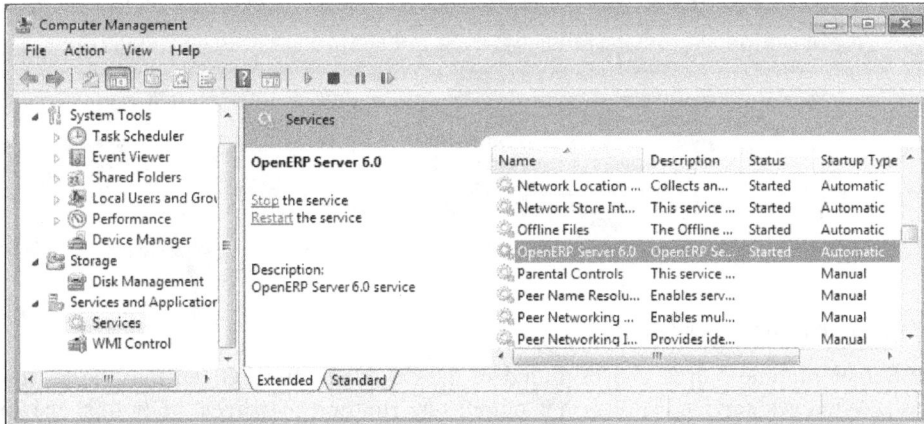

*OpenERP Server 6.0 in the Services list*

Here, you can define how the service should act in case of server failure. Access the service's properties by double-clicking `OpenERP Server 6.0` in the list.

*Recovery tab to set service failure response*

The Computer Management logging service offers additional information about the execution of the OpenERP Server, for example, the startup or shutdown information of the service.

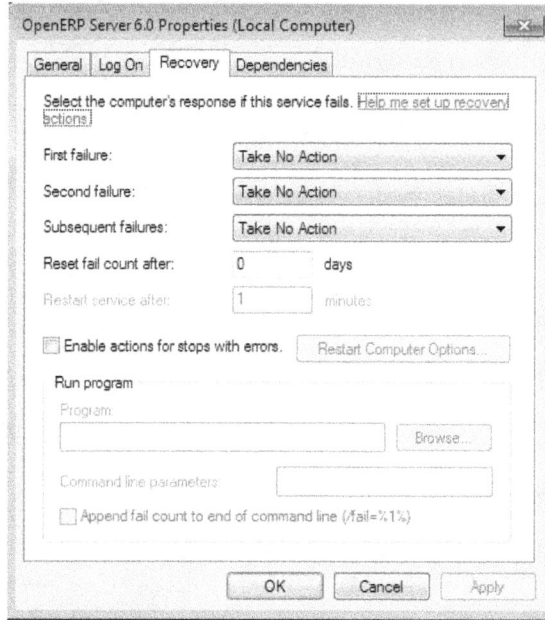

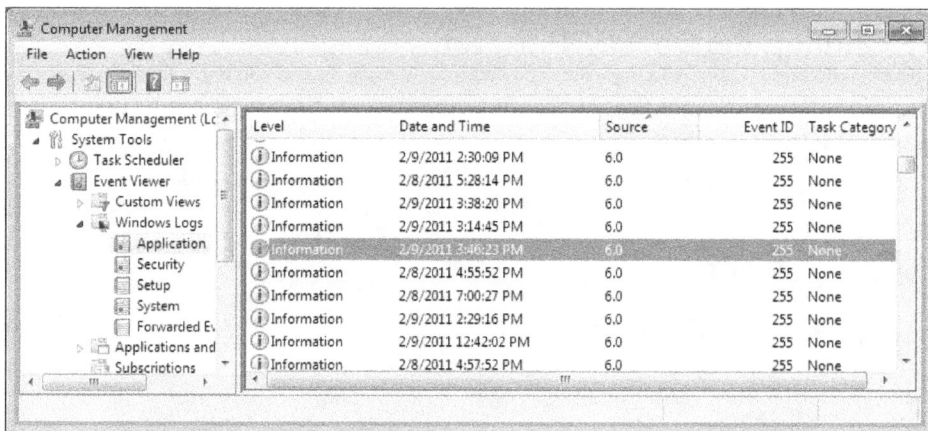

*Server information in Windows Logs list*

OpenERP Server runtime output can be found in the default logfile. Given that the server is now running as a Windows service, it does not output any runtime messages. For this, the logfile is the only option. Access it from the *Start* menu, through the `View log` link in the group of shortcuts for OpenERP Server 6.0. Alternatively, use the path `C:\Program Files\OpenERP 6.0\Server\openerp-server.log`.

*OpenERP Server log file*

You can find out whether OpenERP Server is running by invoking *Windows Task Manager*. When you look at the *Processes* tab, you will see `OpenERPServerService.exe` and `openerp-server.exe`, both having `SYSTEM` as their user (to see these, *Show processes from all users* must be enabled in the Task Manager).

---

The services in Windows Task Manager

### 8.3.5 Congratulations, you have successfully installed OpenERP Server

For more information, please take a look at *Additional Installation Information and Troubleshooting* (page 210), where you can find some troubleshooting examples.

## 8.4 OpenERP Client Installation

You must install, configure and run the OpenERP Server before using the OpenERP Client. The client needs the server to run. You can install the server application on your computer, or on an independent server accessible by network.

## 8.4.1 Downloading the OpenERP Client

The OpenERP Client can be downloaded from OpenERP website's download page.

Under *Windows Auto-Installer*, choose **Client** to download the OpenERP Client standalone.

## 8.4.2 Installing the OpenERP Client

Click the executable installation file you have just downloaded, and proceed with the following steps:

- 1. **Select installation language** The default is English. The other option is French.

- 2. **Welcome message** Carefully follow the recommendations given in this step.

- 3. **Licence Agreement** It is important that you accept the GNU General Public License to proceed with installation.

- 4. **Select folder for installation** By default, OpenERP Client is installed in C:\Program Files\OpenERP 6.0\Client. To install in a different folder, browse for a different location(folder) in this step.

- 5. **Create shortcuts** Select a folder in the *Start* menu where you would like to create the program's shortcuts.

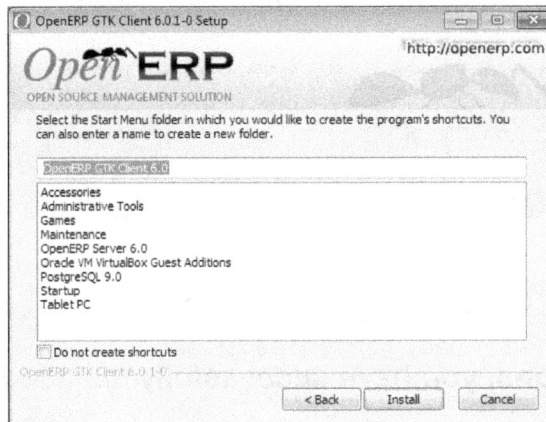

*Create Start Menu Shortcuts*

- 6. **Install** The automatic installation of OpenERP Client begins and you can view its progress.

- 7. **Finish** On successful installation of OpenERP Client, you will get an appropriate confirmation. Click *Finish* to close the setup wizard.

*End of Configuration Wizard*

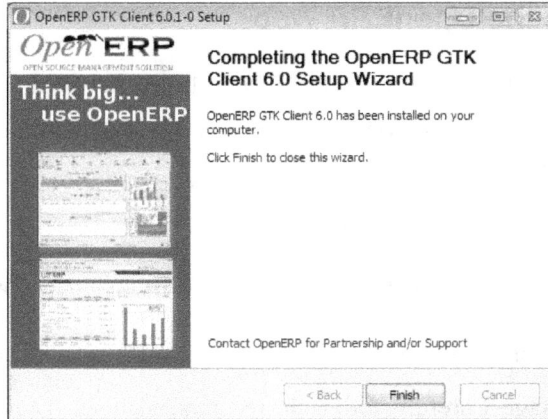

### 8.4.3 Starting the OpenERP Client

The installation program creates shortcuts in the main program menu and on the desktop, which you can use to start the client. Be sure to have an OpenERP Server running somewhere (on your computer or a distant server) to be able to use the client software.

Log in to `openerpdemo` database using default username and password:

- Username = admin

- Password = admin

Enjoy!

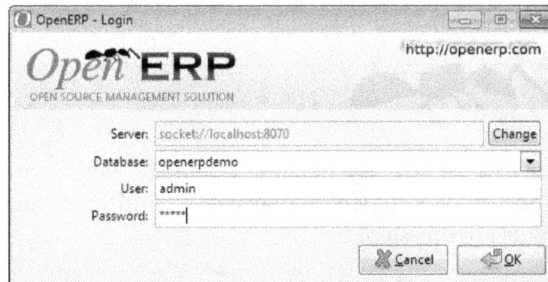

*Connecting to the Demo Database*

## 8.5 OpenERP Web Installation

You must install, configure and run the OpenERP Server before using the OpenERP Web. The web client needs the server to run. You can install the server application on your computer, or on an independent server accessible by network.

### 8.5.1 Downloading the OpenERP Web

The OpenERP Web can be downloaded from OpenERP website's download page.

Under *Windows Auto-Installer*, choose **Web** to download the OpenERP Web standalone.

### 8.5.2 Installing the OpenERP Web

Click the executable installation file you have just downloaded, and proceed with the following steps:

- 1. **Select installation language** The default is English. The other option is French.

- 2. **Welcome message** Carefully follow the recommendations given in this step.

- 3. **Licence Agreement** It is important that you accept the OpenERP Public License (OEPL) Version 1.1 to proceed with installation. This licence is based on the Mozilla Public Licence (MPL) Version 1.1.

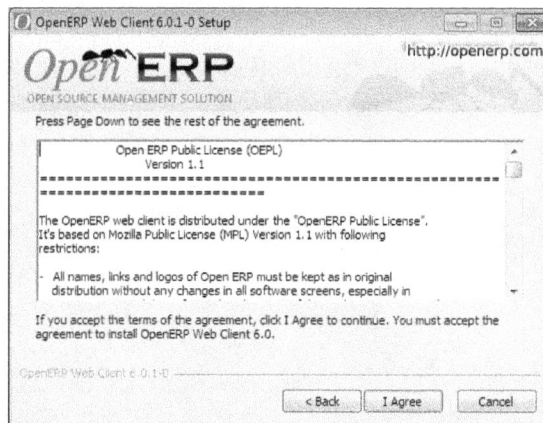

*OpenERP Public Licence*

- 4. **Select folder for installation** By default, OpenERP Web is installed in C:\Program Files\OpenERP 6.0\Web. To install in a different folder, browse for a different location(folder) in this step.

- 5. **Create shortcuts** Select a folder in the *Start* menu where you would like to create the program's shortcuts.

*Create Start Menu Shortcuts*

- 6. **Install** The automatic installation of OpenERP Web begins and you can view its progress.

- 7. **Finish** On successful installation of OpenERP Web, you will get an appropriate confirmation. Click *Finish* to close the setup wizard.

The Windows service for OpenERP Web Server is also installed and is set up to start the server automatically on system boot.

---

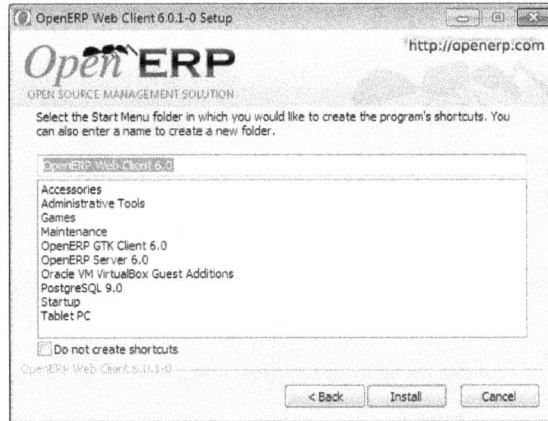

## 8.5.3 Starting the Web Client

The web server being initialized and the settings saved, you can start the OpenERP Web Client.

Use a web browser of your choice to connect to OpenERP Web. If your web client is installed on the same computer as the server, you can navigate to http://localhost:8080 to connect to the OpenERP web version. If the server is installed on a separate computer, you must know the name or IP address of the server over the network and navigate to http://<server_address>:8080 to connect to OpenERP.

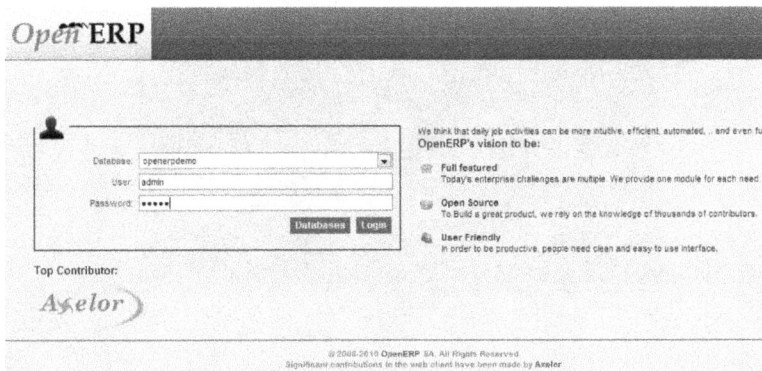

Figure 8.6: *Web Client at Startup*

# 8.6 Troubleshooting and Windows Complementary Install Information

## 8.6.1 PostgreSQL Administration

### OpenERP Server Connection Error with PostgreSQL

If you are initializing a database from the command-line with a custom username/role (-r) and password (-w), ensure that you have created a corresponding PostgreSQL user for the same. Otherwise you may encounter error messages as shown below:

*User authentication failure*

You may also face another problem similar to this situation:

*Database connection failure*

In this case, check if the service `postgresql-9.0 - PostgreSQL Server 9.0` is running in the Services Manager (*Control Panel → System and Security → Administrative Tools → Services*).

*PostgreSQL 9.0 in the Services list*

You can edit the service configuration to start PostgreSQL as a service on system boot. This is usually the default.

*Configure PostgreSQL 9.0 service*

If your PostgreSQL service is running, but you get connection errors, you can restart the service.

*Restarting the service*

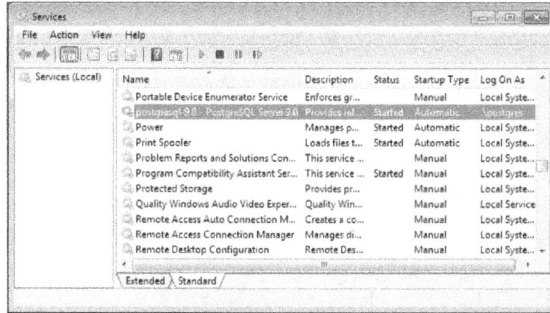

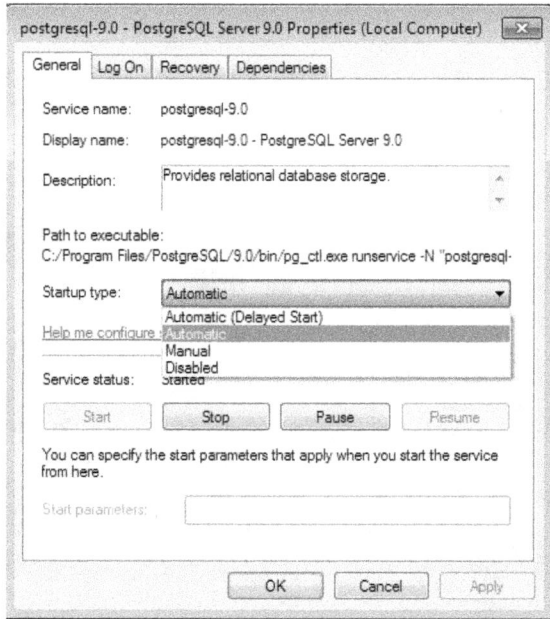

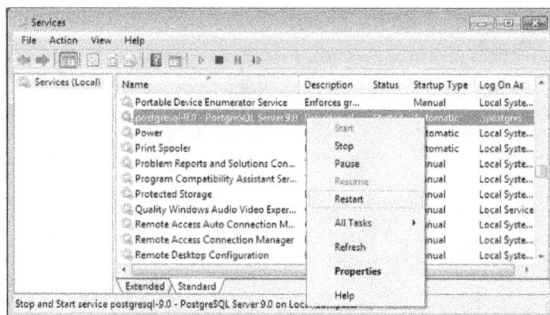

# Index